Richard Yates and the
Flawed American Dream

Richard Yates and the Flawed American Dream

Critical Essays

EDITED BY JENNIFER DALY

McFarland & Company, Inc., Publishers
Jefferson, North Carolina

LIBRARY OF CONGRESS CATALOGUING-IN-PUBLICATION DATA

Names: Daly, Jennifer, 1981– editor.
Title: Richard Yates and the flawed American dream : critical essays /
    edited by Jennifer Daly.
Description: Jefferson, North Carolina : McFarland & Company, Inc.,
    Publishers, 2017. | Includes bibliographical references and index.
Identifiers: LCCN 2017038002 | ISBN 9781476668253 (softcover : acid free
    paper) ∞
Subjects: LCSH: Yates, Richard, 1926–1992—Criticism and interpretation.
Classification: LCC PS3575.A83 Z85 2017 | DDC 813/.54—dc23
LC record available at https://lccn.loc.gov/2017038002

BRITISH LIBRARY CATALOGUING DATA ARE AVAILABLE

ISBN 978-1-4766-6825-3 (print)
ISBN 978-1-4766-2957-5 (ebook)

Front cover illustration of Richard Yates by Christian Bloom (pen and ink
on paper, colorized digitally, 2008)

Printed in the United States of America

McFarland & Company, Inc., Publishers
  Box 611, Jefferson, North Carolina 28640
    www.mcfarlandpub.com

Table of Contents

Acknowledgments

The idea for this collection was first raised back in 2012 when I was beginning work on my Ph.D. at Trinity College Dublin. Having listened to me lament the relative lack of resources then available on Richard Yates, my supervisor suggested I do something to fix it. For what isn't the first time, and most likely won't be the last time either, my thanks to Professor Stephen Matterson for pointing me in the direction of a really good idea. Dara Downey's brain, as always, was useful to pick. Thank you, too, to all of my friends and colleagues at Trinity College Dublin and in the wider American Studies community in Ireland for their support and encouragement.

All of the contributors to this volume deserve the highest praise and gratitude for their stellar work. I have been fortunate to work with gifted academics who have challenged my readings of Yates, presented new and incisive analysis on a somewhat neglected writer, and who all demonstrated constant, infectious enthusiasm for the project from the word go.

And, as always, the final mention has to go to my family. Parents Jim and Bridget, sisters Elizabeth and Barbara, and best niece in the world Lucy: you are all my favorites.

Introduction

JENNIFER DALY

In the last apartment he occupied before his death in 1992, Richard Yates pinned an Adlai Stevenson quotation on the wall above his writing desk. It read, "Americans have always assumed, subconsciously, that every story will have a happy ending" (Bailey 2003, 581). Yates consciously and deliberately wrote against this assumption as he repeatedly grappled with the dominant themes of American life in the middle of the twentieth century. As a writer, Yates was primarily concerned with what he saw as the flawed American dream, and the stifling conformity and artificiality it engendered in the country's citizens. In an interview with the literary journal *Ploughshares* in 1972, Yates discussed the title of *Revolutionary Road*, noting that the title was "meant to suggest that the revolutionary road of 1776 … our best and bravest revolutionary spirit had come to something very much like a dead end in the '50s" (Yates 2011). Yates's characters inhabit an America where the dream is atrophied, but still holds power over almost every aspect of life. Time and again, he addresses themes of exceptionalism, identity, the nature of work, the difficulties inherent in marital and parental relationships, failures to communicate, and outsized dreams that refuse to fit the life of the person dreaming them. Although Yates is very clearly a writer of the mid–twentieth century, in many ways these are timeless themes in American fiction, and are certainly issues that are still alive and relevant in cultural discussions today.

Yates's characters struggle to fit into a society that demands they be successful in every facet of their lives, that they be content to conform to the social and cultural mores of the time; and all this they must somehow do without ever compromising their own sense of individuality. Moreover, throughout all of his work there is a constant engagement with what it means to be a writer. With Yates, there is a sense of compulsive dedication to the role of the writer that meant he personally would rarely live in relative comfort, and his characters would never achieve the stereotypical happy ending that many readers of fiction expected. Indeed, his desire to work out the fundamental problems with American life as he saw them resulted in one reviewer criticizing him for repeatedly treading the "same half-acre of pain" (Towers 1981). The world that Yates wrote about is slightly grubby. His characters try too hard to be what they are not, and often feel that other people have found out the secret of attaining a fabulously glamorous and wealthy life—something that is always, infuriatingly, just out of reach for them. There is no sense of the escapism that comes with some fiction writing. Yates persistently placed the reality of life, complete with all its flaws and heartaches, at the center of his work, something that was perhaps too uncomfortable for many readers to identify with.

Ultimately, all of his books were out of print for many years. Yate's biographer, Blake Bailey, reflected on the reasons for this when he observed that "it's fun to identify with handsome, heedless romantics who come to a bad (but glamorous) end, or stoical mavericks who are graceful under pressure, or sensitive youths who are too fine for this world, so Fitzgerald and Hemingway and Salinger stay in print" (Bailey, *Harvard Review* 2003). Yates and his characters were not seen to be fashionable enough, or sufficiently exciting to ever engage the reading public fully. Yates wrote about ordinary people leading what they believed to be less than ordinary lives, struggling to be content with their lot. The only excess in his stories is in how far his characters go to delude themselves that their wildest dreams are attainable. This struggle to be content is something that remains relevant to this day and now, some twenty-five years after his death, a reengagement with the writing of Richard Yates is timely and necessary. Here is a writer who, even at the supposed height of his powers, was somewhat overlooked because, on the surface, his fiction was just more of the same in a long line of postwar suburban complaints. And yet, as the essays in this collection attest, Richard Yates was a writer of remarkable skill and depth, who probed deep into the American psyche in an attempt to unpick the knots of a constricting, conformist dream. As such, a critical reappraisal of his work is long overdue.

Born in Yonkers, New York, in 1926, Yates's childhood was unsettled and disrupted from an early age as his parents divorced when he was just three years old. Yates and his sister would then spend their formative years moving from place to place with their mother, Ruth, as she searched for a home that satisfied her requirements as something of an artist with pretensions to greatness. More often, though, these moves were quite sudden and precipitated by a need to escape unpaid rent and bills. In spite of this instability, from a young age Yates knew that he wanted to be a writer. For a time he attended an elite school outside Hartford, Connecticut. His years at the Avon Old Farms School saw him eventually overcome his own awkwardness and shame at the relative poverty of his family compared to his fellow students, and become the editor of the school newspaper, *The Avonian*. He performed so well in this role that he was allowed to act as editor without the supervision of a staff member (Bailey 2003, 59). Yates bought into a stereotype of sorts with regard to how he saw himself as a writer and how he should conduct himself. Affecting the pose was something he worked hard at, taking up smoking at a young age to complete the picture (as he saw it). His dedication to the task of producing the school paper was remembered by many of his fellow students and alumni who often commented on how impressed they were with the quality of the work he turned out.

Yates's relationship with his mother was troubled. Ruth Walden Maurer, or Dookie as she preferred to be called, was flighty and restless and often heavily reliant on Yates for emotional and financial support. When he was a small boy she used him as a model for some of her artwork—something Yates later fictionalized as intensely uncomfortable and embarrassing in *A Special Providence*. His ambivalent attitude to her is evident in much of his writing, with the mother figure often being a source of frustration and conflict. And yet Yates was also deeply sympathetic to his own mother even though he devoted a significant portion of his writing to cataloguing her flaws and was often caustically critical about her behavior. Characters based on Dookie are sloppy, brash, oblivious drunks who depend on others to bail them out. These women are terrible mothers who emotionally manipulate their children and their (usually former) husbands, and never ever see beyond their own pretensions. But in response to a question from a student at a reading about what he personally thought of Alice Prentice in *A Special Providence*, a character who was clearly based on his own mother, he replied "Oh, I don't know […] I guess I sort of love her" (Bailey 2003, 36). For all of her flaws, he could still identify with her and see much of himself in her. This tendency recurs throughout much of Yates's writing; alongside the almost brutally honest depictions of characters denying the scope of their abilities is an undercurrent of empathy. Yates does not pity these characters, nor do his narratives display any sympathy for them in the midst of their delusions, but there is an acknowledgment that "they can't help being the people they are" (245).

Yates himself was troubled throughout his life with health problems, both mental and physical. He experienced a number of mental breakdowns that increased in severity as he got older, and often resulted in his being institutionalized for extended periods of time. He also spent months in the hospital in 1950 after he developed advanced tuberculosis. This particular stint in hospital was not as bad as previous visits, as his colleagues at Remington Rand clubbed together to buy him a set of books to keep him occupied. Blake Bailey notes that,

> as his future publisher Seymour Lawrence put it, Halloran became Yates's "Harvard, Yale, and Princeton" … while Yates would forever remain a slow, insecure writer with

a wildly inflated idea of what he'd missed by way of college, his eight months in the TB ward began a lifelong process of autodidactic recompense.... Some of the writers he got around to reading there ... included Dickens, Tolstoy, Dostoyevsky... [114].

Yates never did get to go to university. It was something that he felt the lack of all throughout his life, often berating his students in later years for not fully appreciating how lucky they were to "live in the world of ideas" before having to get a job (Yates [1976] 2008, 33). Characters such as Emily Grimes, and her father Walter, in *The Easter Parade* illustrate Yates's bitter-sweet, and at times overly romantic, attitude to the university experience. Emily is urged by her father to make the most of her time in college as she will never have that intellectual freedom again once she enters the world of work. Walter is shown to be slightly diminished in the eyes of his daughter when he tells her that he only spent one year at college before getting a job. Pookie, Emily's mother, had always boasted of how he had "gone through Syracuse" (32), implying that he had the full university experience, in an attempt to appropriate some of the social and cultural kudos this would gen-erate.

Similar to his feelings of inadequacy as a result of his perceived lack of higher education, Yates enlisted in the military during the Second World War but was always uncomfortable with how he had, to his mind, failed as a sol-dier, an experience played out in the character of Robert Prentice in *A Special Providence*. Yates joined up in 1944, somehow passing the physical exam, and then proceeded to demonstrate almost comedic ineptitude as a soldier (Bailey 2003, 77–78). He saw a little combat action before falling ill, and was even-tually honorably discharged in 1946 (87).

Yates married twice, and although both unions ended acrimoniously, he was a devoted father to his three daughters. Nonetheless, his relationships with, and attitude towards, women in general were contradictory on many levels. He desired the attention of women, and often tried to cultivate the aura of the rakish author who could attract any woman he wanted. But his deep insecurities about his abilities as a writer, the psychological scars he bore from his turbulent childhood, combined with his mental health issues and his recurrent impotence made him intensely needy in any relationship. Yates viewed women in a very traditional manner, and could be horribly sexist in his opinions of women writers, once telling a female writer he was in competition with for an award that she should not win it because "you're a girl, and you've got a baby" (245).

Yates was rarely able to support himself and his family solely through fiction writing. He worked as a copy writer at Remington Rand for many years. He also tried his hand at writing Hollywood screenplays on several occasions, which invariably left him feeling exploited and frustrated. Unwill-ing and unable to churn out work that he considered below par, Yates would agonize over his screenplays, pouring detail into them, and refining them until he was completely satisfied with their artistic merit, only to see them gutted by studio producers. His ultimately unfilmed adaptation of William Styron's *Lie Down in Darkness* was considered to be so accomplished that it was published by *Ploughshares* in the expectation that doing so might anticipate a studio finally committing to filming it. However, as George Bluestone noted in his introduction to the screenplay, even if it was never filmed its publication would "at the very least make an astonishing document available to the public" (Yates 1985, 8). In keeping with so much of Yates's career, the critical approval of his work proved much more difficult to translate into financial success. So desperate was Yates to make ends meet that he even ended up at one point writing speeches for Robert Kennedy while he was attorney general, an experience which provided the basis for his unfinished final novel *Uncertain Times*. An ardent Adlai Stevenson supporter, Yates almost actively disliked the Kennedys but developed a grudging respect for Bobby during his stint as a speechwriter. Towards the end of Yates's life, as his physical and mental health deteriorated, he would move from place to place taking teaching positions at various universities. These teaching roles, however, were sources of immense internal conflict for Yates. Convinced that one could not be taught how to write, at the same time Yates desperately needed the money these positions brought and so was forced to muddle his way through semester after semester of teaching and marking, frustrated in the knowledge that it was eating into precious writing time as he found he was unable to write and teach at the same time. In teaching others how to write, he was actively impairing his own ability to produce the work he wanted.

He began his writing career in earnest with a number of stories which would go on to form the basis of his first short story collection, *Eleven Kinds of Loneliness*, which was first published in 1962. It was not an easy process. Yates agonized over every word, and struggled to place his stories, with his agent Monica McCall tolerating Yates's increasingly despairing pleas while she fielded rejection after rejection from numerous magazines and publishers. Yates's lifelong ambition was to have one of his stories published in *The New Yorker*, but this would become an almost darkly comic saga as they rejected every story he submitted, eventually suggesting that it would be best for all concerned for him to stop trying. Ironically, *The New Yorker* did finally publish a Yates short story—"The Canal"—but only some eight years after his death. His major breakthrough came with the publication of *Revolutionary Road* in 1961. Hailed as a modern classic, the time seemed ripe for Yates to capitalize on the success of *Revolutionary Road*, but it would be another eight years before he published his second novel, *A Special Providence*, and while it was generally well-received as a solid but unspectacular sophomore effort, it did not capture the same attention as his first novel. In many ways, Yates was always slightly out of fashion, either ahead of or just behind what was in vogue. While *Revolutionary Road* highlighted something of a moment in American literature, by the time *A Special Providence* appeared, the literary scene had moved on. Similarly, the reading public lacked any interest in a wartime novel which appeared, in many ways, to celebrate the military life at a time when American society was riven with unrest and protests against America's involvement in Vietnam. Time and again in his subsequent fiction, Yates would return to the domestic dramas of ordinary characters, people he referred to as "running around trying to do their best" (Bailey 2003, 17). It was not the stuff of sensational bestsellers.

Yates's view of American society, and the challenges citizens faced in trying to find a place within it, was bleak, resulting in his characters retreating into fantasies to help them cope. This is encapsulated in characters such as Alice and Robert Prentice in *A Special Providence*. Alice refuses to give up on her belief that she and her son are uniquely entitled to a more fashionable life than they have, something which frustrates Robert: "why couldn't he let her have her illusions? That was what her wounded, half-drunk eyes had seemed to be saying throughout his interrogation: Why can't I have my illusions? Because they're lies, he told her silently in his mind" (Yates 2008, 16). This idea of deploying illusions as coping mechanisms is a recurring theme throughout Yates's writing. We see it in *Revolutionary Road* with Frank Wheeler's daydreams about the idyllic life he thinks he should be leading; it is present in the carefully cultivated façade Emily Grimes projects in *The Easter Parade*; it is evident in short stories such as "The Best of Everything" in Grace's studied movements as she tries to bring the fantasy of marriage to life; it is clear from the repeated descriptions of characters behaving as if they were actors in a movie, or view themselves as stars in a film of their own lives. Images, surfaces, and projections are all central to how Yates constructs his fictional worlds, but there is always a slight chink in the construction which, to paraphrase Bob Prentice's description of his writing technique in "Builders," will let the light in (Yates 2008, 221).

Yates has often been described with that most damning of faint praise: that he is a writer's writer. Richard Ford has described *Revolutionary Road* as a "cultish standard" (Ford 2000) and regularly refers to Yates as an unfairly overlooked American writer, going so far as to include a Yates short story in both volumes of the collections of American short stories he edited for *Granta*. Other contemporaries of Yates championed his work during his many fallow years in an effort to help him with financial and artistic difficulties, hosting readings, arranging paid writing work, and creating teaching posts to keep him afloat. Somewhat surprisingly, considering the differing styles, and presumably attitudes, they both had, Yates had a strong literary friendship with Kurt Vonnegut. Andre Dubus III was also an ardent champion of Yates's writing and a devoted friend for many years. Yates's own health problems and slow writing speed contributed to his failure ever really to capitalize on any success he might have had during his lifetime. Indeed, in spite of the efforts of his agent, Monica McCall, and his publisher Seymour Lawrence, Yates would always find himself struggling to make ends meet, never comfortable, always under pressure to produce work that was, for him, a loved and loathed obsession.

He was fiercely loyal to his concept of what it meant to be a writer even when this was to the detriment of his physical and mental health. Visitors to his invariably shabby apartments often noticed the circle of crushed cockroach carcasses around the chair at his writing desk (Bailey 2003, 4). It can even be argued that, to a certain extent, Yates reveled in the role of the tortured artist; much of the tragedy of his later years can be seen as self-inflicted. As mentioned earlier, he took up smoking at a young age in order to make himself look tough, and harden up what he thought to be his soft features. This habit would go on to cause him numerous health problems, including the emphysema he suffered with towards the end of his life. Somewhat dramatically, his smoking habit was also the cause of a number of house fires from which he was lucky to escape with only minor injuries. The ferocious cough he developed as a result of his smoking habit was legendary, and yet when he eventually did decide to give up cigarettes (by which time he was in constant need of oxygen) he found it remarkably easy. His drinking was not so straightforward. Throughout his life, Yates's alcoholism would prove to be his undoing, both personally and professionally. It exacerbated his bipolar disorder, and the toxic combination of alcohol with the strong prescription medication he took sparked a number of serious breakdowns that saw him hospitalized for lengthy periods. Yates never would accept the advice of the many doctors who treated him throughout his life, who urged him to stop drinking, dismissing them as quacks as he accepted yet another prescription for anti-psychotic medication. All of his personal relationships were adversely affected by his dependence on alcohol, with his already depressive tendencies heightened to an alarming degree when he drank to excess.

In terms of writers he respected, Yates was a devoted admirer of F. Scott Fitzgerald. Students in his classes recalled his declarations "now that is fucking good writing!" after reading aloud from *The Great Gatsby* (Bailey 2003, 326). Fitzgerald was Yates's hero; indeed, Yates went so far as to say that were it not for Fitzgerald he would never have become a writer. *Gatsby* was Yates's bible, the text he kept coming back to, and he always considered its final passages to be the best produced by any writer (600). He also regularly referred to Anton Chekov, Gustave Flaubert, and Ernest Hemingway in his classes as examples of masters of the craft of writing.

The critical reception of Yates's work was mixed. *Revolutionary Road* was almost universally hailed as a classic, and his short story collections were well-reviewed. *The Easter Parade* also drew positive reviews, although Yates personally dismissed this praise as he considered it to be one of his less successful books owing to its relative shortness and the speed with which he wrote it. His other work invariably attracted the category of review reserved for minor writers who know their strengths and never move beyond them. He was also the subject of what can only be described as a hatchet job from Anatole Broyard, once a friend of Yates's, who was a former writer-turned-reviewer for the *New York Times* and regularly used his position to settle scores with old friends and writers.

Yates would eventually pass away at a VA facility in Alabama in 1992. Interest in his writing, and even knowledge of who he was, dwindled to such an extent that by the time Blake Bailey approached the Yates family about writing a literary biography, his daughter Monica was moved to ask whether any of his books were still in print (most of them were not). Since then there has been something of a flurry of interest in Yates and his work. Vintage reissued all of his books, including the two short-story collections, in paperback in 2007 and 2008. Also in 2008, acclaimed director Sam Mendes finally brought a film adaptation of *Revolutionary Road* to screen, starring Kate Winslet and Leonardo DiCaprio. Both were nominated for several prestigious acting awards, and the movie brought a new audience to the novel and the work of Yates, with Winslet explicitly mentioning him in her Golden Globes acceptance speech. At the same time as this increase in popular interest in Yates, there has been a simultaneous emergence of academic interest in the writer, resulting in his works appearing on reading lists for university courses in Ireland, the UK, and the U.S., and he has also been the subject of a number of postgraduate theses and Ph.D. dissertations. Discussions of his writing have been included in books such as *Beyond the Grey Flannel Suit: Books From the 1950s That Made American Culture* (2004) by David Castronovo, and popped up in Catherine Jurca's *White Diaspora: The Suburb and the Twentieth-Century American Novel* (2001). More recently, he has been the subject of a monograph by Kate Charlton-Jones, *Dismembering the American Dream: The Life and Fiction of Richard Yates* (2014), one of the first full-length academic readings of Yates's work. And yet there is still something of a dearth of meaningful critical analysis on the work of Richard Yates, and no identifiable community of Yates scholars in the same vein as his heroes F. Scott Fitzgerald and Ernest Hemingway, both of whom have their own specific societies of devotees. The aim of this collection then, which is the first critical edition on Yates, is to bring together a range of voices and readings that will stimulate debate and open up new areas of analysis on his work.

The essays in this collection examine some of the major themes in Yates's writing and also make the case for his consideration as a significant American writer of the twentieth century. There is also a conscious effort to widen the analysis of Yates's writing to include his lesser-known works. Almost all of Yates's fiction is covered here in some fashion, signaling a shift in focus from the rightly lauded *Revolutionary Road*, which tends to be the center of most critical analyses of Yates. Two essays here concentrate specifically on *Revolutionary Road*. Joanna Wilson looks at the issues surrounding mental illness and ideas of control as manifested in the novel, while Rory McGinley takes the much-derided picture window at the center of the Wheelers' house and uses it to analyze suburban life in mid–twentieth century America. Beyond *Revolutionary Road*, Rona Cran maps the turbulent life of Emily Grimes in *The Easter Parade* to examine how location and place are important factors in the formation of identity. Chloé Avril interrogates Yates's use of disgust as a political tool in *Cold Spring Harbor*. Sophie A. Jones discusses the idea of autofiction and autobiography primarily in *Disturbing the Peace* and *A Special Providence*. Helen Turner provides a comparative reading of marriage and the American Dream in Yates's writing and that of his hero, F. Scott Fitzgerald. Another gap that this book addresses is the fact that Yates's short fiction is often overlooked in terms of critical discussion. Kate Charlton-Jones looks at the representation of children in his short stories. Also in relation to Yates's short stories, Karl Wood examines the representation and performance of masculinity. Finally, Rubén Cenamor discusses issues of masculinity in Yates's fiction and the writer's troubled, and possibly misunderstood, relationship with feminism.

Taken as a whole, this collection is not only an introduction for readers of Richard Yates's writing, one that demonstrates the breadth of his vision, but it also stimulates analysis of his fiction in new and different directions. These essays demonstrate that he is not just a chronicler of suburban fiction or of middle-class malaise or a masculinity crisis. These elements are all present in his writing, but Yates is a challenging writer of the American experience on many different levels that all deserve examination. At the time of writing, issues of American identity, of what it is to be "truly" American are front and center in national and international debates. A writer such as Richard Yates articulates the complexities of certain aspects of American identity in ways that are still all too relevant today. In his 1972 interview with *Ploughshares*, Yates admitted that

> in my more arrogant or petulant moments, I still think *Revolutionary Road* ought to be famous. I was sore as hell when it first went out of print [...] I can't honestly claim that my stuff has been neglected; it's probably received just about the degree of attention it deserves. I simply haven't published enough to expect more [Yates 2011].

In the subsequent years, Yates would eventually become more productive in terms of his fiction, although he would always feel that he had never fully realized his potential. In spite of this, it is hoped that the readers of these essays, and of the fiction of Richard Yates, will see things differently—that here is a writer who not only demands our attention, but is worthy of it.

BIBLIOGRAPHY

Bailey, Blake. 2003. "Poor Dick: Looking for the Real Richard Yates." *Harvard Review* Issue 25.
_____. 2003. *A Tragic Honesty: The Life and Work of Richard Yates.* New York: Picador.
Ford, Richard. 2000. "American Beauty (Circa 1955)." *The New York Times.* April 9. www.nytimes.com/2000/04/09/books/essay-american-beauty-circa-1955.html.
Towers, Robert. 1981. "Richard Yates and His Unhappy People." *The New York Times.* November 1. http://www.nytimes.com/1981/11/01/books/richard-yates-and-his-unhappy-people.html?pagewanted=all.
Yates, Richard. (1961) 2007. *Revolutionary Road.* London: Vintage.
_____. (1962) 2008. *Eleven Kinds of Loneliness.* London: Vintage.
_____. (1969) 2008. *A Special Providence.* London: Vintage.
_____. (1976) 2008. *The Easter Parade.* London: Vintage.
_____. 1985. *Lie Down in Darkness.* Ploughshares.
_____. 2011. "From the Archive: An Interview with Richard Yates." By DeWitt Henry and Geoffrey Clark. *Ploughshares* 37.3.

Revolutionary Road
Mental Illness and Socio-Political Control

JOANNA WILSON

In the 1960s a group of psychiatrists attacked their discipline from within, asserting that diagnoses of mental illness were nothing more than a repressive tool used to quash those who refused to conform to social norms. One of the most well-known of these men, labeled anti-psychiatrists, was Dr. R.D. Laing who claimed that "psychiatry can so easily be a technique of brainwashing, of inducing behavior that is adjusted" (1976, 12). These comments were made at a time when diagnoses of mental illness were reaching epidemic levels in America. A major contributing factor was the sheer volume of returning service personnel seeking treatment for what would now be termed Post Traumatic Stress Disorder and other mental illnesses following their exposure to the horrors of the Second World War.[1] Psychiatrist Thomas Szasz claimed that by 1961—the year *Revolutionary Road* was published—"seventeen million persons [were] allegedly suffering" (1961, 14), and furthermore, that "mental illness [was] said to be the nation's number one health problem" (13). Szasz's carefully worded comments belie his repudiation of these statistics, and his belief that diagnoses of mental illness were not medical issues, but rather could be reduced to "problems in living" (13). Szasz believed that, where one's personal beliefs or conduct were deemed socially undesirable (if one were a Communist, for example), one could easily be judged insane and removed in order to restore collective harmony. Psychiatrists like Szasz and Laing viewed psychiatric diagnoses not as neutral medical facts, but instead as a powerful tool of social and political enforcement and control.

Psychiatric debates like these would have been significant to Richard Yates, and these issues relentlessly permeate his fiction. Yates suffered from mental illness throughout his life, and it has been posited that this could have been inherited from his mother, known as Dookie, who (it is suspected) suffered

11

from manic depression like her son (Bailey 2004, 22). In his biography of Yates, Blake Bailey describes how as a youngster, the author would experience periodic episodes of "sudden brooding depression" (54–55) and later "psychotic episodes," for which he was prescribed a cocktail of drugs (375). On several occasions these nervous outbursts were so severe that Yates had to be sedated, like John Wilder in his 1975 novel *Disturbing the Peace*, and hospitalized in psychiatric institutions that Yates later scathingly referred to as "bughouses" (O'Nan 1999, 7). In his first novel, *Revolutionary Road*, Yates tackles this issue of mental health head-on. In tandem with the antipsychiatric rhetoric of the time, *Revolutionary Road* very clearly destabilizes and complicates the boundaries between what is considered sane and insane, and seeks to resituate these apparent medical issues within a socio-political context. Characters like John Givings and April Wheeler force the reader to examine the supposedly scientific nature of these diagnoses, and give credence to the possibility that, as Dana Cloud points out, mental illness was not a natural phenomenon but an artifice invented "so as to enable society to intervene in the private lives of subjects, regulating their behavior and disciplining them for their transgressions" (1998, 11). Cloud's assessment derives from Foucauldian observations that in centuries gone by "madness" was not "linked to medicine" and, therefore, was not understood to be treatable (Foucault 2001, 70). Instead the insane could be "mastered only by discipline and brutalizing" (70) and should be kept separate from society in squalid conditions for the preservation of common decency.

Even into the late eighteenth century, those suffering from conditions variously classified as "insane, alienated, deranged, demented [or] extravagant" were locked away in order to safeguard familial respectability, rather than for the treatment of inmates (62–63). Many parallels exist between the barbaric treatment of those incarcerated historically for their unusual conduct, and mental patients locked away in the postwar period, detained under the rubric of protection from self-harm as illustrated by Yates. Jeffrey Schaler has drawn attention to the unconstitutional nature of such detentions, arguing that "persons considered 'a threat to self and others' effectively lose their entitlement to a trial without being tried," and are thereby "deprived of liberty by the state when committed to a mental hospital" (2004, xvi). These misgivings are echoed directly in Yates's narrative when, during a discussion on John Givings's hospitalization, the narrator ponders "Could a man be forcibly committed to the nuthouse just like that? Didn't it sound fishy somehow, from a legal standpoint?" (64). *Revolutionary Road* steadfastly engages with these ideas, confronting and challenging readers' expectations and beliefs on the ethics and empirical reliability of psychiatric nosology, and the forcible treatment of patients. Yates's narrative ultimately creates a space for dialogue over the nature and human cost of a harmonious and functioning democratic society.

These are undoubtedly highly contentious issues. Responses to the various anti-psychiatric theories that espoused these ideas during the 1960s were often hostile, and sometimes even inflammatory, particularly from within the medical profession. Those who doubted the scientific nature of psychiatry were dubbed "extremely ignorant" by the editor of *Psychiatric Quarterly* in 1962 as part of a thinly veiled diatribe against Szasz (Bigelow 1962, 754), while Nick Crossley has claimed that Laing's 1967 anti-psychiatric work, *The Politics of Experience*, pushed him "beyond the bounds of [psychiatry's] acceptance" (1998, 884). One of the most outrageous pronouncements in *The Politics of Experience* posited that

> [t]here is no such condition as schizophrenia, but the label is a social fact and the social fact a political event. This political event occurring in the civil order of society, imposes definitions and consequences on the labelled person. It is a social prescription that rationalizes a set of social actions whereby the labelled person is annexed by others, who are legally sanctioned, medically empowered, and morally obliged, to become responsible for the person labelled [1977, 100].

These assertions represented a full-scale attack on empirical understandings of psychiatry as a bona fide scientific discipline, and the ethical implications of forced institutionalization. Laing's argument here explicitly positions psychiatry as a tool of social and political control. Despite protest from colleagues, the questions these anti-psychiatrists posed are important in challenging orthodox psychiatric methodologies that deny the historically relativist nature of what is considered normal—and therefore acceptable—and what is not.[2]

During times of political and/or social turbulence, individuals expressing dissatisfaction or challenging the nascent (and therefore unstable) social zeitgeist are often punished particularly harshly. This is, I argue, the predicament faced by the postwar suburban residents of *Revolutionary Road,* and of John Givings and April Wheeler in particular. Several critics have agreed, linking increasing levels of widespread anxiety and the spread of therapeutic discourse and psychiatric influence to times of rapid change. Aubry has commented that during the nineteenth century, despite "personal happiness [appearing to be] far more attainable than ever before," the "various conditions associated with modernity—the rise of crowded urban centers filled with strangers, the emergence of bewildering new high speed communication and transportation technologies, and a sense of disorientating and rapid social and cultural change—helped produce in the 1800s an outbreak of … 'nervous disorders'" (Aubry and Travis 2015, 7).

Industrialization and concurrent urbanization irrevocably changed the landscape of the 1800s, and this transformation resulted in increased psychological distress as citizens struggled to adjust at the same pace as the changes occurring around them. Though Aubry is referring to the process of industrial modernization that occurred in the late 1800s, I would argue that the post-Second World War era witnessed similar seismic shifts with regards to class, prolific de-urbanization, and concurrent mass suburbanization on the outskirts of the once great cities.

The rapid changes of the immediate postwar years such as the "thinning of community ties; [and the] vehement emphasis on the patriarchal nuclear family," along with a "sense of depersonalization and a loss of self in huge corporate workplaces and other mass institutions" (Herman 1995, 263) each contributed to a sense of anxious alienation and uncertainty in the years following the Second World War. This engendered a need to conform to precarious new social structures within communities in pursuit of personal security and well-being, in addition to the wild proliferation of reassuring therapeutic discourse throughout middle- to upper-class American culture. By utilizing the American suburbs as his setting Yates deftly reveals the mechanisms of social control that drive these conformist environments, and thereby exposes the illusory nature of freedom and autonomy existing therein.

Suburban communities were represented in starkly dichotomous ways by academics and the media in the post–Second World War era, hailed both as a familial idyll and as an inherently dangerous site asphyxiated by blandness and homogeneity. The iterative nature of mass-produced housing and lack of privacy between neighbors was viewed as anathema to individual well-being and subjective integrity. Researchers published texts warning of these various dangers. Among the most influential were William H. Whyte's *The Organization Man* and David Riesman's *The Lonely Crowd*. Whyte and Riesman were both sociologists concerned with the impact of the new corporate way of life coming to dominate America, including within the domestic sphere. Catherine Jurca has commented that the suburbs represented the "residential analogue of the corporation" (1999, 85), and Whyte and Riesman both feared that these environments, as part of a new corporate culture, were reducing the autonomy of individual Americans. Whyte argued that suburbanites were "imprisoned in Brotherhood" (2002, 365), required to maintain strict adherence to the codes of responsibility that consumed all areas of domestic life. Riesman argued that the combination of corporate success and suburbanization was leading to a growth in "other-directed" citizens. The term "other-directed" is defined by one's willingness to align oneself with a changeable greater good, by seeking guidance from those around oneself on how to behave. Riesman wrote that

> what is common to all other-directed people is that their contemporaries are the source of direction for the individual [including the mass media].... This source is of course 'internalized' in the sense that dependence on it for guidance in life is implanted early. The goals toward which the other-directed person strives shift with

that guidance: it is only the process of striving itself and the process of paying close attention to the signals from others that remain unaltered throughout life [1974, 21].

Rather than having a strong appreciation of heritage or an authoritarian background for behavioral guidance as in the previous periods (defined respectively by "tradition direction" (11) and "inner direction," (14)) this new individual sought instead to harmonize with the collective for the greater good, regardless of the changes and shifts this obliged him or her to comply with. This collective leaning "permits a close behavioral conformity" (21), and was undoubtedly useful as a tool for the development of a harmonious social cohesion during a tumultuous era. Nevertheless, Yates's narrative demonstrates how underneath the surface there existed an underground pervasive anxiety within the suburban populace over the growing dissatisfactions in their quotidian experience.

Many suburban residents remained essentially dissatisfied in spite of the improved living standards in these newly developed communities. Some felt a "deep, gnawing sense of personal emptiness" that has been connected to increased economic activity as citizens desperately sought the happiness promised in advertisements by spending newly disposable incomes on goods and services (Cushman 1995, 216). Yates's *Revolutionary Road* effectively demonstrates this dichotomy between the expectations upon residents to internalize and conform to the romanticized rhetoric of the suburbs, and the intrusive reality of ever increasing personal reservations. Frank Wheeler, Yates's protagonist in *Revolutionary Road*, is vocal in his derision of the suburbs, performing regular monologues in front of selected friends and family on the subject. During a party one evening he laments, "It's as if everybody'd made this tacit agreement to live in a state of total self-deception. The hell with reality! Let's have a whole bunch of cute little winding roads and cute little houses painted white and pink and baby blue; let's all be good consumers and have a lot of Togetherness and bring our children up in a bath of sentimentality" (Yates 2007, 66).

Frank's words are a direct and powerful critique of the postwar era, but they function solely as performance. The reader is aware that, although Frank may criticize his environment, he does so as a way to separate himself from those he views as inferior. As Jonathan Tran has argued, "people who live in the suburbs often fancy themselves better than suburbia, having themselves transcendentally adjudicated the emptiness of [its] false promises" (2009, 199). The reassurance that they, the Wheelers and their friends alone, "get-it" produces seductive "pleasures of knowing" (190), that bolster and gratify their sense of superiority. The satisfaction this produces functions as a form of pressure valve. Instead of protesting against the impossibility of personal fulfillment through consumption and suburban conformity, these citizens continue to thrive in their present environment without posing a threat to the longevity of the status quo through genuine dissent in the form of peaceful protest or violent resistance. In times of frustration, they engage in this kind of vapid discourse then return, sated, to their mundane lives within the community they verbally railed against.

Tran suggests that by allowing these episodes of performative dissent, the dominant ideology of the time is in fact secured: "It is the ruse of freedom … that makes life 'tolerable,' the condition *sin qua non* that renders life amongst the powers at least palatable, while disguising power's true genius" (195). The true genius of this dominant power is that no one can escape its mechanisms: one may recognize the social, political, and economic structures that bind and perpetuate it, but ultimately one cannot bypass it. John Givings, Yates's "real certified insane person" (Yates 2007, 182), is particularly important here: in his behavior he "reveals freedom to be an illusion, power everywhere, and institutionalization the ineluctable condition of being" (Tran 2009, 203). John's delight in his hospital clothing in particular reinforces this knowledge. Unlike Frank Wheeler, he knows the impossibility of genuine individual agency, and by refusing to take off his hospital dress, he functions as a signifier for the literal institutionalization of those inside the asylum, and the figurative cultural chains that bind those who are supposedly free.

Yates's narrator consistently undermines Frank's position as dissenter against the zeitgeist of the times throughout *Revolutionary Road*, reinforcing the performativity of his outbursts. This becomes especially apparent when April offers to relocate their family to Paris to escape the claustrophobic culture vacuum of postwar suburbia. Frank has, the narrative infers, always thought of himself as an intellectual with an as yet undiscovered artistic flair located "somewhere in the humanities" (Yates 2007, 22). April further bolsters this self-inflated confidence, based on nothing more than Frank's "performance in … beery, all-night talks" (22) and that he is "intelligent-looking" (7). However when April offers to take a full-time job overseas to allow Frank to pursue this "exceptional merit" (21) in a more conducive environment he baulks, fearing his inadequacies will be discovered and his masculinity destroyed by his wife's financial independence: "he was trying to conceal from her, if not from himself, that the plan had instantly frightened him" (109). The revelation of Frank's interior narrative here allows the reader privileged access to what is left unspoken throughout Yates's text, and it is quite often these tacit thought patterns within *Revolutionary Road* that are the most revealing of characters' true natures. The employment of free indirect speech swiftly undermines Frank's superficially blasé response—"he chuckled and shook his head"—to his wife's suggestion (109). Although Frank attempts to patronize his wife's plans, brushing them off as unrealistic and impractical, Yates's narrative perspective hints at Wheeler's true reason for pooh-poohing the suggested trip, allowing the reader superior access to Frank's motivations and destabilizing Wheeler's projected self-image. Yates's narrator continues, describing Frank's vision of himself "hunched in an egg-stained bathrobe, on an unmade bed, picking his nose" (109) in a Parisian apartment as April returns home from work looking polished, accomplished and professional in comparison, highlighting Frank's underlying awareness of his own shortcomings, and lack of belief in his constructed image of himself as the stifled intellectual.

Frank is almost uniquely concerned with constructing a façade of exceptionalism around himself and his family, but the narrative consistently demonstrates this to be nothing more than artifice. When the family move into their new suburban home, described as "a sweet little house" (29), Frank is instantly on the defensive, seeking to deflect the curse of suburban banality from their new family home. The Wheelers install a bookshelf directly in front of the picture window in order to give passers-by the impression that therein resides a learned and cultured family, set apart from their stultified neighbors: "their solid wall of books would take the curse off the picture window" (30). Again, the narrative undermines this surface image by continuing on to state that the only well-used corner of the living room was the "province of the television set" that alone "showed signs of pleasant human congress," and that the bookshelves remained neglected (31). The symbolism of the picture window is deeply important to the suburban context. These windows were a ubiquitous feature of post–Second World War housing, and were intended to create an airy space within the family home. Instead, social commentators of the time asserted that these large, front-facing windows created a disturbing continuity between hitherto discrete private and public spheres. Whyte sardonically claims that "even the architecture" of the suburbs has become "functional" in the "battle against loneliness" (2002, 352), including the picture window and a lack of doors inside the home. In addition, Spigel argues that the picture window embodied the "central dilemma" over "the increasingly blurred boundary between public and private worlds" (2001, 1) engendered by the suburban lifestyle and established within the built environment of the home a disturbing "continuity of interior and exterior" (32).

The transparency conferred by the prevalence of the picture window created a scene for the outsider looking in, framing the goings-on within the family home, particularly at night. This enforced a means of social control as neighbors could conduct fleeting surveillances of their peers, ensuring codes of conduct were being adhered to. The resultant liminal space was considered disconcerting by those who prioritized privacy and interiority. For Whyte, within the suburbs, "privacy has become clandestine" (2002, 353), and the desire to spend time alone is characterized as a worrying indication of "some inner neuroses" (352). The picture window therefore becomes a talisman for this new style of communal living with its emphasis on the presented image or façade. In his frustrated unhappiness with the unsatisfactory actuality of suburban life, Frank barely controls his violent desires to destroy the window, and by extension, the vacuous life it represents. The narrator describes his feelings of "sinking helplessly into the cushions and the papers and the bodies of his children like a man in quicksand" (Yates 2007, 56), and his struggle to restrain himself from "doing what suddenly seemed the only thing in the world he really wanted to do: pick […] up a chair and throw […] it through the picture window" (57). Frank's children and the cushions overwhelming him represent the ties of suburban adulthood; the cushions are indicative of the soft, affluent, and comfortable lifestyle that has sapped his masculine potency, whilst his children demand he occupy the role of responsible and attentive father, something Frank is chronically unable to do.

Frank's impulse control, along with his adherence to middle-class social ethics, protects him from a diagnosis of insanity. As Szasz argues, "we call people mentally ill when their personal conduct violates ethical, political, and social norms" (1973, 23). By carefully guarding his personal conduct and his constructed image, Frank seeks assimilation with his social milieu, thereby avoiding the pit falls that others like John Givings are trapped by. John Givings is a fundamentally revealing character, described by Jonathan Tran as a "dark hope, [the] one who authentically refuses the world's terms" (2009, 203) and pays the ultimate price for that refusal. John is labeled by April Wheeler as a "real certified insane person" (Yates 2007, 182) after he is confined to a mental hospital following a violent outburst in his parents' home. Despite their reservations about meeting John in person, the Wheelers find him to be "sort of nice … intelligent … brilliant…. He's the first person who's really seemed to know what we're talking about" (192). The Wheelers and John have a striking amount in common, particularly in their views on rampant consumerism and suburbanization. Indeed, during their first meeting John denounces the vapidity of the contemporary moment, arguing that

> you want to play house, you got to have a job. You want to play very *nice* house, very *sweet* house, then you have to get a job you don't like. Great. This is the way ninety-eight-point-nine per cent of the people work things out…. Anyone comes along and says "Whaddya do it for?" you can be pretty sure he's on a four-hour pass from the State funny-farm [187].

John's assertion cuts right to the core of capitalist ideology: in pursuit of consumer pleasure, one must sacrifice oneself in the process, submitting to a corporate lifestyle where one's individuality is consistently eroded in lieu of the greater economic good. In order to perpetuate this system, individuals who feel empty and unhappy because of their unfulfilling employment and lack of real autonomy must be persuaded, through advertising and other consumerist ideology, that pursuing material wealth and purchasing unnecessary or luxury goods (including, one could argue, the procurement of therapeutic services) will replace this inner sense of despair. Cushman has claimed that the postwar years were characterized by a "striving for self-liberation through the compulsive purchase and consumption of goods [and] experiences" (1995, 211), while Szasz asserts that "as soon as people have more money than they need ... they will expect to be 'happy'" (1961, 75). John's comments reveal the futility of this continual struggle for relentlessly deferred personal satisfaction.

Here John represents the Foucauldian madman. In *Madness and Civilization*, Michel Foucault argues that after the fifteenth century the figure of the madman was "no longer simply a ridiculous and familiar silhouette in the wings: [instead] he stands center stage as the guardian of truth" (2001, 11). Foucault continues, "if folly leads each man into a blindness where he is lost, the madman on the contrary, reminds each man of his truth" (11). R.D. Laing similarly argues in *The Divided Self* that "the cracked mind ... may let in light which does not enter the intact minds of many sane people whose minds are closed" (1976, 27).[3] Interpreted this way John—in his supposed madness—illuminates the power structures at play within democratic capitalist ideology, subversive knowledge that his sane contemporaries suppress. The insane, in this context, exist in order to reveal the anxieties and insecurities that permeate under the carefully constructed surface of postwar utopia, and which Yates frequently draws attention to through his utilization of free indirect style. During the postwar years it was understood that mental health "could be manufactured (and illness prevented) [when] the environmental conditions were favorable" (Herman 1995, 253), but John's diagnosis and violent incarceration demonstrate that anxieties over madness and sanity remain regardless, even in affluent and comfortable surroundings. John's supposed neuropathologies attest to the failure of this purported landscape of exceptionalism.[4]

Furthermore, although John's criticisms of the suburban context are in the same vein as Frank's, John is the one punished by the system for his refusal to assimilate into polite middle class society. The critical difference between the two men can be reduced to verbal performance versus authentic protest: while Frank may be an orator against the status quo, in reality he continues to co-operate with, and even reassert, the social codes at play in the suburban context through his daily behaviors. This contrast also explains the lack of sympathy the reader feels for either Frank or April Wheeler; despite the tragic end of the novel, the Wheelers exemplify falsehood, duplicity, and inauthenticity. Their excessive (and often absurd) dependence on a carefully crafted image of exceptionalism is continually demonstrated to be false by Yates's narrator, particularly in descriptions of their conduct. In an ultimately unsuccessful attempt to persuade April not to abort her third pregnancy, Frank begins a bizarre campaign of self-conscious behaviors intended to impress his wife with his affected masculine aura: "[W]hen he lit a cigarette in the dark he was careful to arrange his features in a virile frown before striking and cupping the flame (he knew, from having practiced this at the mirror of a blacked-out bathroom years ago, that it made a swift, intensely dramatic portrait)" (Yates 2007, 219).

Frank complements this vision of manhood by "keeping his voice low and resonant" (219), and being extra fastidious in his grooming to cultivate the required presentation. The reader, however, knows these are empty gestures. Yates's narrator continually employs free indirect style to convey the inner thoughts of the characters, and to destabilize their fabricated outward appearances. In the same passage, Frank admits to himself that "he found he had made all his molars ache by holding them clamped for too long for an effect of grim-jawed determination," and that he felt a "certain distaste" with himself "for having to resort to such methods" (219). Yates's narrative style therefore deftly deconstructs Frank's created image and, in sharp contrast, demonstrates the subversive reality that the "real certified insane person" is, in fact, the novel's most veracious character.

That John is punished so harshly for seeking to live outside social norms raises grave questions for the psychiatric profession. John's character forces readers to reassess the central assumption of psychiatry, and medicine more generally, that illnesses are scientific facts and immune from cultural or political influence. Aubry explains that, for those challenging this assumption, "categories designed to identify mental illnesses were not ... neutral scientific descriptions of actual pre-existing conditions" (Aubry and Travis 2015, 9). These pathologies are not, this argument maintains, simple and irreducible facts, but rather symptomatic of a wider and "coercive, ideologically motivated taxonomy designed to extend legitimacy and legal rights to those who adhered to social conventions while marginalizing those labelled deviant or subversive" (9). In this reading one could assert that psychiatric diagnoses are in fact being utilized to justify the incarceration of anyone who challenges or seeks to subvert dominant power structures. Givings is acutely aware of the political nature of his diagnosis, and his proclamation to Frank that "[a]nyone comes along and says 'Whaddya do it for?' you can be pretty sure he's on a four-hour pass from the State funny-farm" (Yates 2007, 187), clearly highlights this cognizance. John relishes his revelatory position, knowing that under the guise of insanity he is able to pose disruptive questions and behaviors that would otherwise be unthinkable, giving him an air of authenticity that others (the Wheelers and the Givingses alike) fundamentally lack. As a "madman" John is uniquely able to behave as he chooses. He has no credibility as an apparently free agent and so, ironically, his delineation as insane affords him a greater political freedom than his "sane" counterparts.

Givings takes full advantage of this dichotomous position as both the most free and simultaneously most overtly institutionalized in Yates's cast of characters. In addition to voicing his beliefs in the futility of personal happiness under the capitalist system, John delights in horrifying his mother with his flagrant disregard for manners and decorum, something Mrs. Givings is especially attuned to. He asks for a high-ball glass for sherry during a visit to the Wheelers' home, for example, which makes his mother "want [...] to die" (185), but most appalling, for Mrs. Givings, is John's choice of dress. Instead of wearing the "good shirts and trousers, his fine old tweed jacket with the leather elbows, [or] his cashmere sweater," John insists upon wearing his hospital clothes during visits home, which his mother deduces he does for "spite" (185). John's sartorial choices are inherently political. In his study of asylums and other institutions Erving Goffman argues that by stripping a new patient of their own clothes, cosmetics, and other belongings with which they routinely maintain their appearance, the institution (the asylum or otherwise) is deliberately causing a "personal defacement" (1968, 29), through which the patient's autonomous identity is directly threatened. The uniform provided by the institution in place of the patient's own clothes further diminishes their subjectivity, shared as it is with countless others, and constitutes a metaphorical violence against personhood. Cooper agrees, arguing that within the asylum "bodies are assiduously cared for but individual personalities are murdered" (1967, 109). In retaining his uniformed identity outside of the hospital setting, John is demonstrating this attack on his personal integrity, and the wider artifice of political freedom that exists within American society. By forcing others to view his institutionalized status, John is externalizing his position as the "sacrificial scapegoat" of the community (Szasz 1971, 267), forcing his neighbors to witness the violence they have sanctioned against him.

John deliberately upsets his mother who is devoted to the upkeep of the façade of respectability and polite gentility. Mrs. Givings is exposed throughout the narrative as extremely duplicitous, lacking integrity in place of a well-mannered veneer. At one point in the novel she bursts into tears, distraught over the loss of her youth and the possibilities that went with it. However, just as quickly as her tears began, they stop, and "all she had to do was go into the bathroom and blow her nose and wash her face and brush her hair" (Yates 2007, 165) to regain her outward composure. Her unsettled interiority is kept private; she goes downstairs "jauntily" (165) to join her husband, avoiding any discussion of her outburst. Again here the narrative utilizes free indirect style to expose the superficiality of Mrs. Givings's apparently sunny disposition. The reader is given a privileged insight into her thoughts and secret actions, and in order to increase the appearance of inauthenticity in her deportment, the narrator mimics her speech patterns, destroying her thin and nervously guarded attempts to keep her dissatisfaction with her life a secret. The narrator reports her "high, high hopes" and that she was "terribly, terribly, terribly disappointed" when the Wheelers declare their intention to move, mirroring her tendency toward unnecessary exaggerations (165). John's delight in tormenting his mother is a localized expression of his revulsion at the deluded nature of society that Frank Wheeler refers to as the "state of self-deception" (65). By relentlessly upsetting his mother, and insisting on dressing as a patient, John is accentuating his institutionalization by making it visible. By refusing to participate in the construction of a façade of freedom and acceptability he actively draws attention to the violence done to him by the social establishment.

In spite of his deliberate, and at times violent, rejection of polite society, John is in fact integral to its longevity. Aware of his inability to escape the cultural ideology of the time, John relishes his outward representations of the prison experienced by all. Instead of residing in a well-maintained suburban home and being confined by social codes of acceptability, John dramatizes the impossibility of ever fully relinquishing the chains of responsibility through his clearly visible punishment. In his rueful acceptance of the lunatic role, John in fact helps to perpetuate the system he seeks to protest against and ultimately to escape. David Cooper explains that our understanding of madness requires "others [to be] elected to live out the chaos that we refuse to confront in ourselves" (2001, *viii*) and this is precisely the function that John undertakes within *Revolutionary Road*. Instead of confronting and working to understand the contradictions Frank labels as "self-deceptions," (Yates 2007, 65) these doubts and anxieties are instead externalized onto the figure of the madman, who is punished for everyone's secret transgressions. Givings functions as a warning to readers of *Revolutionary Road* of what may happen if one steps out of line, while simultaneously demonstrating the impossibility of a real alternative. Either one is "imprisoned in Brotherhood" as Whyte puts it, or one is physically institutionalized as mad for protesting against the suffocating status quo.[5]

If John Givings's only alternative to this chronic and lifelong self-delusion is imprisonment in madness, April Wheeler's fate is perhaps even bleaker. April is fundamentally dissatisfied with her dual roles as wife and mother, viewing both as an impediment to her independence and the reason for her squandered potential. April rails against the traditional gendered behaviors expected of women during the post–Second World War years, feeling trapped and alienated from her inner desires. For Deborah Chalmers, "it is now acknowledged that the built environment [of suburbia] tends to institutionalize … patriarchal relations" (1997, 87), as these communities helped keep women isolated in the domestic space as housewives and mothers, whilst their men were free to commute to cities for work. Indeed, Robert Fishman has argued that "the new suburban house of the 1950s ... existed precisely to isolate women and the family from urban economic life" (1987, 195). April represents one of the myriad unfulfilled housewives of the postwar years, confined to their homes and gendered roles.

In 1963, two years after *Revolutionary Road* was first published, Betty Friedan's study into the overwhelming dissatisfaction with the domestic role experienced by housewives nationwide appeared. In *The Feminine Mystique* Friedan wrote that although women were leaving college earlier than ever before in an enthusiastic pursuit of marriage and motherhood, the domestic bliss they envisaged never materialized, and reality was far more grueling than anticipated.[6] Friedan interviewed many women who reported losing their sense of self in the process, with one saying she had

> never had any career ambitions. All I wanted was to get married and have four children. I love the kids and [my husband] and my home. There's no problem you can even put a name to. But I'm desperate. I begin to feel I have no personality. I'm a server of food and a putter-on of pants and a bedmaker, somebody to be called on when you want something. But who am I? [2010, 10].

This frightening and disorientating experience was repeated over and over again in Friedan's research, and was so prevalent and insidious that she referred to it as the "problem with no name" (11). April Wheeler is a classic example of Friedan's bored and unsatisfied suburban housewife. A reluctant mother and an unhappy wife, she deludes herself that she is satisfied and that her husband is the remarkable man she convinced herself he was when they met. By the end of the novel this façade crumbles, and she tells him that he is nothing more than a "wonderful talker" (Yates 2007, 290), cutting through Frank's deluded and rapidly eroding sense of self as an intellectual. April realizes the error she made in marrying Frank, understanding finally that she had acquiesced to a sentimental and overly romanticized vision of their initial flirtation that should have ended long ago, and now "all honesty, all truth, was ... far away [and] ... hopelessly unattainable" (304).

Many of the women Friedan interviewed confessed to feeling alone and deeply isolated in their distress, believing themselves to be defective. Unhappy housewives were "so ashamed to admit [their] dissatisfaction that [they] never knew how many other women shared it" (Friedan 2010, 8). Doctors and psychiatrists were overwhelmed with patients presenting with a vague but pervasive experience of discontent, depression, and anxiety, but despite their similar symptoms, women largely concealed these thoughts, shamed by the suffocating feeling that they were in some way to blame, or simply ungrateful, in spite of their comfortable and financially secure lives. Women who refused to accept their apparent biological destiny to be housewives and mothers were considered dubious and unnatural, and April Wheeler can be read as a classic example of repressed postwar femininity. For Friedan, women who sought an alternative path to motherhood and housewifery during the postwar years were interpreted as having rejected their fundamental "nature as women, which fulfils itself only through sexual passivity, acceptance of male domination, and nurturing motherhood" (60). April's desire to terminate her pregnancies is both repugnant and incomprehensible to Frank; her reluctance towards motherhood is understood as the "most unnatural of conjugal problems, a wife unwilling to bear [a] child" (Yates 2007, 220).

April's disinclination towards her role as housewife and mother is rationalized by Frank as symptomatic of psychiatric disturbance, brought on by her non-traditional upbringing. April was raised by a group of aunts. Her only relationship with her father was a fleeting and unsatisfactory one, while her mother gave her up as a new-born, only visiting occasionally during her formative years. Frank attempts to excuse April's supposedly unnatural reluctance to bear children, viewing it as intrinsically linked to these unorthodox early years: "[w]asn't it likely, after all, that a girl who'd known nothing but parental rejection from the time of her birth might develop an abiding reluctance to bear children?" (225). Concern over the lasting impact on children's mental health from unhealthy or unusual family dynamics was rife during the post–Second World War years, and Frank's comments draw direct attention to this anxiety. Deborah Weinstein has commented that postwar psychotherapists "attempted to use therapeutic means to address social ills such as delinquency and prejudice [by] attributing these ills to pathological families" (2013, 5), and that media outlets, particularly television, regularly disseminated diatribes on the dangers of overbearing mothers and absent fathers. In 1959, Weinstein writes, a television show was aired titled *The Fine Line* that starkly advised viewers that the "seeds of insanity could be lurking in your own home" (1). The family became the front line in the defense against madness, and Frank's rationale that April's childhood spent away from her parents and surrounded by women was responsible for her reluctance to engage fully with her gender-defined destiny would have been understandable to readers of Yates's text, published just two years after *The Fine Line* aired.

This threat posed by dysfunctional families was also understood as one of the root causes of mental disturbance by several anti-psychiatrists of the time. Cooper argued that a combination of overbearing, domineering mothers and weak or absent fathers resulted in mentally distressed offspring denied personal autonomy by their parents.[7] He argues that in the early stages of a child's development, "if the mother fails to generate the field of reciprocal action so that the infant learns how to affect her as another, the child will lack the precondition for the realization of his personal autonomy" (1970,

36). Essentially Cooper argues that children of these suffocating parents are prevented from developing a discrete identity, and must forever instead live lives alienated from their interiority. In Cooper's terms, this meant that the child's "being-for-others" dominates his "being-for-himself" (69), with catastrophic and long-term consequences. This flawed state of affairs led to a child who could only assert themselves through violent protest against the family unit, forceful resistance that Cooper interpreted as "the method in madness, the secret sense of nonsense" (65). In these cases, according to Cooper's theory, the child would thereafter be diagnosed as mentally ill, and removed to an institution predominantly as a way to reassert the familial balance of power.[8]

In this interpretation, the illness is not located within an aberrant individual, but instead positioned externally and generated incrementally through "disturbed group behavior" (43). Likewise, R.D. Laing and Aaron Esterson sought to demonstrate through interviews with British schizophrenics and their families that "the experience and behaviour of schizophrenics is much more socially intelligible than has come to be supposed by most psychiatrists" (1964, 13). Again, like Cooper, Laing and Esterson are suggesting that what has been understood as inchoate psychotic episodes are, in actuality, grounded in youngsters' logical protests against untenable domestic lives.[9]

Although these ideas are problematic, they offer a useful perspective on the familial relationships in *Revolutionary Road*.[10] John Givings's violent outburst at his parents' home can be interpreted under Cooper's rubric as a rational but drastic reaction to his mother's claustrophobic need for control. If John views the suburbs as a locus of delusion and conformity, his parents' home becomes representative of this oppressive ideology, especially since his mother is the local real estate agent, required to propagate the suburban dream to potential new clients on a daily basis. His destruction of their material possessions—"furniture, pictures off the wall, dishes" (63)—and the intentional destruction of his birth certificate both revolt against the identity she attempts to construct for him. After a walk with the Wheelers, and without his parents, April comments to her husband, "Wasn't it funny how much more sane [John] seemed once we got him away from her?" (2007, 192). John's behavior is markedly different when he spends time unsupervised with his peers, walking with the Wheelers, and when he is subject to his mother's fussing. When John is permitted to be autonomous, he becomes reasonable and calm, but when he is forced into the role of the tightly controlled child (despite being an adult), he lashes out both physically and verbally in an attempt to reassert his own identity as Cooper predicted.

In the Wheeler home, April's rejection of her role as a nurturing mother is, for Frank, a direct result of her unconventional family background. Going directly against what he believes to be the natural feminine attitude, Frank understands this rejection as a clear indication of mental instability. Although he is careful not to utter these words directly, the narrative voice tells us that "he managed to say it several times in several different ways" (Yates 2007, 224). Frank's desire to believe that his wife is ill rather than consider that she does not want to bear his children leads to his suggestion that she seek help from the medical profession in an attempt to resolve their conflict. He tries to persuade her, arguing that "assuming you *are* in some kind of emotional difficulty, assuming there *is* a problem of this sort, don't you see there *is* something we can do about it? ... We ought to have you see a psychiatrist" (226). That Frank's only response is to medicalize April's protest is telling. He ignores any other legitimate reason for April's unwillingness to have more children, and instead tells her she is mentally defective.

April understands the motivation behind this will to marginalize and discredit any protest against the expected behaviors of her gender. Indeed, she tells Shep Campbell after their tryst that her unhappiness with her life stems from "my own Emotional Problem" (257). The capitalized "E" and "P" demonstrate the ideology at play here. April's unhappiness is categorized as a personal issue; there is no recourse allowed to blame society for her sadness. Instead, she must internalize it, and bear the shame herself. It is she who is damaged and ungrateful for her lot, rather than the society that has let her down and forced her into a repressive and meaningless life and marriage. Cloud points out that "the therapeutic, as a situational, strategic discourse ... dislocates social and political conflicts onto individuals or families, privatizes the experience of oppression and possible modes of resistance to it, and translates political questions into psychological issues to be resolved through personal, psychological change" (1998, *xix*).

Simply put, it is far safer for the dominant socio-political ideology of the time to label unhappiness or dissatisfaction with the status quo as an emotional and, therefore, highly individualized problem, rather than conceding the legitimacy of these experiences as rooted in an unsatisfactory or repressive society. Rose argues that "the therapeutic worldview is a smoke and mirrors game, inviting people to believe their problems lie in themselves, not in the world, and encouraging them to adjust their attitudes rather than fight against injustice" (1990, 11). By removing those who defy social convention, all challenge is effectively negated, and the system can continue undisturbed.

Richard Ohmann has argued that this relentless shifting of blame back to the apparently flawed individual in order to protect the dominant ideology has a vibrant history in novels of this period. Texts like Sylvia Plath's *The Bell Jar*, for example, explicitly address this tension between private desires, and the pressures of social expectation with particular emphasis on the female experience (1983, 213). Plath's protagonist, Esther Greenwood, finds herself having to choose between motherhood and marriage, or a brilliant career. The mutually exclusive nature of these options is conjured up by the analogy of a fig tree upon which grow ripe fruits, each representing a different choice. Greenwood describes how upon "every branch, like a fat purple fig, a wonderful future beckoned and winked," but as she stalls in making her selection "the figs began to wrinkle and go black, and one by one, they plopped to the ground" (Plath 2005, 73). As a woman, Esther can choose only one destiny: wife and mother, or career woman, not both. Her gendered body roots her to restrictions that her male counterparts never have to submit to. Esther ends up in psychiatric care as a result of her recurrent mental distress related to this female dialectic. Ohmann summarizes this strategy of individualization by stating "myth, ideology, and experience" taught the newly enlarged middle-classes that nothing would bar the way to personal satisfaction through wealth and national exceptionalism during these golden years of American prosperity; therefore, "it was easy to nourish the suspicion that any perceived lack was one's own fault. If unhappy, one must be personally maladjusted ... social contradictions were easily displaced into images of personal illness" (1983, 212). The climax of *Revolutionary Road* reinforces this propensity to situate blame with the aberrant individual. When April Wheeler dies following a late-term home abortion attempt Frank, who had been determined to prevent the termination, exclaims "she did it to herself" (Yates 2007, 320), absolving himself and society more generally for its part in her decision and subsequent violent demise.

In 1948 American psychiatrist C.C. Burlingame ran for president of the American Psychiatric Association, and declared in a speech that psychiatry was a "scientific medical [discipline] and not one ... trying to tell everyone else what to do and how to live" (qtd. Herman 1995, 8). By the 1960s, however, this could no longer be taken for granted. Those labeled "Anti-Psychiatrists" challenged the prevailing opinion that psychiatry was a neutral and empirically driven discipline akin to medicine, arguing instead that the "theoretical concept" of mental illness functions in the same way that "deities" and "witches" did in the past (Szasz 1973, 12). In this radical reading, mental illnesses occupy a faux-explanatory function that aims to control the population, and punish transgressors for their perceived misdemeanors. In *Revolutionary Road*, both John Givings and April Wheeler represent the need to marginalize or discredit those who refuse to align themselves with the zeitgeist of the time. April recoils from motherhood, and chooses physical violence against the fetus inside her and her own (accidental?) death instead of submitting to the ideology of traditional gendered behaviors demanded of her by the postwar context. John Givings is punished for exposing the self-delusions and underlying anxieties hidden close to the surface of suburban life. Just as Foucault describes the post–fifteenth century madman as the "guardian of truth" (2001, 11), Givings forces his family and neighbors to confront the ruptures in the dominant ideology of the time, and revels in his knowledge of freedom as a false construct for both himself, his fellow inmates, and those outside the walls of the institution. Yates's novel, read alongside the theories of those skeptical of psychiatry's scientific neutrality, demands that we as readers probe the meaning of mental illness and ask ourselves where medicine ends, and socio-political control begins.[11]

NOTES

1. Herman claims that "the number of psychiatric cases in VA [Veteran Association] hospitals almost doubled between 1940 and 1948" and that by "April 1946 … forty-four thousand out of a total of seventy-four thousand" VA patients were suffering from "neuropsychiatric" disorders (1995, 242–243).

2. The term anti-psychiatry is an overly simplified taxonomy; in fact, Szasz "vehemently refuse[d]" the term, while David Cooper, who first used the term, came to "regret" having done so (Miller 2005, 19).

3. It is known that Laing was deeply impressed by Foucault's conception of madness, so much so that Laing (along with David Cooper) edited the first English translation of *Madness and Civilization* in 1961.

4. Robert Beauregard argues that "life in the suburbs was a mark of American exceptionalism and a model to which all nations could aspire" (2006, 6).

5. John Givings explicitly refers to himself and his fellow patients as "prisoners" (Yates 2007, 282), reinforcing this sense of physical and ideological incarceration.

6. Friedan states that a hundred years before "women had fought for higher education; now girls went to college to get a husband. By the mid-fifties, 60 per cent dropped out of college to marry, or because they were afraid too much education would be a marriage bar" (2010, 6).

7. In *Psychiatry and Anti-Psychiatry* Cooper asserted that, in families with schizophrenic children, "the mother of the patient was usually … emotionally manipulative, dominating, over-protective and yet at the same time rejecting person, while the father was seen as characteristically weak, passive, preoccupied, ill, or in some other sense 'absent'" (1970, 56). No mention is made of a reverse situation where the father might be the overdomineering parent, nor does Cooper acknowledge the gender bias inherent in his observations.

8. Cooper argued that, as a result of the child's protest, "His dramatic assumption of free personal agency threatened the whole structure of the family's existence: it had to be invalidated by the invention of an illness" (73).

9. Laing and Esterson's case study with the Abbott family reinforces Cooper's theory as noted above. In this instance the daughter of the family was understood to be unwell as a result of her desire for increased responsibility and autonomy, which the parents interpreted as "symptoms of illness" (1964, 32).

10. Although Cooper asserts that his case study (Eric V) is driven to madness by his overbearing family, many other explanations for his breakdown seem equally possible, including various neuropathologies. Nevertheless, this perspective seems to support what I believe Yates's narrative indicates in relation to Mrs. Givings and her son in particular. It is for this reason I have chosen to include Cooper's theory above.

11. It is important to note the problematic and often criticized nature of the anti-psychiatric arguments that have been utilized above; these are not taken at face value but are clearly applicable to Yates's narrative as demonstrated. Furthermore, this paper does not dispute or seek to diminish the often debilitating nature of mental illness as experienced by vast sections of the population, but simply seeks to question the political foundations of medical interventions into the psychiatric well-being of individuals.

BIBLIOGRAPHY

Aubry, Timothy, and Trysh Travis, eds. 2015. *Rethinking Therapeutic Culture*. Chicago: The University of Chicago Press.

Bailey, Blake. 2004. *A Tragic Honesty: the Life and Work of Richard Yates*. London: Methuen.

Beauregard, Robert. 2006. *When America Became Suburban*. Minneapolis: University of Minnesota Press.

Bigelow, N. 1962. "Sass for the Gander." *Psychiatric Quarterly* 36, no. 1–4: 754–66.

Chalmers, Deborah. 1997. "Women's Experience of Suburban Development." *Visions of Suburbia*. Ed. Roger Silverstone. London: Routledge.

Cooper, David. 1970. *Psychiatry and Anti-Psychiatry*. London: Paladin.

_____. 2001. "Introduction." In *Madness and Civilization: a History of Insanity in the Age of Reason* by Michel Foucault, trans. by Richard Howard. London: Routledge.

Crossley, Nick. 1998. "R.D. Laing and the British Anti-Psychiatry Movement: A Socio-Historical Analysis." *Social Science & Medicine* 47, no. 7: 877–889.

Cushman, Philip. 1995. *Constructing the Self, Constructing America: A Cultural History of Psychotherapy*. Cambridge, MA: Perseus Books.

Fishman, Robert. 1987. *Bourgeois Utopias: The Rise and Fall of Suburbia*. New York: Basic Books.

Foucault, Michel. 2001. *Madness and Civilization: A History of Insanity in the Age of Reason*. Translated by Richard Howard. London: Routledge.

Friedan, Betty. (1963) 2010. *The Feminine Mystique*. London: Penguin Books.

Goffman, Erving. 1968. *Asylums: Essays on the Social Situation of Mental Patients and Other Inmates*. London: Penguin Books.

Herman, Ellen. 1995. *The Romance of American Psychology: Political Culture in the Age of Experts*. Berkeley: University of California Press.

Jurca, Catherine. 1999. "The Sanctimonious Suburbanite: Sloan Wilson's the Man in the Gray Flannel Suit." *American Literary History* 11.1: 82–106.

Laing, R.D. 1976. *The Divided Self*. London: Penguin Books.

_____. 1977. *The Politics of Experience and the Bird of Paradise*. London: Penguin Books.

Miller, Gavin. 2005. *R.D. Laing*. Edinburgh: Edinburgh University Press.

Ohmann, Richard. 1983. "The Shaping of a Canon: U.S. Fiction 1960–1975." *Critical Inquiry* 10, no. 1: 199–223.

O'Nan, Stewart. 1999. "The Lost World of Richard Yates." *The Boston Review*. 1 October. https://bostonreview.net.

Plath, Sylvia. (1963) 2005. *The Bell Jar*. London: Faber and Faber

Riesman, David. 1974. *The Lonely Crowd*. London: Yale University Press.

Rose, Nikolas. 1990. *Governing the Soul: The Shaping of the Private Self*. London: Routledge.

Schaler, Jeffrey A. 2004. "Introduction." In *Szasz Under Fire: A Psychiatric Abolitionist Faces His Critics*. Edited by Jeffrey A. Schaler. Chicago: Open Court.

Spigel, Lynn. 2001. *Welcome to the Dreamhouse: Popular Media and the Postwar Suburbs*. Durham, NC: Duke University Press.

Szasz, Thomas. 1961. *The Myth of Mental Illness: Foundations of a Theory of Personal Conduct*. New York: Harper & Row.

_____. 1973. *Ideology and Insanity*. London: Calder & Boyars.

Tran, Jonathan. 2009. "The Otherness of Children as a Hint of an Outside: Michel Foucault, Richard Yates and Karl Barth on Suburban Life." *Theology and Sexuality* 15, no. 2: 189–209.

Weinstein, Deborah. 2013. *The Pathological Family: Postwar America and the Rise of Family Therapy*. London: Cornell University Press.

Whyte, William H. (1956) 2002. *The Organization Man*. Philadelphia: University of Pennsylvania Press.

Yates, Richard. (1961) 2007. *Revolutionary Road*. London: Vintage Books.

Playing Suburbia in *Revolutionary Road*

Rory McGinley

At the turn of the 21st century, the *New York Times* ran an article entitled "Suburbia Outgrows Its Image in the Arts" (Freedman 1999, 1) to lament the persistence of the cheerful utopia that is portrayed in the television series *Ozzie and Harriet* (1952–1966), and the materialistic anomie that is evident in the literature of Sloan Wilson and Rick Moody. Freedman's article maps out the polarities of domestic contentment or dystopian ennui that have endured and become synonymous with cultural interpretations of the topic. In a wider context, the author's recognition of this dialectic is concurrent with the discernible advancement in the re-assessment of fictional portrayals of suburbia. Critical studies, such as Catherine Jurca's (2001) *White Diaspora: The Suburb and the Twentieth-Century American Novel*, Robert Beuka's (2004) *SuburbiaNation: Reading Suburban Landscape in Twentieth Century American Film and Fiction*, and Jo Gill's (2013) *The Poetics of the American Suburbs* have shortened the gap between the polarities Freedman identifies to provide more nuanced readings of suburban fiction and poetry. Beuka's and Gill's work, particularly, has re-analyzed the persistence of symbolic and meta-phoric tropes, such as the picture window and the grey flannel suit, that have often been used to consolidate static and collective readings of the environ-ment. These approaches have provided a counterpoint to regressive inter-pretations of the era by divesting the setting of its stereotyped associations to engage in a more dynamic relationship with the suburban landscape. More broadly, their work has attempted to recover established suburban texts by challenging a critical consensus that has frequently viewed all fictional engagement with the setting in terms of indictment.

Since *Revolutionary Road* (1961), Richard Yates has, somewhat unfairly, been viewed as a critic of postwar suburbanization. Shortly after the novel's publication, *The Chicago Tribune* printed what would be the most damning review of the novel—within the mainstream periodicals at least—as Warren E. Preece (1961) voiced exasperation that another book had added its name to a very tired canon: "As one in a long and rapidly lengthening line of novels concerned with the problem of marriage in suburbia, this book offers nothing unusual" (129). Such a synopsis must still carry some weight. In the blurb to Vintage's (2007) recent re-issue, *Revolutionary Road* is described as an "evocative portrayal of the opulent desolation of the American suburbs," while Richard Price (2009) opens his introduction to a trio of Yates's books with the claim that he is the "poet laureate of the Age of Anxiety, a master purveyor of the crushed suburban life" (ix). This lingering categorization may have its genesis in the ideological context of *Revolutionary Road*'s release in which a number of works, including Lewis Mumford's (1961) *The City in History*, were upheld as sharp critiques of the setting.

In keeping with recent revisionist approaches to suburban narratives, this chapter will argue that a reading of *Revolutionary Road* from a perspective of suburban indictment severely limits and restricts our understanding of the topic in his seminal text. This chapter will take a similar approach to Robert Beuka in as much as the "troubled nature of suburban place identification [...] fuels the contentious social dynamics" (2004, 16) of suburban fiction: in *Revolutionary Road*, Yates upholds the proposition of suburbia as a troubling point of identification rather than as a metonymic location loaded with ideological association. To advance this argument, I will focus on the author's treatment of one of the most prominent symbols of suburbia: the picture window. Gill suggests that the picture window should be read more broadly within the context of the Cold War and its relationship to a "concomitant rethinking of boundaries between intimate, private spaces and shared, public domains" (2013, 134). This rethinking opens up a more complex interpretation of these boundaries in which suburbia is viewed as a "highly charged site for the testing and transgression of these binaries," while such reconsideration uncovers an environment that embraces a "marginal, liminal, in-between space" (Gill 2013, 156). The extent to which the picture window plays a prominent role in *Revolutionary Road* has been somewhat overlooked by Yatesian scholars, with Antonia Alexandra Mackay providing the only extended analysis of its presence in the novel. For Mackay, it represents a "highly complex architectural device," which, in turn, "creates a barrier between inside and outside, and a transparency between interior and exterior" (2013, 131). Just as the picture window heightens notions of observation and privacy, it sets up various composite points of self-reflexivity within the text. My analysis builds on this notion to argue that Yates's deployment of the trope should also be viewed in connection to, and as an extension of, the theme of performativity in the novel.[1] The heightened valorization of the suburban household results in the increased theatricality of the living room, caused by the frequent exposure of the Wheelers' picture window. Yates's treatment of such will be shown to complicate the connection between suburban inhabitants and one of its most recognizable symbols: it transcends a separation of private and public spaces to set up a far more dynamic relationship with the suburban environment.

Postwar Suburbia

Even though America had experienced a similar demographic repositioning after World War I, suburban expansion post–World War II was unprecedented in terms of volume and its signification of broader cultural and political change—an ideological push towards the domestic and restratification of gender roles; legislation that prioritized GI housing; Cold War containment and concerns over privacy. The publication of Yates's first novel arrived at the endpoint of suburbia's most rapid expansion in the postwar period. Between 1934 and 1954 the suburban population increased by 75 percent, while the country's overall rose by only 25 percent (Donaldson 1969, 4). If the baby-boom following the end of World War II necessitated an upsurge in new houses across the country, suburban plots, with the promise of extra space, became the perfect location: of the 13 million homes constructed from 1950 to 1960, 11 million were built in the suburbs, a scale that placed suburban growth at six times that of cities (Creadick 2010, 123). The Servicemen's Readjustment Act (1944)—commonly known as the G.I. Bill—which created the Veterans Administration mortgage program, signified the most important step in the development of housing, as it allowed more potentially high-risk clients, such as young homebuyers without guaranteed long-term financial security, to purchase homes. By 1960, the total number of suburbanites reached approximately 50 million; five years later it soared above 60 million (Donaldson 1969, 4).

Such a vast demographic repositioning did not come without a barrage of cultural criticism and, notably, a recurrence of the critiques levied at suburbia in the 1920s. Mumford's (1961) *The City in History*, awarded the National Book Prize that year, claimed postwar suburbanization had produced a "low-grade uniform environment from which escape is impossible" (175). His critique condemned suburban estates for their unvarying developments in which little regional differentiation could be made. Claims of spatial claustrophobia extended to the particular structural make-up of suburban homes, particularly the lack of distinction between public and private spaces in new housing estates. A large part of this criticism drew from sheer numbers. In *The Suburban Myth*, Scott Donaldson (1969) cites the example of Irving, Texas, which saw its population rise from 2,621 in 1950 to 45,489 in 1960, underlining the scale of acceleration of suburbanites finding residence in self-contained pockets of land (70). On top of the uniform profile of the developments, there was said to be little space between houses, giving rise to the close proximity of inhabitants. In *The Organization Man*, Whyte (1956) warns that the "more accustomed one becomes to the homogeneity, the more sensitized is he to the small differences" (312). In Levittown, Pennsylvania, Whyte asserted residents were becoming increasingly cognizant of any modification to the standard ranch-house design: in one illustration, he observes how one owner mounted a small gargoyle on top of his house, an act which resulted in residents driving out of their way to show visitors (312).

Privacy and Suburbia

Privacy became a central tenet and concern of postwar American culture, yet there remained confusion as to how it could be achieved. Deborah Nelson (2002) suggests that its cultural deployment always carried with it a concomitant association in Cold War Studies, where ambivalence surrounding privacy arrived hand-in-hand with the "ubiquitous" (xxi) metaphor of containment. Nelson (2002) traces the term to the 1947 foreign policy directive outlined by George Kennan, in which the diplomat detailed the threat of prospective Soviet expansion set against the libertarian domestic ideology of the U.S. This set up a diametric opposition between the countries' respective domestic ideologies: "The sanctity of the private sphere was generally perceived to be the most significant point of contrast between the two regimes. The potency of American democracy in cold war rhetoric was, therefore, not its cultivation of a vibrant and free public discourse but its vigilant protection of private autonomy" (Nelson 2002, xiii).

This distinction came to the public fore in the infamous Kitchen Debate between Russian Premier Nikita Khrushchev and American Vice President Richard Nixon in 1959. Fashioned as an impromptu meeting in the display kitchen of a split-level suburban home, political debate was discarded as Nixon extolled the virtues of the American household. Discussing the respective merits of household commodities, Nixon upheld the argument that the American lifestyle remained true to ideals of freedom in which the suburban home, with its designated areas for husband and wife, plus the technological appliances available, stood as a realization of domestic liberty. Nixon proclaimed: "To us, diversity, the right to choose [...] is the most important thing. We don't have one decision made at the top by one government official[....] We have many different manufacturers and many different kinds of washing machines so that the housewives have a choice" (May 1998, 17).

Nixon's carefully worded speech steered attention from the perceived vulnerability of the American military to the security, freedom, and enfranchisement of those living in a model suburban household (18). The distillation of the Cold War conflict was thus brought squarely to the domestic realm, with Malvina Lindsay (1959) of *The Washington Post and Times Herald* stating in a front-page headline, "U.S. Typical Home Enters Cold War" the following day (1). The perceived freedom (and at the same time, privacy) afforded to American suburban residents provided a political message antipodal to the totalitarianism of the Soviet Union. As with the demographic movement of the 1920s, suburban dispersal, set against the city, offered something of a quest towards a pastoral ideal to offer residents space and retreat.

Yet this preoccupation with privacy also became one of the central concerns of suburban criticism, with the lack of space afforded framed within a Cold War narrative of containment. Nelson comments, "The suburban home was supposed to offer the opportunity to live out the democratic dream of privacy in postwar America. And yet, at the same time, true to the paradox of postwar privacy, suburban homes in the earliest and most influential accounts of suburban life were associated with a profound deprivation of privacy as well" (2002, 85).

Suburbia, then, occupied a somewhat liminal position as a place of retreat—in that it represented dispersal from more heavily populated urban areas—and one that also brought with it a foreclosing of privacy. Mackay suggests that the enclosed form of suburban houses, with areas designated to instill a sense of togetherness, also heightened feelings of insularity: "Indeed, the very lay-out of suburban spaces meant family space and family 'togetherness' functioned as a form of containment, where private spaces (the home) served only one purpose—to protect from the outside (the public space) and therefore segregate any outside influence, in effect containing the inhabitants" (2013, 131).

As such, readings of the claustrophobic nature of suburbia condensed and centered upon some of its most salient aesthetic features that were seen to contribute to issues of containment, perhaps none more so than the picture window (Beuka 2004, 258). Structurally, suburban homes were designed with picture windows holding a prominent, street level position, contrasting with the vertical form of urban apartments. As Creadick (2010) notes, the picture window became a central part of this narrative of containment due to its dual aspects of "proximity and exposure" (124), ocular features John Keats (1956) explored and used as the title metaphor in *The Crack in the Picture Window*.

Consumable and Visible Symbols

A cohort of postwar suburban critics has recognized the significance and persistence of the metaphoric attachment to the picture window. Bennett Berger's (1961) *The Myth of Suburbia* suggested images of suburbia had been evoked primarily to denote a consumable "way of life for the non-suburban public" (315). Berger adds, "one source of the peculiar susceptibility of suburbia to the manufacture of myth is the fact a large supply of visible symbols are ready at hand" (315) and identifies patios, barbecues, lawnmowers and picture windows as the most malleable and frequently referenced images. Benjamin Stroud (2009) advocates a similar position in terms of the residual significance of such symbols and argues that the image of the suburb has subsumed a more complex reading of the environment, where interpretations begin from "afar as a collective while fixing on only a few details, like barbecues and picture windows, to underscore a similarity of manner" (18). Drawing on humanistic geography, Beuka (2004) believes a more dynamic reading of suburbia would exist if we could separate the idea of the environment from its reality, arguing that a "reductive, two-dimensional vision" has persisted because of an investment in "symbolic meanings" (5).

Just as the picture window remains a representative trope of suburban imagery—and one which has been consistently latched on to in suburban commentaries and critiques—it has been re-defined in a more fluid context of observation and as a device, or aperture, for the suburbanite to reflect on their identity. For Jo Gill (2013), one of the first articulations of this can be found in the work of Phyllis McGinley. Referring to her poem "View from a Suburban Window," taken from the collection *Times Three: Selected Verse from Three Decades with Seventy New Poems*, McGinley (1960) situates the suburban window as a reciprocal point of interior and external vision. There is a panoptical element to the vantage point of the suburban viewer when positioned at the window, while it also functions as a point of contemplation, a "lens or mirror through which the suburbanite studies herself and the abstract conditions of her own existence" (Gill 2013, 104). This reading of the picture window instates a more spatially conscious analysis of its function within the suburban home, and understands it to hold a far more active relationship with the viewer. Updike (1963), similarly, delineates the lack of privacy in his poetry collection *Telephone Poles and Other Poems*. In "Suburban Madrigal," which appeared in *The New Yorker* in 1959, each observation occurs from the vantage point of a window. The intense intimacy of this becomes apparent when the narrator speaks of placing his car in front of his neighbor's house, an act that would "violate his windows" (Updike 1959, 100).

(No) Escaping the Picture Window

Frank and April Wheeler's introduction to the Revolutionary Hills Estate does little to suggest their environment will be distinguishable from the standardized suburban milieu as Yates ([1961] 2007) quickly outlines many of the established aesthetic features, with sustained focus on the picture window. While the estate agent, Mrs. Givings, stresses that their house is disconnected from the great hulking split-levels in the estate, the Wheelers' habitat is constructed as prototypically suburban. The couple are shown around a "sweet little house" with a "sweet little setting," the development is "simple" with "clean lines" and "good lawns" that are "marvelous for children" (29). We are told that their house has a "prim suburban look" with an "all too-symmetrical living room," and as a final allegorical signpost to the reader, an "outsized picture window" (30). Inside, the description moves on to the neatly-aligned floorboards, perfectly-balanced doors, and flawless bathroom. The window increasingly governs Yates's description; April states, "Of course it does have the picture window; I guess there's no escaping that," to which Frank replies: "I guess not. Still, I don't suppose one picture window is necessarily going to destroy our personalities" (30). Here, the affective power of the picture window is implied, along with its encaging presence. The narration suggests its reflective potential too, as the "outsized central window" stares "like a big black mirror" (29). Such a description intimates its reflectivity yet it is complicated by the fact that the window is darkened, which relates, in part, to its foreboding aesthetic appearance, but also seems to suggest the gaze will be transmitted from outside the house (almost like a one-way police mirror).

The initial description of the picture window in *Revolutionary Road* establishes its reflective power and in turn outlines how it will hold an active presence in the Wheelers' household. This is apparent in its subsequent mention in the text, when Frank reads the newspaper cartoons to his children: "When the funnies were finished at last he struggled to his feet, quietly gasping, and stood for several minutes in the middle of the carpet, making tight fists in his pocket to restrain himself from doing what suddenly seemed the only thing in the world he really and truly wanted to do: picking up a chair and throwing it at the picture window" (56–7).

Here, Frank's realization that he is playing the role of prototypical suburban husband compels him to shatter the image by breaking the picture window. This current of reflection is complicated shortly after when Frank returns home from his affair with Maureen Grube. Approaching the house, Frank is met with a romanticized suburban scene as April hurries from the kitchen to wait for her husband in the carport, clothed in a cocktail dress, and enters the house to be greeted by a cake and the chorus of happy birthday from his wife and children. The image has been framed with the knowledge that when Frank nears the house he notices the "curtains were drawn in the picture window" (102), thus obscuring the vision of domestic harmony that awaits him. As Mackay observes, the drawn curtains have a dual effect on Frank: they cut him off from "surveying the family unit within the home and distancing himself from family togetherness," yet at the same time also offer "him a reflection of his own subjectivity (a blankness)—a constant site of tension for his character" (2013, 131). This tension uncovers Frank's inability to reconcile the reflection of his suburban self (as suburban father reading to his children) with that of his subsequent dislocation from the role.

This dislocation and fluidity of reflection continues throughout the novel as Frank uses the picture window to visualize a series of different images:

> Catching sight of his walking reflection in the picture window, he had to admit that his appearance was not yet as accomplished as hers [127].
> Sometimes ... he could glare at the window and see the brave beginnings of a personage [127].

When April mentions Frank is fluent in French, he ponders:

> If he'd looked at the window at that moment he would have seen the picture of a frightened liar [131].

And finally, after their meeting with John Givings:

> He took a deep drink, standing at the picture window and watching the last of the sunset. "I guess that means we're as crazy as he is" [192].

These four points of reflection each operate on separate levels. In the first, Frank considers it in relation to his wife. In the second he traces the vague contours of a self, followed by a reflection of insincerity in the third and, finally, in comparison to John Givings.

Living Room as Theater

This focus on the picture window and its pervasive power in the household becomes increasingly pronounced as the Wheelers begin to react to its encaging presence. Various critics have noted the theatrical current that runs throughout *Revolutionary Road*: David Castronovo and Steven Goldleaf (1996) connect this to Erving Goffman's (1959) *The Presentation of Self in Everyday Life*. For the critics, Yates and Goffman analyze the idea of social performance, public behavior and the projection of self (Castronovo and Goldleaf 1996, 16). Kate Charlton-Jones (2014), similarly, believes Yates's fiction displays a "more complex view of selfhood that is perhaps subconsciously informed by the likes of Mead and Erving Goffman" (77). Ola Jönsson (2014), meanwhile, posits that the opening performance "becomes an extended metaphor in the novel for the strictly regulated 'script' or code of affects and behavior in Revolutionary Hill, where characters play designated roles of husbands, wives, parents" (59–60). If the Laurel Players performance at the beginning sets the novel for the theatrical undertones of its central characters, notions of performance are heightened when the Wheelers' suburban home begins to displace the theater as the arena in which they begin to exhibit and negotiate their roles. As with the picture window, the television became a malleable symbol of the postwar suburban environment and one that came to signify an intrusion into personal space. Mumford ([1961] 2006) warned of such an intrusion in *The City in History*, predicting that that "within the cabin of darkness before a television set … every part of this life … will come under supervision" (299). Updike ([1960] 2006) adopts a similar critique in *Rabbit, Run*, and uses imagery that echoes Mumford's. Moving through Wilbur Street at the beginning of the novel, Rabbit looks through the "broad living-room windows," which uncover the "silver patch of a television set the warm bulbs burning in kitchens, like fires at the backs of caves" (Updike 2006, 15). Rabbit's vision assimilates the picture window with that of the television, coordinating the two as viable points of observation and supervision. Lynn Spigel (1997) outlines this connection from a slightly different angle when looking at the metaphors of postwar domesticity to argue that the suburban home increasingly became characterized by the "theatrical quality of everyday life" (220). Spigel furthers this to suggest that theatricality stood as the key metaphor for defining suburban family relations: "the husband may be an audience to the wife, or the wife to the husband, or the older child to both" (220). This theatricality is, in part, attributable to the very artifice on which suburban life is founded, where would-be suburbanites left multiethnic or mixed-class urban areas to pursue a lifestyle in a "prefabricated social setting" (221). Spigel broadens this connection to argue that home magazines often featured suburban households with "glamorous backgrounds" that were appropriate for enacting "spectacular scenes" (221). This was often visualized by adopting features of the homes of Hollywood celebrities to further "enrich its theatrical status" (221). Creadick (2010) meanwhile, designates an even stronger connection, arguing that "television effectively extended the eye of the 'picture window' across the nation" (125). The picture window had allowed for a gaze "knowing, yet passive […] critical, but also covetous," a practice that had extended to and allowed the normalization of television viewing, of "watching and being watched" (125). This was in part due to the remarkable rise of televisions within American family life: in 1946, 0.02 percent of American households owned a television; by 1960, this figure had reached almost 90 percent (Creadick 2010, 5).

We see on two levels how Yates constructs the living room as the platform on which these scenes will be played out. Firstly, the passage to the

Wheelers' front door has been rendered inaccessible by the poor condition of the stone path (45). As such, visitors must enter via the kitchen, meaning the front of the house holds no practical purpose other than spectacle. As Charlton-Jones (2014) notes, the path provides a "literal means by which the Wheelers' friends will cross their threshold, a literal means by which the Wheelers' suburban performances can be enacted" (26). Remaining incomplete for the entirety of the text, the path is both a narrative indicator of the "fractured nature" (Charlton-Jones 2014, 26) of the household and one that denotes a defective point of observation: with the Wheelers unable to view their visitors as they approach the house, they must enter through the kitchen door.[2] Rendered inaccessible by the broken passageway, the living room's interiority is valorized—for both spectator and inhabitants—with its furnishings, on first description, fashioned as props. On their first viewing of the house, April switches on the light and the "living room exploded into clarity. In the first shock of light it seemed to be floating, all its contents adrift" (Yates 2007, 30). The room has a "tentative look," as the wall of books obediently competes with the picture window, yet "might as well have been a lending library" (31). The furnishings, "chairs, coffee table, floor lamp and desk, they stood together like items arbitrarily grouped for auction" (31). Their arbitrariness and tentative form yields similarities with props compiled for a stage production, comparable to a mise-en-scène, while the glaring light illuminates the room for external observation. Nelson (2002) identifies this notion of the suburban home's plasticity in Anne Sexton's poem "Self in 1958," where the speaker opens with the lines "I live in a doll's house with four chairs, a counterfeit table, a flat roof and a big front door" (88). The depersonalized furniture results in an unavoidable paradox where, although the house is "divorced from the public" it is "neither private nor individual" (Nelson 2002, 88). The arbitrary arrangement of the Wheelers' living room also picks up on the difference between a lived-in home and occupied house, a theme of suburban literature that stretches back to Theodore Dreiser's (1900) *Sister Carrie* and Sinclair Lewis's (1922) *Babbitt*. This discordance is outlined at the very beginning of Lewis's text when we are told that what Babbitt encounters in Lewis' novel is a disjuncture, as Catherine Jurca (2001) identifies, that uncovers the difference between "material and spiritual shelter, structure and sentiment, suburban house and home" (4).

The living room as theatrical arena thus serves as the backdrop to the Wheelers playing out a number of highly-stylized performances. Immediately prior to proposing the Parisian move, April apologizes for her behavior (the reader is aware that this is done solely as a pretense for what is to come). The scene runs:

> "Forgive you for what, April?" They were standing alone on the living room carpet, and she took a tentative step toward him.

"Oh, for everything," she said. "For everything. The way I was all weekend. The way I've been ever since I got mixed up in that awful play. Oh, I've got so much to tell you, and I've got the most wonderful *plan*, Frank. Listen" [105].

April's movement, the tentative step, is framed as a succinct stage direction, while her apology is not articulated in the text: the scene cuts directly to Frank's question. The interconnection between *The Petrified Forest* and the living room is denoted by the direct reference to her role in the play, and April's lilting, excited lines are delivered in a performative manner. While Frank identifies the picture window as a means of reflection and subjectivity, April utilizes the living room as a stage, and it is an environment in which she gradually becomes the more dominant of the two. During the heated argument concerning the prospect of abortion, the passage runs:

She began to move stiffly around the living room in a way that always meant trouble. He had learned early in the courtship, or the campaign, that this room was the worst possible place for getting his points across. All the objects revealed in the merciless stare of its hundred-watt light bulbs seemed to support her argument; and more than once, on hot nights like this, their cumulative effect had threatened to topple the whole intricate structure of his advantage: the furniture that had never settled down and never would, the shelves on shelves of unread or half-read or read-and-forgotten books that had always been supposed to make such a difference and never had; the loathsome, gloating maw of the television set [221].

There is an acknowledgment firstly, that April has retained the living room as a site of control. The illuminated room recalls the imagery associated with the final rehearsal of *The Petrified Forest*, where the "blinking" floodlights engulf the empty auditorium (3). Yates recalls the objects he outlines in the initial mise-en-scène, items that remain disconnected from the rest of the room. The theatrical, framed tone of the description is rounded off with a reference to the television, which is given an anthropomorphic profile in its mocking presence: a concession, in part, to the commodification of the Wheelers' household and its assimilation with every other suburban home. On a figurative level, the "gloating maw" also suggests a form of mimicry, as if the Wheelers are playing out roles in a TV show.

Kitchen v. Living Room

If the living room is a site in which Frank senses he is losing control, we see how he redirects and extends the platform of performance. As Nelson observes, the kitchen (despite Nixon's assertion that autonomy resides in housewives' freedom to choose their electrical appliances) became an intense site of surveillance and containment for women (2002, 87). Betty Friedan (1963), of course, outlined the vacuity of the suburban housewife's role in the

1950s, relating the enclosing space of the kitchen to the stifling of female identity. This can, in part, be attributed to the spatial configuration of suburban homes, with the open-plan set-up allowing for no form of privacy. Prototypical suburban kitchens were designed to be both accessible to the rest of the house and set up in such a way that housewives could do their washing up and cooking with a minimum of movement (Gill 2014, 64).

In *Revolutionary Road*, Frank begins to gravitate towards the kitchen in an attempt to regain some semblance of authority in the text. When April first informs Frank she is pregnant, the scene is played out in the kitchen; the description is focalized from Frank's gaze: "He found her in the same tense, high-shouldered way she had paced the stage in the second act of *The Petrified Forest*. From the living room came the muffled strains of horn and xylophone, interspersed with the shrieks of midget voices; the children were watching an animated cartoon on television" (206).

Again, the performative intonation is conveyed through the television sounds emanating from the living room and there is a further recall of the theater production. Displaced from the living room, April's image is recast in much the same light as her shaky performance during *The Petrified Forest*. This breakage of front is furthered in the subsequent image and directly connected to that of her responsibilities as a housewife: "the perfection of her curtain-call smile began to blur and moisten into a wrinkled grimace of despair and her breathing became as loud as the boiling vegetables on the stove" (206). There is a direct assimilation, too, with the image we are presented when Frank visits April backstage, at which point he observes the "small replica of her curtain-call smile" (15). Backstage and in the kitchen, April's performance is hesitant, her curtain-call smile unconvincing. Shortly after, when Frank finds the syringe that April intends to use for the abortion, he carries the package "through the living room, swiftly past the place where the children watched their cartoon [...] and into the kitchen" (209). Once more, note the prominence of the living room and television, yet the action is displaced from here—and thus obscured from observation—as Frank marches purposefully to the kitchen with the syringe. Prop in hand, the scene, played out at a distance from the picture window, marks the point in which Frank re-establishes some semblance of authority in the text. The kitchen, existing as both a contradictory realization of the housewifery freedom and an enclosing space of femininity, is centered, swiftly, to the latter with Frank's possession of the syringe, a symbolic move that marks a clear domestication of April's sexuality.

The close of the novel contains two further allusions to the living room and its connection to the picture window, both of which are worthy of consideration. The first occurs when Jennifer views her parents from the garden: "She walked up close to the picture window and was peeking inside. They were still sitting on the sofa, leaning a little toward each other, and her mother was nodding and her father was talking. It was funny to see his hands making little gestures in the air and his mouth moving and moving, with no sound coming out" (236). This scene has strong echoes of *The Great Gatsby* when Nick observes Tom and Daisy after Myrtle's death in Fitzgerald's novel: "He was talking intently across the table at her and in his earnestness his hand had fallen upon and covered her own. Once in a while she looked up at him and nodded in an agreement[....] There was an unmistakable air of natural intimacy about the picture and anybody would have said that they were conspiring together" (1925, 113).

Nick views the pair from the pantry window as they sit opposite each other at the kitchen table and, like the scene in *Revolutionary Road*, the husband actively outlines instructions. We can detect, too, the contrasting awareness of both narrators: Jennifer only has the capacity to view their interaction as "funny" due to the fact her parents are muted, while Nick Carraway—so infamously within and without—is able to pick up on the closeness of Tom and Daisy at this point and, cognizant as to what has come before, the conspiratorial nature of the scene. Flaubert's presence, too, lives on in the control exhibited in the third person narrative as it repositions itself, yet maintains the requisite distance from both characters. This is the only time the point of observation is transferred as we view Frank and April arguing from outside of the house—prior to this, the reader is a silent and invisible presence within the living room. Significantly, it is Jennifer, (recall Spigel's definition of the theatricality of the suburban household) who observes her parents. While before the television denoted a metonymic and theatrical backdrop to their arguments, Frank and April become characters controlled by notions of performance yet seem without any script to follow. The reader (or their daughter) is not privileged with any dialogue; all we are afforded is the vision of two gesturing silhouettes.

During their final argument, Frank struggles to deal with April's hysteria and, as with the previous scene, there is a further disintegration in the code of performance:

> He wondered what to do. In the movies, when women got hysterical like this, men slapped them until they stopped; but the men in the movies were always calm enough themselves to make it clear what the slapping was for. He wasn't. He wasn't, in fact, able to do anything at all but stand there and watch, foolishly opening and shutting his mouth [290].

Without a designated role to follow—how does the suburban sitcom Dad comfort a hysterical wife?—Frank searches for a cinematic reference point to guide his actions. The final break from performance is realized as Frank voices what is, up until this point, his only sincere line in the novel, as indicated in Yates's use of omniscient narrative: "The great pressure that began to be eased inside him now, as he slowly and quietly intoned his next words, made it seem that this was a cleaner breakthrough into truth than any he had ever made before" (291). Note how "seem" acts as a crucial qualifier to the scene too; at this point he believes a point of resolution has been reached, which is undercut by the strength—and knowledge—of the narrative voice. Frank then reveals his true feelings about April's wish to have an abortion: "I wish to God you'd done it" and, to close, he departs the scene on the "perfect exit line" (291–2). Following this, April runs to the woods, resisting his calls to return home. Frank observes April from the kitchen window: "Once he was in the kitchen he gave all his attention to the grim business of keeping watch on her through the window, standing—or crouching, and finally sitting on a chair—far enough back in the shadows so that she wouldn't be able to see him" (293).

As suggested, the kitchen is a domain in which Frank possesses the most power; this vantage point, of watching yet remaining unseen, strengthens his position. April is now purely the subject of her husband's surveillance and aims to obscure his point of observation by hiding in the woods. This is played out, critically, in the encaging arena of the kitchen, a room he has utilized as a means of domesticating her role, but now there is no need to enter when she is cooking dinner, or arrive with a prop (the syringe) to do so.

When April returns, we are presented with their final interaction in the living room: "Then she came into the living room and turned on the lights and the exploding glare caused them both to blink and squint. What he felt, above all, was embarrassment. She looked embarrassed too, until she walked across the room and lay down on the sofa with her face out of sight" (294). As before, April has entered the room and switched on the lights, almost as if illuminating the auditorium. While this has, previously, signaled her looming authority, here she crosses the room to lie prostrate on the sofa. Again, there is no dialogue, yet this time the living room as theater has lost one of its characters with April's face now obscured from vision. The living room scene has suggested a close to the role April has played—all that seems to be missing is the direction "April departs"—yet her withdrawal is signified in two further movements. The morning after their final argument, Yates presents us with a breakfast scene that could have been lifted from an idealized suburban catalogue: "The table was carefully set with two places for breakfast. The kitchen was filled with sunlight and with the aromas of coffee and bacon. April was at the stove, wearing a fresh maternity dress, and she looked up at him with a shy smile" (296).

April looks to have adopted, or fulfilled, the role of suburban housewife that has previously been so ill-fitting. After a momentary pause, Frank accepts the scene as it is presented and April feigns interest in the meeting her husband will hold with Pollock that afternoon (Yates revealed in the 1972 *Ploughshares* interview that he felt this to be the strongest scene he had ever written). As he prepares to leave for work, Frank, under the impression that a truce has been struck after the night before, states, "I mean it was a swell breakfast…. Really; I don't know when I've ever had a—a nicer breakfast" (298). Following his departure, the focalization of the narrative switches, for the first time in the novel, entirely to April: "April Johnson Wheeler watched her husband's face withdraw, she felt the light squeeze of his hand on her arm and heard his words, and smiled at him" (300). The narrative therein concentrates on April as she makes all the necessary preparations for the home abortion. If we bridge the two scenes together, the novel has reached a point of closure in its exposition of performances: the breakfast episode functions almost as an encore to the couple's interaction in the living room, with April constructing a scene of idealized domesticity during their final scene together in the kitchen. We see one last glimpse of April's curtain call smile, bringing us back to her casting in *The Petrified Forest*, completing the circularity of the novel's engagement with performance.

"The Toyland of Pastel Houses"

In her study of confessional poetry in mid-century America, Gill identifies a number of recurring tropes used to signify a suggestive context or point of realization in the suburban environment. For Gill, metaphors such as "lamps and stars (and occasionally of street and moonlight) help to situate the action in a liminal dawn or dusk timeframe, poised between night and day" (2013, 157). This period of uncertainty allows for an "exploration of polarities, between the micro- and the macrocosm, the personal and the public, the immediate and the historical, the margin and the center" (157). After April's self-induced abortion and subsequent death, we are taken to a point where Frank approaches his house and, in a scene that can be seen to align with Gill's conception of a liminal point, Yates's protagonist reconsiders his suburban setting. Moving through the Revolutionary Hill Estates, where "proud floodlights" illuminate front lawns, Frank scrabbles through the woods to view his home, and the narration runs: "Then he saw the house— really saw it—long and milk-white in the moonlight" (Yates 2007, 324–5). This revised perception of his home, as if he is viewing it for the first time, is set against the "toyland of […] pastel houses" of the estate (323). At first depicted as a constructed and artificial setting, with the living room akin to a show home, there is a sense that it is now something animate in the shadow of April's death. As critic Tim Foster (2012) notes astutely, this inversion is furthered as Frank attempts to clean the crimson carpet, colored by his wife's

blood (66). Moving through the rooms, he is able to hear his wife's voice—
"How could she be dead when the house was alive with the sound of her and
the sense of her?"—as she narrates and explains the abortion method:

"I thought that would be the simplest way to handle it."

"I thought you could just wrap the towels up in newspaper and put them
in the garbage, and then give the tub a good rinsing out. Okay?" (324)

This anthropomorphic description again counteracts the sterile environment Yates initially outlined, as April's voice—which remains muted in
the closing two scenes in the living room—now percolates through the house.
As her voice begins to disperse and fade, when he has cleaned the last of the
blood, Frank is left with "nothing to do but walk around and turn on lights
and turn them off again" (324), recognizing that her figure would immediately—as it had before—become visible upon the room's illumination. The
passage closes with Frank, who has hidden in the closet to avoid Shep, carrying April's suicide note to sit "in the darkness by the picture window" (325).
Foster (2012) sums up the position of Yates's protagonist to claim, "In the
narrative's climax, it is only through a literal separation from his domestic
arrangements that Frank is released from the ideological hostility he feels
towards the suburban environment" (64). The pretense with which he has
constructed his anti-suburban persona has collapsed to uncover Frank's complete reconsideration of his suburban environment, a contemplative point
that takes place beside the picture window at the close of dusk.

Revolutionary Road *as Suburban Text*

Reconsideration of Yates's treatment of suburbia is pressing in light of
the recent critical appreciation of the topic, with scholarly attention showing
authors of suburban fiction and poetry engaged in a more complex relationship with the environment than previously recognized. This advancement is
of particular interest to Yatesian scholars due to the fact that *Revolutionary
Road* was placed within the suburban genre, a categorization that shaped and
ultimately limited its commercial and critical potential on release. Well known
to Yates critics is the fact publishers Atlantic-Little, Brown rejected the first
draft of the novel on the grounds that it was "one of the many imitators of
The Man in the Gray Flannel Suit" (Bailey 2003, 178). The similarities weren't
lost on Yates who, reflecting on the first draft of the novel, admitted the
Wheelers were very earnest, "thin […] sentimental" and reminiscent of characters from a "Sloan Wilson novel" (Bailey 2003, 178) Despite clear reservations—from both publisher and author—about pushing the novel towards
the suburban market, Atlantic–Little, Brown, after accepting the title, proposed the following blurb: "*Revolutionary Road* is a novel about suburbia,"

an opening line that was eventually revised. While Yates stressed that he wanted the text to represent a clear departure from topical critiques of the environment, the blurb contained, much to Yates's chagrin, references to "commuters," "the suburbs," and "Suburban life." Diverting the novel from the suburban genre was also a strategic way of broadening *Revolutionary Road*'s prospective audience: if the literary market had been saturated by novels about suburbia, suburbanites themselves would surely be exhausted by the number of fictional critiques of the topic, thus lessening the book's appeal to a rapidly-increasing consumer group. It is apparent that Yates did not want *Revolutionary Road* associated with suburban texts—he had spent enough time loosening the novel's ties with *The Man in the Gray Flannel Suit* for it to be an issue once more—but felt the copy did little to distinguish or disentangle such a connection.

Following discussions with Yates and his agent, Monica McCall, and publisher, Seymour Lawrence, Atlantic–Little, Brown altered the first lines of the blurb to read: "It probes modern American marriage and suburban living to a depth heretofore unexplored. It is not, however, anything so tame as just another book about suburbia or infidelity." The opening line seems to stand as a compromise between author and publisher; suburbia is still mentioned at the outset, but with the caveat that Yates's novel provides a fresh approach in its exploration of the setting. There is a similar sentiment to the second line, although it does take a rather confused position as to whether it is, or is not, about suburbia and marriage. Whether it came across to readers as a somewhat contradictory disclaimer, the blurb offered an amorphous outline of the text. The direction of this promotional strategy must be seen to have shaped how the novel was appropriated on first entry to the market with *The Chicago Review*'s Warren Preece (1961) one critic who expressed his exasperation at a further addition to the suburban in his piece "Another Fictional *Exposé* of Suburban Living."

The strength of this categorization may be seen to have influenced more contemporary readings of the novel: critics such as Catherine Jurca (2001) have argued that the text "brilliantly defines the postwar suburbanite as the antisuburbanite, whose existence is a protest against everyone else's putative conformity" (148). Such identification situates Yates's novel alongside Wilson's as a suburban critique with the Wheelers an exemplar of the American couple at odds with their conformist habitat. Yet this approach equates the downfall of the Wheelers' relationship with the potentially destructive effects of suburbia: a correlation that critically misconceives Yates's intention in the text and sidesteps the more nuanced manner in which he treats the suburban environment.

During his interview with *Ploughshares*, Yates provided his own response to the fact *Revolutionary Road* has been frequently referenced as an anti-suburban polemic: "The book was widely read as an anti-suburban novel, and that disappointed me. The Wheelers may have thought the suburbs were to blame for all their problems, but I meant it to be implicit in the text that that was their delusion, their problem, not mine" (1972, 1). Voiced in 1972, these remarks suggest that the reception of the novel did not assimilate with Yates's intention. Rather than an anti-suburban exposition, *Revolutionary Road* should be regarded as a text that cautions against an implicit acceptance of its perceived effects, the source of which is not suburbia itself, but the controlling and troubling impact of one of its most prominent symbols: the picture window. Yates's use of the window sets up a fluid interplay of observer and observant, a site of contemplation and an interstice through which the Wheelers' living room becomes a platform of display and performance. Yates's employment of this, as Mackay asserts, creates a complex interplay of spatialities within the text that can be placed, more broadly, in relation to cultural discussions of surveillance. For Mackay the picture window serves no "gender designed function, but instead, creates a troubling fluidity and mobility of surveillance" (2013, 131). Such an assessment recognizes its recurring presence and is in line with more progressive conceptualizations of our relationship with the longstanding images associated with the suburban landscape. My reading suggests that, in light of the kitchen scenes in the text, Yates does hint at the prescriptive categories of suburban gender and the ways these are spatially dependent, yet does not necessarily relate these to the picture window. This analysis has extended the signification of the picture window to show that it not only functions as a site of surveillance but also heavily influences the stylized performances of Frank and April throughout the novel. The circularity and recurrence of this is denoted through the persistent references to *The Petrified Forest*, with the picture window the aperture through which Frank and April play out the disintegration of their suburban marriage. This approach argues for a more spatially conscious reading of the picture window in Yates's novel and is informed by the recent re-conceptualization of its symbolism in suburban literature. Not only does this loosen the somewhat binary or staid ties to its presence within *Revolutionary Road*, but it can be seen to outline a more progressive appreciation of its function within postwar suburban fiction.

NOTES

1. Performativity, of course, relates to a broad range of disciplines and is a loaded concept that must be unpacked for the forthcoming discussion. I extend my reading of suburban privacy to show that both the picture window and television denoted points of intrusion into the suburban home, resulting in the living room becoming a platform for domestic theatricality. This interpretation draws upon Lynn Spigel's (1992, 136) contention that this increased exposure was similar to watching the "family in the theatre next door." In my analysis, I view Yates's protagonists as exhibiting a heightened awareness of their roles in the suburban setting, with the living room displacing the theater as the platform for their performance.

2. As the Givings approach for their second visit, the Wheelers are not alerted of their arrival. "The house had a strangely unwelcoming look, as if they weren't expecting visitors. She knocked again, and this time she made a visor of one hand and pressed it to the pane, to see inside. The kitchen was empty […] but just then Frank Wheeler came lunging in from the living room, looking awful[….] She saw at once that he hadn't heard her knock and didn't know she was there: he hadn't come to answer the door but in desperate escape from the living room, possibly from the house itself" (284).

BIBLIOGRAPHY

Bailey, Blake. 2003. *A Tragic Honesty: The Life and Work of Richard Yates*. New York: Picador.
Beuka, Robert. 2004. *SuburbiaNation: Reading Suburban Landscape in Twentieth-Century American Fiction and Film*. New York: Palgrave Macmillan.
Castronovo, David, and Steven Goldleaf. 1996. *Richard Yates*. New York: Twayne Publishers.
Charlton-Jones, Kate. 2014. *Dismembering the American Dream: The Life and Fiction of Richard Yates*. Tuscaloosa: University of Alabama Press.
Creadick, Anna. G. 2010. *The Pursuit of Normality in Postwar America (Culture, Politics, and the Cold War)*. Boston: University of Massachusetts.
Donaldson, Scott. 1969. *The Suburban Myth*. New York: Cambridge University Press.
Fitzgerald, F. Scott. (1925) 1991. *The Great Gatsby*. New York: Cambridge University Press.
Foster, Tim. 2012. "Escaping the Split-level Trap: Postsuburban Narratives in Recent American Fiction." Dissertation. University of Nottingham.
Freedman, Samuel. 1999. "Suburbia Outgrows Its Image in the Arts." *The New York Times*. 28 February.
Friedan, Betty. (1963) 2010. *The Feminine Mystique*. London: Penguin Books.
Gill, Jo. 2014. "Anne Sexton's Poetics of the Suburbs." Ed. Mark Jackson. *Health and the Modern Home*. London: Routledge.
_____. 2013. *The Poetics of the American Suburbs*. New York: Palgrave Macmillan.
Hanlon, Bernadette, John R. Short, and Thomas J. Vicino. 2010. *Cities and Suburbs: New Metropolitan Realities in the U.S.* New York: Routledge.
Henry, DeWitt, and Geoffrey Clark. 1972. "An Interview with Richard Yates." *Ploughshares* Vol. 1, no. 3.
Jönsson, Ola. 2014. *Suburbia Rewritten: Masculinity and Affect in Contemporary American Literature*. Uppsala: Uppsala University.
Jurca, Catherine. 2001. *White Diaspora: The Suburb and the Twentieth-century American Novel*. Princeton, New Jersey: Princeton University Press.
Mackay, Antonia Alexandra. 2013. *City, Suburban and Pastoral Spaces and the Formation of Identity in Cold War America, 1945–1965*. Oxford: Brookes University Press.
May, Elaine Tyler. 1998. *Homeward Bound: American Families in the Cold War*. New York: Basic Books.
Mumford, Lewis. *The City in History*. Quoted in *The Suburb Reader*. 2006. Becky Nicolaides and Andrew M. Wiese, eds. New York: Routledge.
Nelson, Deborah. 2002. *Pursuing Privacy in Cold War America (Gender and Culture Series)*. New York: Columbia University Press.
Preece, Warren E. 1961. "Another Fictional Expose of Suburban Living." *Chicago Tribune*. 5 March.
Price, Richard. 2009. Introduction to *Revolutionary Road, The Easter Parade, Eleven Kinds of Loneliness*. New York: Everyman's Library.
Spigel, Lynn. 1992. *Make Room for TV: Television and the Family Ideal in Postwar America*. Chicago: The University of Chicago Press.
_____. 1997. "From Theatre to Space Ship, Metaphors of Suburban Domesticity in postwar America." In *Visions of Suburbia*, ed. Roger Silverstone. London: Routledge.
Stroud, Benjamin. 2009. *Perilous Landscapes: The Postwar Suburb in Twentieth-Century American Fiction*. Ann Arbor: University of Michigan Press.
Updike, John. 1959. "Suburban Madrigal." *The New Yorker*. 25 April.

_____. (1960) 2006. *Rabbit, Run.* London: Penguin Classics.
Whyte, William H. (1956) 2002. *The Organization Man.* Philadelphia: University of Pennsylvania Press.
Yates, Richard. (1961) 2007. *Revolutionary Road.* London: Vintage Publishing.

The Geography of Identity in *The Easter Parade*

Rona Cran

"New York was an inexhaustible space, a labyrinth of endless steps, and no matter how far he walked, no matter how well he came to know its neighborhoods and streets, it always left him with the feeling of being lost."
—Paul Auster, *City of Glass*

This essay provides a new reading of Richard Yates's heavily autobiographical 1976 novel, *The Easter Parade*.[1] By delineating the importance of place within the novel—an area that has provoked a good deal of discourse with respect to his first book, *Revolutionary Road* (1961), but which has not been explored in *The Easter Parade*—I demonstrate that Yates's topographical specificity contributes to the narrative beyond the realism for which he is famous. In particular, the network of real and imaginary places depicted within the novel actively shapes and fosters the existential loneliness of Yates's characters, which is closely connected to the experience of place. My overall aim is to particularize David Castronovo and Steven Goldleaf's observation that in his "notation of the suburbs, Manhattan, and the Midwest, Yates produces his most comprehensive account of American unhappiness" (1996, 124).

Yates was famously accused of lambasting the suburbs in *Revolutionary Road*, a charge that he said "disappointed" him (*Ploughshares*, n.p.). It is important to clarify from the outset, therefore, that my contention here is not that Yates holds accountable any of the locations he uses for the events that transpire within their limits, or that his characters in any way lack agency as a result of the locations in which they live. Rather, it is to suggest that his work meaningfully explores the formative influence of place, in the understanding that life—and fiction—is simultaneously shaped by and played out against it. As Foucault put it, "we do not live in a homogenous and empty space, but in a space that is saturated with qualities" (1984, 46). As inhabitants of a variety of psychic, social, and physical places, the constitution of our subjectivity is necessarily affected by their form, structure, and shifting intersections, as this chapter will discuss. The geographer J. Nicholas Entrikin, in his seminal work *The Betweenness of Place* (1991), for instance, argues that "place is both a center of meaning and the external context of our actions" (7). Literary scholar Robert Beuka, whose work makes reference to Entrikin, further demonstrates that meaning is shaped by place, contending: "place is more than simply the passive physical backdrop against which the stuff of life (or fiction) is played out, instead often emerging as a 'center of meaning' in our lives" (2004, 3). For Allan Pred, too, place is always more than just "an inert, experienced scene" (1984, 279), while for Tim Cresswell "place is not just a thing in the world but a way of understanding the world" (2004, 11). Ashild Lappegard Hauge, an environmental psychologist whose persuasive essay on the subject of "place-identity" acknowledges that the word "place" lacks specificity when compared with "more precise words like 'dwelling,' 'landscape,' 'city,' or 'neighborhood,'" but also argues that there is "a need for a common term for the physical environment in relation to the social, psychological and cultural meanings attached to it" (2007, 44). Doreen Massey, a geographer whose *Space, Place, and Gender* (1994) carefully explores the instability of place as a political concept, also contests the "view of place as bounded [...] as singular, fixed and unproblematic in its identity" (1), contending instead that places should be viewed as "open and porous," with "unfixed, contested and multiple" identities (5). The American philosopher Edward Casey, finally, argues that "where we are—the place we occupy, however briefly—has everything to do with what and who we are (and finally, *that* we are)[....] Our immediate placement [...] counts for much more than is usually imagined. More, for instance, than serving as a mere backdrop for concrete actions or thoughts. Place itself is concrete and at one with action and thought" (xiii). Clearly, the growing body of work devoted to the study of place by literary scholars, geographers, philosophers, and psychologists is rich in its implications and wide in its range, but encompasses a unifying argument: that place functions as both a physical backdrop and a determining force, and is essential to the establishment of subjectivity.

These viewpoints clearly owe a debt to phenomenology. Initially focusing on cerebral, "transcendental" structures, phenomenology later moved to explore lived experience within daily human life, with Heidegger arguing that human existence and human consciousness are linked (*Being and Time*, 1927), and Merleau-Ponty reunifying the body and the mind (*Phenomenology of Perception*, 1945). As a result, the importance of place—specifically of the physical and emotional home, or dwelling—gained philosophical traction, with Heidegger suggesting that an authentic existence is one which is embedded in place (*Building Dwelling Thinking*, 1951). In particular, Heidegger argued that human beings "are" to the extent that they "dwell," using the word "bauen" to mean "building" not just in terms of construction but with reference to the spectrum of human endeavor, placing emphasis on preserving, nurturing, cherishing, and protecting. Our failure to "dwell" successfully results in a failure to build (again, referring to the whole range of human productive activity): or as Heidegger put it, "Only if we are capable of dwelling, only then can we build" (2).

Reading *The Easter Parade* with these ideas in mind, it becomes clear that the novel is a sustained examination of the effect of place on human (and particularly female) endeavor, with the failure to dwell and the condition of rootlessness at its core. Whether in urban, suburban, domestic, external, or transitional spaces, behavior and place are repeatedly shown to be intimately connected, and identity relational, as Yates articulates the diverse and metamorphic perspectives of his characters by carefully positioning them in relation to their physical surroundings. The cumulative effect of the vast catalogue of places Yates both references and invents is a comprehensive vision of the near meaningless entrapment of a "dislocated, disordered, and psychologically stifled" group of people (Castronovo and Goldleaf 1996, n.p.). Although, as Castronovo and Goldleaf suggest, Yates uses "the locales of New York and its suburbs as markers of time" (129), these markers are in no sense demonstrative of progress. Viewed on a map, it becomes clear that the movement from place to place of Yates's protagonists is more akin to that of wild animals trapped in cages. As children, Emily and Sarah Grimes "change homes so often" (Yates 2008, 12) that they lose track of the number of times they move, and yet they remain confined to suburbia until their late teens, during a period of their lives ironically described as "memorable" (3). Later, as Emily moves from place to place, up and down the island of Manhattan and sometimes beyond, we realize that her repeatedly thwarted plans for independence are a palimpsest of her mother's, with both women seeking (and failing to find) salvation by compulsively changing their geographical coordinates. Sarah, by contrast, pathologically roots herself to a singular place in an attempt to create a permanent sanctuary in order to resist the kind of dispersal that Gaston Bachelard suggests must occur when one lacks a place to call home: "[w]ithout it," he writes in *The Poetics of Space*, "man would be a dispersed being. It maintains him through the storms of heaven and through those of life. It is body and soul" (1994, 7).

*   *   *

The novel begins in Tenafly, in suburban New Jersey, where the newly divorced Pookie, a thinly disguised variant of Yates's own mother, Dookie, attempts "to launch a career in suburban real estate" (Yates 2008, 3). Yates's protestations notwithstanding, *Revolutionary Road* has taught readers to be wary of suburbia (and of real estate agents), particularly when New York City is supplanted, as it is in both novels to luckless effect. In many ways, Pookie is the embodiment of William Upksi Wimsatt's definition of the suburbs as being "founded on fear, conformity, shallowness of character, and dullness of imagination" (2001, n.p.). More significant, however, are the unstable connotations of the real estate business, a profession founded on and sustained by human itinerancy. Pookie sets her two daughters on migratory pathways, which for one ends in domestic violence and death (Sarah becomes a troubling variant of Rapunzel, trapped by her handsome but brutal prince within the claustrophobic foliage of Great Hedges) and for the other, Emily, ends in penury, social limbo, and psychological breakdown, defined by a string of addresses and an almost total absence of friends and family.

The Easter Parade's opening line—"Neither of the Grimes sisters would have a happy life" (Yates 2008, 3)—sounds like the beginning of a fairytale by Straparola, Perrault, or the Brothers Grimm. As in many of those tales, in which characters' lives, memories, ideas, and interpretations are shaped by the places in which they find themselves (dwelling or failing to dwell but nonetheless being-in-the-world), Yates's protagonists both embody and are embodied by place. The mutual physicality of this relationship—the interface between bodies and places—is key in Yates's novel, for two reasons. The first is that, as M.R. Barral writes, "it is because of the body that man can speak of space at all. [...] It is always through the body that I make contacts, either with the world and things in the world or with other subjects in the world" (1969, 175). Throughout the novel, pivotal moments of epiphany and revelation, usually concerning Emily's existential self-doubt or crippling self-awareness, occur as a result of realized corporeality: direct physical contact with or within a specific place. Examples include the steel pipe in a neighbor's yard that cuts Sarah's head and leads to Emily's realization of her "unfathomable dread of being alone" (Yates 2008, 10); after Walter Grimes's death, "the cool, shuddering glass of the limousine window" (41) that precipitates Emily's uncertain and introspective tears "for poor, sensitive Emily Grimes whom nobody understood, and who understood nothing" (42); or the visual impact of two bicycles, one with a child's seat, in Emily's nephew Peter's garage, in the closing pages of the novel, which provokes Emily's final furious outburst and her subsequent exhausted confession: "I've never understood anything in my whole life" (226).

The second reason is that place also functions as the objective correlative, a concept that preoccupied Yates throughout much of his writing life.[2] As in *Revolutionary Road*, the third person narrative in *The Easter Parade* is vocalized chiefly through the main protagonist—in this case, Emily Grimes.

While the narrative is usually closest to Emily's perspective, we also receive glimpses of Sarah and Pookie's perspectives. But although we have access to their interior thoughts, and to the kinds of words and phrases that seem to originate from the characters, moments of genuine interiority are rare. Emily and, occasionally, Sarah insincerely say "I see" in response to situations they struggle to understand, but their failure to actually see is countered by Yates's pansophical narrator, who maintains a wry, distant perspective throughout, navigating the liminal space between objectivity and judgment when moments of interiority open up.[3] In a subtly interventionist style that perhaps owes a debt to E.M. Forster's narrator in *Howards End* (1910), Yates's narrator is simultaneously measured and mocking—whether relating Pookie's search for "'nice' communities to live in, whether she could afford them or not" (7), or Emily's daydreams about "riding in that splendid old car with her hair blowing attractively in the wind" (25), or Sarah's studied greeting to her mother and sister upon their arrival at Great Hedges: "Welcome to the House at Pooh Corner" (45). Kate Charlton-Jones notes that in *Revolutionary Road*, "many voices collide to create the picture of the fractured 'subject' at work on his chosen role" (2014, 25); in *The Easter Parade* the images of our fractured subjects are created via the colliding of many places. Yates uses a variety of places, and the webs of meaning that form between them, to evoke the emotion and embody the behaviors of his protagonists, whether in the reclaimed swampland of suburban New Jersey; in Great Hedges, a disintegrating estate on Long Island; in a grotesque evening tableau of Times Square; in a dirty hotel in Hell's Kitchen; in "a once-grand, shabby old 'floor through' on the south side of Washington Square" (Yates 2008, 17); in "the raucous labyrinth of the Port Authority Bus Terminal" (218); in an "odd-looking" house in Iowa City (96); in an overpriced and underwhelming cocktail bar in London; in Central Islip Psychiatric Center's "bewildered maze of trees and buildings" (172); or in a wholesome suburban driveway in New Hampshire. The novel's constant shifting (or parade) from place to place provides an illusion of progress, and functions as what T.S. Eliot called "a skillful accumulation of imagined sensory impressions" (1997, 86), used in this case to evoke the sense that all Yates's characters are outsiders, spurned by every community they attempt to join. Emily in particular is emotionally as well as literally itinerant, and while she tends to think of herself as willfully nomadic, Yates repeatedly uses her environment to communicate a status closer to that of the refugee, as she is forced from place to place first by her mother and then by her own "unfathomable dread of being alone" (Yates 2008, 10). Sarah, meanwhile, in her struggle to overcome her damagingly peripatetic childhood and form a meaningful attachment to a place she can call home, grows almost pathologically attached to Great Hedges, in spite of "the mildew, the chill, the ancestors staring from the walls, the smell of garbage in the kitchen," not to mention the abuse she endures there (168).

Urban places of significance in the novel include primarily the numerous apartments in which Emily resides in Manhattan, as well as Central Park, where she loses her virginity, and the Manhattan streets, from City Hall to the Upper East Side, where she encounters the many ghosts of her past and finally catches a horrifying glimpse of her aging face in a plate-glass window. Noteworthy suburban or non-urban places include the cottage, main house, and apartment above the garage on the Wilsons' Long Island estate that Pookie clumsily names Great Hedges, but also the numerous rented houses between which Emily and Sarah are shunted as children, the bungalow in Iowa City, the grounds of Central Islip, where both Sarah and Pookie are incarcerated, and Peter's driveway, in which the possibility for redemption might be found. The novel also features a number of key liminal, or transitional, spaces, where key narrative moments occur *between* places and within moving vehicles. Such spaces include the train that the young Sarah takes during her privileged visits to the city to visit Walter Grimes, the limousine that transports Emily to and from Walter's funeral, the 5th Avenue bus, taxi, and IRT local that frame her first sexual encounter, and Andrew Crawford, Howard Dunninger, and Peter Crawford's cars.

The American critic J. Hillis Miller makes the following useful argument in his 1995 book *Topographies*:

> A novel is a figurative mapping. The story traces out diachronically the movement of the characters from house to house and from time to time, as the crisscross of their relationships gradually creates an imaginary space. This space is based on the real landscape, charged now with the subjective meaning of the story that has been enacted within it. The houses, roads, paths, and walls stand not so much for the individual characters as for the dynamic field of relations among them [19–20].

The Easter Parade performs just such a mapping. Its topographical specificity is a rhetorical gesture that enriches a network of places with the deep meanings of a relational, if unstable, identity. As Doreen Massey observes, if "the spatial is thought of in the context of space-time and as formed out of social interrelations at all scales, then one view of a place is as a particular articulation of those relations, a particular moment in those networks of social relations and understandings" (1994, 5). *The Easter Parade*, read thus, is less a procession than a ground, a space in which Yates can muster the troops of his own life (including his mother, his wife, himself) and present them for inspection. But the novel is a literal mapping as well, providing the reader with an effective archive of recognizable or semi-recognizable places, much like a film. With a few exceptions, the places featured are easily identifiable on a map, as well as being well-known within the context of American literature and culture, from Greenwich Village to Central Park, Columbia

University to Hell's Kitchen, Iowa City to the Hamptons. A large number of the places used in the novel will reach beyond it, in a "conversion of seen into scene," to quote Stephen Heath (83), prompting many readers to remark "I know that place!" or "I've been there!," a beguiling experience of place that satisfies a desire for reference but that also blurs the line between fiction and reality. The effect of this is that the novel becomes a textual heterotopia—a unique place, according to Foucault, with both mirroring and distorting properties, capable of inverting or unsettling other places and troubling our understanding of them. Once again the word "parade" demands to be understood less as a procession than as a reflective space or ground, like Foucault's mirror: "it makes the place that I occupy, whenever I look at myself in the glass, both absolutely real—it is in fact linked to all the surrounding space—and absolutely unreal, for in order to be perceived it has of necessity to pass that virtual point that is situated down there" (1984, 47). It is on this unsteady ground, and within this textual heterotopia, that the novel's action is played out, or mapped, beginning and ending in uncertainty.

* * *

Sarah and Emily Grimes start life in the city of New York, but are dragged by their single mother to one rented suburban house after another. In addition to emotionally destabilizing the girls—"remember how awful it was when we were little?" (Yates 2008, 130)—this involuntarily nomadic lifestyle has the effect of rose-tinting both their absent father, Walter Grimes, and New York City where he lives. Walter "writes headlines," Sarah tells her schoolmates, articulating it in such a way that "it made clear they ought to be impressed" (3). Even though Walter's achievements are demonstrably over-inflated by Sarah—as well as by Walter's own admission, and by the girls' visit to the *Sun* newspaper plant, where the physicality of the production is portrayed as far more noteworthy than the paper's intellectual processes—Yates nonetheless indicates that our sympathies should lie with him, and, by extension, with the city. While Pookie is arguably in possession of some honorable motives with regard to good schools and communities, she is presented coolly and with irredeemable suspicion—she is shallow, insincere, and pretentious—while Walter, in spite of his obvious failings, is portrayed as funny, self-aware, and good with children. Leaving the *Sun* plant after their visit, the two girls and their father walk hand in hand "across City Hall Park in the spring sunshine" (5), a positive, uplifting image that is consistent with Emily and Sarah's view of the situation rather than the reader's, but the intention of which is to transcend interiority and influence the reader in Walter's—and in New York's—favor. The trip to the city is ultimately disappointing—even through their rose-tinted lenses the girls can understand that their father is "only a copy-desk man" (6)—but although "it wasn't much to take back to Tenafly"

(6) Yates conveys a sense that suburbia, as a place on its own terms, is not enough for the girls, and that they need to be sustained, somehow, by stories from the city. This need not only indicates the perceived remoteness of the suburbs in Sarah and Emily's minds, but it also calls to mind Lewis Mumford's view that "in breaking away from the city, the part became a substitute for the whole" (1961, 486).

This sense of truncation pervades the initial suburban section of the novel, with the places depicted—Tenafly, Larchmont, Bradley, Armonk, and a couple of unnamed others—seeming to "narrow the outlook and dull the imagination" (Wimsatt 2001, 11). In spite of Pookie's purported intentions—nice communities and good schools—her children nevertheless seem to experience not so much "middle-class advantages" as "middle-class abasement": the "material benefits, however 'great,' are cultural and spiritual handicaps" (Jurca 2001, 4). Suburbia, in many ways, resembles another kind of heterotopia—that of the cemetery:

> an "other" place with respect to ordinary cultural spaces, and yet it is connected with all the locations of the city, the society, the village, and so on, since every family has some relative there[....] [From the 19th century] they no longer constituted the sacred and immortal wind of the city, but the "other city," where each family possessed its gloomy dwelling [Foucault 1984, 48].

Emily feels these cultural and spiritual handicaps and abasements particularly strongly, and will spend the rest of her life reacting against them, but for Sarah the problem lies not in the circumstances of a suburban existence but in the "curse" (Yates 2008, 14) of her near constant displacement. Her solution as an adult is to adopt a half-life, or semi-death, at Great Hedges, where she undergoes a voluntary process of fossilization, embracing a metaphorical version of "that strange heterochronism that is, for a human being, the loss of life and of that quasi-eternity in which, however, he does not cease to dissolve and be erased" (Foucault 1984, 48).

J. Hillis Miller, referencing Heidegger, writes that "[b]eing rooted in one dear particular place, like a tree or a house, is the proper condition of Dasein, but modern 'man' (das Man, as Heidegger puts it) is uprooted. He drifts from place to place, like the poor Arab tribesman and his tent" (1995, 11). Emily's itinerant approach to life exemplifies her as "modern," and while it prevents her from forming any meaningful relationships with the many places through which she passes, it nonetheless also marks her out as a threat to the social order. She is, as Peter points out, "the original liberated woman" (Yates 2008, 221), or a kind of "invisible flâneuse" (Wolff 1985, 37) trespassing in a traditionally male public world. In particular, her restlessness renders her a threat to the patriarchal order. As Massey argues: "One gender-disturbing message might be—in terms of both identity and space—keep moving!" (1994, 11). In this regard, Pookie's desire to constantly move also takes on greater significance, and her subsequent confinement to an apartment above a garage greater irony, if we look past her pretensions and take into consideration her tendency to "compare herself with the woman in *A Doll's House*" (Yates 2008, 134). The woman, of course, is Nora, a character who embodied Ibsen's opinion on the impossibility, for women, of being themselves and of making progress while living in a society built exclusively by men. The difficulty, as Massey continues, is managing "to [keep moving] while at the same time recognizing one's necessary located-ness and embeddedness/embodiedness, and taking responsibility for it" (1994, 11). This is Emily's failure: while she does "keep moving," and in doing so threatens a settled patriarchal order, she persistently struggles to "take responsibility" and to recognize her "necessary located-ness and embeddedness/embodiedness." She ultimately rejects both her "located-ness" and her liberation, snarling at Peter, "liberated from what?" (Yates 2008, 221).

Sarah, by contrast, cannot or will not keep moving, and is ultimately killed by the patriarchal order in which she exists, meeting her end at the hands of her husband, in a houseful of men, after "twenty-five years of brutality and stupidity and neglect" (224)—a situation worsened by the tacit complicity of her three sons. Traumatized by a childhood spent moving, she thrusts down roots with a troubling vigor, marrying at the age of twenty, and investing her life in a quasi-gothic monstrosity of a house to whose horrors she appears willfully insensitive, simply in order to have a place she can call home. Yates makes clear that in expecting her home to provide sanctuary, she is deluded—and as the decades pass she suffers repeatedly for her romanticism and naivety, with the decaying and hideous Great Hedges providing a persistent example "of a world that is not romantic and whose inhabitants suffer because they want it to be" (Naparsteck 2012, 95). The "House at Pooh Corner" (Yates 2008, 45), as Sarah calls it, contains horrors—from mildew and "gaunt furniture" (46) to domestic violence and death—that are made all the worse by her physical and psychic isolation.

"Our house," writes Bachelard in *The Poetics of Space*, "is our corner of the world[....] [I]t is our first universe, a real cosmos in every sense of the word [...] the house shelters daydreaming, the house protects the dreamer, the house allows one to dream in peace" (1958, 4–6). bell hooks, meanwhile, in *Yearning*, speaks of home as being

> no longer just one place. It is locations. Home is that place which enables and promotes varied and everchanging perspectives, a place where one discovers new ways of seeing reality, frontiers of difference. One confronts and accepts dispersal and fragmentation as part of the constructions of a new world order that reveals more fully where we are, who we can become [1991, 147–8].

As a child, neither Sarah nor Emily is given the chance to experience home in these ways. Deprived of a "corner of the world," Sarah reacts strongly against future threats of dispersal (a reaction that comes at the cost of her life). While Emily attempts to broach the "constructions of a new world order," Sarah retreats to the comforting inertia offered by a suburban home, detaching herself almost entirely from the outside world and using her husband's alleged disdain for "traffic" and unnecessary expense (Yates 2008, 145) as an excuse for never returning. For Lewis Mumford, the "cost of this detachment in space," effected by life in suburbia, where the houses were designed with garages built into them in order to reinforce individual automobile ownership and usage, discouraging pedestrian activity and interaction with the external environment, was "out of proportion to its supposed benefits" (1961, 512). The result, he argued, was "an encapsulated life, spent more and more either in a motorcar or within the cabin of darkness before a television set" (512). An encapsulated life is what Sarah desires, however, and is certainly what she attains –the majority of her courtship with Tony takes place in "a splendid old car" (Yates 2008, 25), before the 1941 Easter Parade in New York leads her straight into the "cabin of darkness" that is Great Hedges, which will be her tomb.

* * *

"On any person who desires such queer prizes," wrote E.B. White in *Here Is New York*:

> New York will bestow the gift of loneliness and the gift of privacy. It is this largess that accounts for the presence within the city's walls of a considerable section of the population; for the residents of Manhattan are to a large extent strangers who have pulled up stakes somewhere and come to town, seeking sanctuary or fulfilment or some greater or lesser grail. The capacity to make such dubious gifts is a mysterious quality of New York. It can destroy an individual, or it can fulfil him, depending a good deal on luck. No one should come to New York to live unless he is willing to be lucky [1991, 19].

In 1940, Pookie, nineteen-year-old Sarah, and fifteen-year-old Emily pull up stakes and head to town, returning to New York City after ten years in the suburbs, seeking a new home and new fulfillment, all three willing themselves to be lucky in their new locale. They move into an expensive apartment off Washington Square Park in Greenwich Village, one of New York's most famous parks and a location rich with literary and (particularly by 1976, when *The Easter Parade* was published) socio-political credentials. Once "the ideal of quiet and of genteel retirement," to quote Henry James (2010, 13), by the mid–twentieth century Washington Square was a densely-populated community space, increasingly functioning as a nucleus for politics and culture. In 1888 Mark Twain and Robert Louis Stevenson had absorbed the sunshine together on a bench in the Square, "like a couple of characters out of story by Henry James" (Stevenson to Clemens, 16 April 1893), and Eleanor

Roosevelt occupied an apartment there between 1942 and 1949. The *New York Times* writer Anatole Broyard described Greenwich Village during the 1940s as having an "immense, beckoning sweetness," humming with a sense of adventure and with "social, sexual, exciting" changes (*Kafka Was the Rage*, 1992, vii). The park had also been the site of political activism from the early nineteenth century, and by the time Yates was writing *The Easter Parade* had become synonymous in the popular imagination with dissent and counter-cultural movements, from the Triangle Shirtwaist Factory Fire protest to anti–Vietnam War demonstrations. Yates, who lived in New York during the 1940s and who had made use of Washington Square in previous works, was clearly aware of the significance of the park as an iconic urban site. It is also, as Jerome Klinkowitz points out, "at the foot of an avenue to the world: Fifth Avenue, to be precise, up which Emily and her first lover ride in an open-topped bus and down which Sarah and her fiancé, the eminently more suitable young Englishman named Tony Wilson, walk in the city's Easter parade" (1986, 43).

Crucially, this culturally and historically rich location also foreshadows and is emblematic of the troubled juncture between private and public places in the novel, as well as between New York City and other places, which Emily tends to treat with disdain—including the patronizingly italicized "*Iowa*"; St. Charles, which is characterized by such startling offerings as "BLOOD AND SAND WORMS" (Yates 2008, 44); and even London, which is dismissed as being "not very different than riding into New York from St. Charles" (110). In an image that brings the interiority and exteriority of Washington Square into communion with each other, Yates describes how "passengers on the double-decked Fifth Avenue buses could peer" (18) into the Grimes' apartment on their journey uptown. This again evokes E.B. White's suggestion that the city "blends the gift of privacy with the excitement of participation" (1999, 22). This is, of course, one of the city's "dubious gifts"—namely, the contradictory and crippling urban isolation common to the crowded works of writers like Dostoevsky, T.S. Eliot, Joyce, and Dos Passos. Yates capitalizes on this trope in his depiction of the peering passengers juxtaposed with the idea of the naïve, enlivened Grimes girls in their "once-grand" (Yates 2008, 17), possibly Jamesian, Washington Square apartment. Although at this stage Greenwich Village is an exciting gateway to the wider world and the girls are young and eager for adventure, the novel's opening folkloric pronouncement that neither will lead "a happy life" (3) still lingers over the text, as does, in all possibility, Yates's famous and similarly gloomy observation about his writing in general: "If my work has a theme, I suspect it is a simple one: that most human beings are inescapably alone, and therein lies their tragedy" (O'Nan, n.p.). Viewed in this light, the duality of the image prefigures the lives of both the Grimes daughters, that of lonely Emily, the city girl who will spend most of her life in a densely populated area, surrounded by people, particularly men, but who will remain almost permanently isolated, and that of Sarah, for whom the desire for stasis and a place she can call home leads her to reject the outside world, choosing "the comfort of Being instead of forging ahead with the (assumed progressive) project of Becoming" (Massey 1994, 119). It is the first indication, too, of the aggressive encroachment on Emily's private world by the exterior forces she initially embraces but later comes to dread, and an ironic prefiguring of Sarah's public-private dilemma: ensconced in the suburb of St. Charles of her own problematic volition, she is ultimately unable to break free from the deadly privacy of Great Hedges and the devastating secrets of her marriage.

This tantalizing communion between public and private places provides Emily in particular with a glimpse of a new form of lived spatiality that begins to fuel her decadent relationship with the city. The proximity of a multitude of strangers to her apartment window is a peculiarly urban phenomenon that, to quote Elizabeth Grosz, "provides the order and organization that automatically links otherwise unrelated bodies: it is the condition and milieu in which corporeality is socially, sexually, and discursively produced" (1995, 104). Not only does the mystique of the city increase in Emily's mind, but it takes on a romantic corporeality, offering the possibility of a poetic immersion in humanity—of which she feels she has been deprived in the suburbs. Before long she herself is aboard the Fifth Avenue bus, passing by and leaving behind her own apartment window as she makes her way uptown in the company of the stranger to whom she will lose her virginity. Desperate to escape her tawdry, discomfiting mother, and to experience something of the urban romance that she perceives has embraced her sister, Emily leaves the apartment to go and see a movie on Eighth Street: "free of the house," she steps into Washington Square in the early evening, wearing a new yellow dress. She finds that the lamps are "glowing in the trees" and she luxuriates in "deep breaths of the gentle air" (Yates 2008, 34). The romance of this crepuscular escape is soon intensified by the appearance of a soldier on furlough from Camp Croft in South Carolina, a man of indeterminate name—"either Warren Maddock or Warren Maddox" (35)—who asks for directions to "the jazz place." This initially unremarkable urban interaction throws Emily into "perplexity"—flustered, she rattles off a jumbled inventory of street names, punctuated by breathless hesitations like "I mean," "I guess," "it's sort of hard to tell you," and "wait." Her detailed knowledge of street-names contrasts sharply with her profound confusion in giving directions, indicating that her rootedness in New York City is largely superficial, and that beneath her excitement she is overwhelmed by the intensity of the urban environment.

She embraces it nonetheless, boarding a Fifth Avenue bus that is presented to her in the manner of an exciting fairground ride, by an out-oftowner who makes her feel like a local. She shrinks away from the railing of the bus in case her mother happens to look out of the apartment window and see her, and embarks up Fifth Avenue with trepidation, finding relief in the fact "that the soldier did most of the talking" (35). Yates proceeds to take her, and us, on a tour of yet more iconic New York locations—the Empire State Building, 42nd Street (where she is kissed, not far from the Roosevelt Hotel where she and her violent brother-in-law Tony will later have their show-down), and Central Park, where she is maneuvered onto the ground "under a rustling tree" (37) for what seems to be a moderately unobjectionable first sexual encounter. The evening reaches an anticlimactic end, however, in Times Square, where the two go for an awkward, emetic, post-coital malted. Wracked with nausea, embarrassment, and disillusionment, Emily sees the city as a monstrous tableau, to which Warren, and everyone else, appears oblivious. Yates's description calls to mind the macabre paintings of Hierony-mus Bosch or Pieter Bruegel: "Everyone they passed looked grotesque, like figures in a fever dream: a leering, bespectacled sailor, a drunken Negro in a purple suit, a muttering old woman carrying four greasy shopping bags" (38). Returning to Washington Square in silence on the downtown IRT local, the reckless enchantment of earlier in the evening has dissipated entirely. The city is now characterized by advertisements and noise, which symbolize a breakdown of communication between the pair and their incipient (and per-manent) parting of the ways, without so much as a goodnight kiss. Worst of all, we learn, they fail to "exchange [...] addresses" (39), an omission of eti-quette far more telling than any other that has occurred during the evening, that highlights once again Yates's preoccupation with the significance of place: people's exact locations are of the utmost importance.

Emily sets out to embrace her urban environment, approaching the mer-curial urban space of Washington Square and the wider New York City with the curiosity and desire of a Dorothy Richardson or Virginia Woolf. She naively trusts "the world to treat her gently," (O'Nan, n.p.), but she quickly falls victim to the deeply urban quandary diagnosed by Georg Simmel in "The Metropolis and Mental Life": although the city may seem to be practi-cally in her living room, urban "bodily proximity and narrowness of space makes the mental distance only the more visible" (1969, 55). Desperate to seem—if not necessarily to *be*—independent, Emily discovers that at the heart of metropolitan life lurks a struggle between autonomy and socio-cultural currents; or, to quote Simmel again, "the deepest problems of modern life flow from the attempt of the individual to maintain the independence and individuality of his existence against the sovereign powers of society" (47). While life may be "made infinitely easy for the personality in that stim-ulations, interests, uses of time and consciousness are offered to it from all sides" (59), one's individuality is swiftly swallowed up by the metropolis, a tide against which it is difficult to swim. As the city becomes increasingly chaotic, surreal, grotesque, and finally absurd, Emily becomes gradually more bewildered and isolated, before finding herself back where she started with nothing to show for it, "inescapably alone" (Yates, quoted in O'Nan, n.p.).

This encounter in Washington Square and the subsequent trip through Manhattan, marks the start of a journey that exemplifies Matthew Beaumont and Gregory Dart's "sense of the metropolis as a site of endless making and unmaking; one in which [...] identities of all kinds are constantly solidifying, constantly liquefying" (2010, x). Within Emily's larger, figurative journey, there also takes place a number of smaller, literal journeys, which play a pivotal role in the solidifying and liquefying not just of identity but of relationships and certain perceptions about the world too. Pivotal moments often take place for Emily because, or within the bounds, of moving vehicles, further emphasizing the instability of her character's place-identity. These partially indeterminate spaces function like Plato's *khôra*, described in his account of the universe, *Timaeus*—namely as figurative vessels located somewhere between becoming and being, in which formative matter is held. The top floor of the Fifth Avenue bus is the location not of her first kiss, or even her first kiss on a Fifth Avenue bus, but of something more opaque and significant: "it was the first kiss of its kind, ever" (Yates 2008, 36). This is a decisive moment, the point of no return for a woman who will become "a prisoner of sexual liberation" (Castronovo and Goodleaf 1996, 133), and the first of many erotic humiliations that will take Emily from Greenwich Village to Barnard College and Columbia University, Hell's Kitchen, Chelsea, the West Twenties, the Upper East Side, and Gramercy Park.

Another, earlier, example of this kind of transport-related narrative flashpoint is brought about by the young Sarah's need for dental work, when the girls are still living in the suburbs. Sarah gets to "ride the train to New York once a week" (Yates 2008, 13) and spend time with her father after visiting the orthodontist. Emily, as a child, is "jealous, both of the orthodontia and the city visits" (14). Decades later, when Sarah comes clean about the frequency of her train journeys, confessing that they were largely just a ruse so that their father could spend time with her, we learn that Emily, "even now, at thirty-six" (135) is still jealous. Sarah's train rides represent a missed connection for Emily, both with the city and with her father; that they are withheld from her (but not her sister) is formative, highlighting simultaneously her isolation and her entrapment.

There are a number of further instances at which the narrative turns on a moment of revelation that takes place inside a vehicle. The unexpected death of Walter Grimes, for example, brings about an epiphany for Emily as she leans against the window of the limousine on her return from his cremation in Westchester County: her realization that the tears she has finally managed to shed are not for her father but are "wholly for herself" (42), provides an early glimpse of her deeply selfish, self-pitying nature. A drive back from Great Hedges with Andrew Crawford, Emily's highly-strung but impotent first husband, leads to yet another pivotal moment on board a moving vehicle. Topographically precise, as ever, Yates's narrator informs us that having "crossed the Queensboro Bridge" and "crawled through traffic to the West Side," they turn "uptown, heading home" (76), when Andrew launches into the extraordinarily venomous speech about his hatred of her body that precipitates their divorce. Later in the novel, Emily raises the possibility that Tony may have killed Sarah while returning from a drive with Howard Dunninger. Yates uses the occasion to highlight Emily's awareness of the precariousness of her relationship with Dunninger, a relationship that is the only thing keeping her from terminal isolation: "Three or four old barns went by, and then any number of suburban developments, and then the beginnings of the Bronx; they were all the way to the Henry Hudson Bridge" when Emily finally realizes that "there were things she would never know about Howard" (196). Once again, Yates uses the passing by of places, both specific and abstract, to reflect Emily's fundamental rootlessness, in addition to prefiguring the futility of her relationship with Howard. Finally, Emily also takes two car rides with Peter, one at the very end of the novel, to which I will return, and one directly after Pookie's funeral, when he drives Emily "down a long straight road" (199) to visit Tony. This is another revelatory journey, both for Emily and for the reader. Driving through "suburban streets so thickly populated that he had to keep braking for stoplights," Emily learns that Great Hedges has been demolished, that Tony has a new wife and a new home, but most importantly that her sister used to tell her children: "Emmy's a free spirit" (201). Such information is deeply moving, and causes "the walls of Emily's throat [to close] up." But of course, once again, Yates is highlighting her profound and irrevocable isolation, as well as her own realization of it. This loving detail has come too late: Sarah is long dead.

Foucault describes a further kind of heterotopia: that of crisis. Heterotopias of crisis, he writes, comprise "privileged or sacred or forbidden places that are reserved for the individual who finds himself in a state of crisis with respect to the society or the environment in which he lives" (1984, 48). He further suggests that such places are "without geographical coordinates," and makes reference to "the tradition of the honeymoon, or 'voyage de noces,'" which, being the socio-cultural and psychic spaces of "the girl's defloration [...] could not take place 'anywhere.'" As well as being akin to the *khôra*, these mobile, porous places—the bus, the train, the car—clearly bear a correlation to this kind of heterotopia. For Emily, an individual in an almost constant state of crisis with respect to her society and her environment, these places are both 'somewhere' and 'nowhere,' liminal and definitive. She herself, meanwhile, calls to mind a different sort of vessel, and yet another kind of Foucauldian heterotopia: the ship. The ship, Foucault argues, "is the heterotopia par excellence": "a floating part of space, a placeless place, that lives by itself, closed in on itself and at the same time poised in the infinite ocean, and yet, from port to port, tack by tack, from brothel to brothel, it goes as far as the colonies, looking for the most precious things hidden in their gardens..." (1984, 49).

*   *   *

Emily also embodies some of the characteristics that Michel De Certeau assigns to New York, in "Walking in the City": she too displays "extremes of ambition and degradation," and "has never learned the art of growing old by playing on all [her] pasts. [Her] present invents itself, from hour to hour, in the act of throwing away its previous accomplishments and challenging the future" (1984, 91). There is a grim pattern to Emily's restless movement from place to place, to her shrugging off of past experience, and to her humiliations and failures, but "unlike the reader," as O'Nan suggests, "she can't see [it]" (n.p.). For her, a literal and emotional migrant, each new place superficially represents a new beginning, and is emblematic of her quest to "embark on a new and better life" (Yates 2008, 117). But Yates ensures that the proliferation of the places she inhabits—"drab" (85) apartment blocks, "temporary" homes (80), "orderly" (81) workplaces—contributes to their ominous non-specificity, until even familiar places such as Greenwich Village start to resemble what anthropologist Marc Augé conceptualizes as "non-places" which "cannot be defined as relational, or historical, or concerned with identity" (1995, 77). Yates gradually compels the reader to a position of elevation above the narrative, and, by extension, above New York, observing both city and text from the kind of height that "makes the complexity of the city readable and immobilizes its opaque mobility in a transparent text" (De Certeau 1984, 91), as well as transfiguring the reader "into a voyeur" (92). The crowds, chaos, and subjectivity of place at street level melts away, and is replaced by an impersonal "wave of verticals" that "lifts up the skyscrapers over Wall Street, sinks down at Greenwich, then rises again to the crests of Midtown, quietly passes over Central Park, and finally undulates off into the distance beyond Harlem" (91). Such a wave resembles in the abstract the peaks and troughs of Emily's life, through which she has proceeded from little death to temporary resurrection time and again. The aim of such a removal from the places which constitute Emily's identity, which occurs concurrently with Yates's depiction of her increasingly gutless treatment of her sister and mother, is to erode our sympathy for her, a literary maneuver that ensures Emily's isolation is complete, and serves to buttress Yates's view of the human experience as irredeemably lonely.

As the novel progresses Emily becomes increasingly concerned with the cleanliness of her living space, as Yates gradually strips her apartments of their particularity and indicates the steady eradication of the uniqueness of the places she occupies. Place ceases to be a medium which signifies that change might be possible for Emily: her locations become anodyne, little more than a sequence of points on a map. As she retreats into her final apartment, unwilling to walk through streets that are now "seething with memories of the dead" (Yates 2008, 218), she ceases to occupy the role of the migrational city dweller capable of subverting geometrical urban planning. What once were "liberated spaces" (De Certeau 1984, 105) are now threatening and over-burdened with the past. As the novel concludes, Yates appears to offer Emily deliverance in her rejection of, and departure from, the city and its increasingly abstract units of place, and her movement toward and embrace of a new place. This final move, Yates appears to suggest, will transform Emily's world into a state that can be dealt with, and permit her "to be lifted out of the city's grasp," her body "no longer clasped by the streets that turn and return it according to an anonymous law" (92). And, indeed, Yates does offer a tantalizingly double-edged denouement, hinting that redemption may, after all, be a possibility for Emily. As *The Easter Parade* draws to a close, the life-in-death connotations of the novel's title are invoked in numerous ways, from a reference to the month of April with all its expectant associations, to the Christ-like figure of Emily's nephew Peter, whose capacity for clemency seemingly knows no bounds, and even in the redemptive-sounding name of the state in which Peter lives and Emily is seeking refuge—New Hampshire. "[R]eturning from a long walk to the Village that she'd forced herself to take" (Yates 2008, 218), Emily remembers Sarah's son Peter, the young priest, and calls him up in the hope of an offer of sanctuary. Offering her the kindness she herself refused to show her sister in her time of need, Peter tells her: "you can stay as long as you like" (220). In spite of Emily's appalling tantrum on her arrival, Peter forgives her without hesitation, kindly telling her: "I think you're probably very tired and need some rest" (226). As he takes her suitcase, and the narrator states conclusively "they were here," it seems that Emily's journey is finally at an end: she may have finally found a place to call home.

But the novel's melancholy opening pronouncement still looms large—neither sister, we have been assured, will "have a happy life." Yates carefully sows seeds of doubt throughout his depiction of the ostensible haven of New Hampshire, not least by drawing attention to Emily's once unthinkable return to the "trees and neat white houses" of suburbia (224). Peter suddenly seems less stalwart and less Christ-like when we recall that his Biblical counterpart actually betrayed Christ on the eve of his crucifixion—and betrayal from him seems all the more likely when his words of forgiveness ("you don't have to apologize") provide a direct echo of those Emily herself used to say to the impotent and infuriating Andrew Crawford.

In breaking away from the city, in which "no sight or sound or smell [...] was free of old associations" (212)—a process begun following her paranoiac retreat into her final apartment in the West Twenties and completed by her flight to New Hampshire—Emily loses her connection with the places which constitute her subjectivity. While she may have been rootless throughout her life, lacking Heidegger's notion of a properly authentic existence as well as the stable identity that grows from sufficient relation to place and culture, Yates has nonetheless used her movement through an extensive list of places to create an emotionally invested network of locations in which her self-conception, however frail, might reside. In short, her final flight costs her whatever small place she had once maintained in the world, and causes her to regress toward the passivity and entrapment of her suburban girlhood, her life once again held precariously in the hands of others.

NOTES

1. Asked about *The Easter Parade*, Yates invoked Gustave Flaubert's remark that "Madame Bovary, c'est moi," saying "Emily fucking Grimes is *me*." He indicated that the story was drawn from his own life, saying that "it was all there lying around. Peter. My poor pretentious mother," with credit due to him largely only because he was "the one who *saw* it" (Bailey, 465).

2. T.S. Eliot used this phrase in the essay "Hamlet and His Problems" (1919), to describe "a set of objects, a situation, a chain of events which shall be the formula of that particular emotion" that the poet hopes to evoke in the reader. When Yates was interviewed by *Ploughshares* in 1972, the interviewers recalled that he would open his class at the Iowa Writers' Workshop, where he taught from 1964 to 1971, with a lecture based on a quotation from Eliot about the objective correlative.

3. This character trait evokes Georg Simmel's observation that "Someone who sees without hearing is much more uneasy than someone who hears without seeing. In this there is something characteristic of the sociology of the big city. Interpersonal relationships in big cities are distinguished by a marked preponderance of the activity of the eye over the activity of the ear" (1912, 26–27).

BIBLIOGRAPHY

Ardener, S. 1981. "Ground Rules and Social Maps for Women: An Introduction." In *Women and Space: Ground Rules and Social Maps*, edited by S. Ardener, 11–34. London: Croon Helm.
Augé, Marc. 1995. *Non-Places: Introduction to an Anthropology of Supermodernity*. London: Verso.
Auster, Paul. 1987. *City of Glass*. London: Faber & Faber.
Bachelard, Gaston. 1994. *The Poetics of Space*. Translated by Maria Jolas. Boston: Beacon Press.
Bailey, Blake. 2003. *A Tragic Honesty: The Life and Work of Richard Yates*. New York: Picador.
Barral, M.R. 1969. "Merleau-Ponty on the Body." *Southern Journal of Philosophy* 7, no. 2: 171–79.
Beaumont, Matthew, and Gregory Dart, eds. 2010. *Restless Cities*. London: Verso.
Benjamin, Walter. 2003. "On Some Motifs in Baudelaire." In *Walter Benjamin: Selected Writings:*

1938–1940, edited by Michael Williams Jennings and Howard Eiland, 313–55. Cambridge, MA: Belknap.

Beuka, Robert. 2004. *SuburbiaNation: Reading Suburban Landscape in Twentieth-Century American Fiction and Film*. Basingstoke: Palgrave.

Broyard, Anatole. 1997. *Kafka Was the Rage: a Greenwich Village Memoir*. New York: Vintage.

Casey, Edward. 1993. *Getting Back into Place: Toward a Renewed Understanding of the Place-world*. Bloomington: Indiana University Press.

Castronovo, David, and Steven Goldleaf. 1996. *Richard Yates*. New York: Twayne.

Charlton-Jones, Kate. 2014. *Dismembering the American Dream: The Life and Fiction of Richard Yates*. Tuscaloosa: University of Alabama Press.

Cresswell, Tim. 2004. *Place: A Short Introduction*. Oxford: Blackwell.

De Certeau, Michel. 1984. "Walking in the City." In *The Practice of Everyday Life*, translated by Steven Rendall. Berkeley: University of California Press.

Eliot, T.S. 1997. "Hamlet and His Problems." In *The Sacred Wood*, 81–87. London: Faber & Faber.

Entrikin, J. Nicholas. 1991. *The Betweenness of Place: Towards a Geography of Modernity*. Baltimore: John Hopkins University Press.

Forster, E.M. 1910. *Howards End*. London: Edward Arnold.

Foucault, Michel. 1984. "Of Other Spaces: Utopias and Heterotopias." *Architecture, Mouvement, Continuité* 5: 46–49.

Grosz, Elizabeth. 1995. *Space, Time and Perversion: Essays on the Politics of Bodies*. New York: Routledge.

Hauge, Ashild Lappegard. 2007. "Identity and Place: A Critical Comparison of Three Identity Theories." *Architectural Science Review* 50, no. 1: 44–51.

Heath, Stephen. n.d. "Narrative Space." *Screen* 17, no. 3: 68–112.

Heidegger, Martin. *Being and Time*. (1927) 2008. New York: Harper Perennial.

_____. *Poetry, Language, Thought*. (1971) 1975. Translated by Albert Hofstader. New York: Harper.

Heidegger, Martin, and David Farrell Krell. 1993. *Basic Writings*. New York: Routledge.

Homberger, Eric, and Christopher Bigsby. 2006. "New York City and the Struggle of the Modern." In *The Cambridge Companion to Modern American Culture*, 314–31. Cambridge, MA: Cambridge University Press.

hooks, bell. 1991. *Yearning: Race, Gender, and Cultural Politics*. London: Turnaround.

James, Henry. *Washington Square*. (1880) 2010. Edited by Adrian Poole. Oxford: Oxford University Press.

Jurca, Catherine. 2001. *White Diaspora: The Suburb and the Twentieth-Century American Novel*. Princeton, NJ: Princeton University Press.

Klinkowitz, Jerome. 1986. *The New American Novel of Manners: The Fiction of Richard Yates, Dan Wakefield, and Thomas McGuane*. Athens: University of Georgia Press.

Lehan, Richard. 1998. *The City in Literature: An Intellectual and Cultural History*. Berkeley: University of California Press.

Massey, Doreen. 1994. *Space, Place and Gender*. Malden, MA: Polity.

Merleau-Ponty, Maurice. 1962. *Phenomenology of Perception*. London: Routledge.

Miller, J. Hillis. 1995. *Topographies*. Stanford: Stanford University Press.

Mumford, Lewis. 1961. *The City in History: Its Origins, Its Transformations, and Its Prospects*. New York: Harcourt, Brace, and World.

Naparsteck, Martin. 2012. *Richard Yates Up Close: The Writer and His Works*. Jefferson, NC: McFarland.

O'Nan, Stewart. 1999. "The Lost World of Richard Yates: Why a Great Writer of the Age of Anxiety Disappeared from Print." *Boston Review*. 1 October. https://bostonreview.net/stewart-onan-the-lost-world-of-richard-yates. Accessed July 19, 2016.

Pred, Allan. 1984. "Place as Historically Contingent Process: Structuration and the Time-Geography of Becoming Places." *Annals of the Association of American Geographers* 74, no. 2 (March): 279–97.

Proshansky, H.M., A.K. Fabian, and R. Kaminoff. 1983. "Place-Identity: Physical World Socialization of the Self." *Journal of Environmental Psychology* 3: 57–83.

Rose, Gillian. 1993. *Feminism and Geography: The Limits of Geographical Knowledge*. London: Polity.

Simmel, Georg. 1912. *Mélanges de Philosophie Relativiste: Contribution À La Culture Philosophique*. Translated by Alix Guillain. Paris: F. Alcan.

_____. 1969. "The Metropolis and Mental Life." In *Classic Essays on the Culture of Cities*, edited by Richard Sennett, 47–60. Englewood Cliffs, NJ: Prentice-Hall.

Stevenson, R.L. 1950. "Stevenson to Clemens, 16 April 1893." *Twainian*, October 1950.

White, E.B. (1949) 1999. *Here Is New York*. New York: The Little Bookroom.

Wimsatt, William Upski. 2001. *Bomb the Suburbs*. Berkeley, CA: Soft Skull Press.

Wolff, Janet. 1985. "The Invisible Flâneuse: Women and the Literature of Modernity." *Theory, Culture & Society* 2, no. 3 (November): 37–46.

Yates, Richard. (1961) 1986. *Revolutionary Road*. London: Methuen.

_____. (1976) 2008. *The Easter Parade*. London: Vintage.

_____. 1972. DeWitt Henry and Geoffrey Clark. "An Interview with Richard Yates." Winter. *Ploughshares*. https://www.pshares.org/issues/fall-2011/archive-interview-richard-yates.

Aversion as Diversion
The Politics of Disgust
in Cold Spring Harbor

CHLOÉ AVRIL

Introduction

Readers of the fiction of Richard Yates can hardly have missed the fact that several key characters have a tendency to recur, in varied forms, in most if not all of his novels and short stories. These characters are fictionalized versions of people who have been central in Yates's own life, including himself. Indeed, Frank Wheeler in *Revolutionary Road* (1961), Robert Prentice in *A Special Providence* (1969), William Grove in *A Good School* (1978) or Phil Drake in *Cold Spring Harbor* (1986) can all be recognized as more or less straightforward portrayals of the author himself as he struggled through deeply trying experiences at different times in his life. Grove's ungainly coming of age, Prentice's involvement in World War II that held, but ultimately disappointed, the promise of making him a man, and Wheeler's (also eventually unsuccessful) struggle not to give up his aspirations and lose himself in the depersonalizing corporate world and conformity-inducing suburbs all become ways for Yates to work through some of his own personal issues. Many more characters can be added to this list, for example the main protagonist of *The Easter Parade* (1976), Emily Grimes, of whom Yates said, in an explicit reference to one of his literary heroes, "Emily fucking Grimes is me" (Daly 2014). When it comes to *Revolutionary Road*, Yates also claimed that "every character in the book was partially based on myself" (2011, 213). Moreover, as his biographer attests, when writing fiction inspired by his own life, "[g]ive or take a few syllables," Yates tended to "[stick] to the facts" (Bailey 2003, 11).

Second to the author himself, the character that perhaps reappears most often in Yates's fiction is the one based on his own mother, Ruth "Dookie" Yates. Dookie resurfaces again and again in different dramatic forms as though a ghost that, no matter how often it is confronted, fails to be satisfyingly exorcised. Yates never tried to hide the source of his inspiration, as can be most clearly seen by the fact that he named the mother figure in his fourth novel, *The Easter Parade*, Pookie, thus leaving a difference of only one letter between the character and her model. In this essay, I wish to focus on one particular version of this figure, namely, Gloria Drake. Gloria, at once the "most compelling and repellent character" (Pei 1986, par. 5) of Yates's last published novel *Cold Spring Harbor* (1986), occupies a central place in a narrative that typically exhibits the ambiguous feelings he harbored towards his mother. In this specific portrayal, the emotion that comes through most emphatically is one of disgust and, in what follows, I will explore its varied facets in order to tease out the implications it has for our understanding, not so much of Gloria herself, but of the other characters who experience it. Ultimately, I am interested in uncovering the social function that disgust fulfills in Yates's narrative. Therefore, rather than locating the resonance of Gloria's portrayal in Yates's autobiography, what will concern me instead is Yates's capacity to dissect his characters' emotional lives in order to reveal unpleasant truths about how—more than external circumstances—it is their own feelings that tend to keep them mired in insecurity and bad faith.

Yates was a keen observer and chronicler of human behavior and the motives that underpin it. This talent was recognized by many of his contemporaries, including writers such as Kurt Vonnegut, Thomas Pynchon, Dorothy Parker and Tennessee Williams, all of whom voiced their admiration for him. The latter for example praised *Revolutionary Road*, Yates's first—and for many also his most accomplished—novel, stating in his review, "Here is more than fine writing; here is what, added to fine writing, makes a book come immediately, intensely and brilliantly alive. If more is needed to make a masterpiece in modern American fiction, I am sure I don't know what it is" (quoted in Venant 1989, 1). Despite such positive critical support however, Yates never achieved the kind of success that many believed he deserved. Indeed, while his first novel was generally well-received—a notable exception being *The New Yorker* in which Yates also unsuccessfully tried to get his short stories published for years (Bailey 2003, 228, 507–509)—it did not sell especially well. Nor did any of the books that followed. All in all, Yates "never sold more than 12,000 copies of any one book in hardback" (O'Nan 1999).

The close autobiographical nature of Yates's fiction in which he kept revisiting the same painful personal experiences may have been a reason for his lack of popularity during his lifetime. One of the readers who expressed concern about Yates's overt autobiographical tendencies in his writing was the novelist and critic Robert Towers, who, in a generally favorable review of Yates's second collection of stories *Liars in Love* (1981), nonetheless complained that Yates seemed "under some enchantment that compelled him to keep circling the same half-acre of pain," and was often unable (especially in his longer fiction) "to escape the prison of an (apparently) autobiographical self into the freely imagined lives of others" (Towers 1981, par. 2). In turn, this also meant that Yates's fiction lacked what came to be more in vogue in the three decades during which he wrote. In *Dismembering the American Dream* (2014), the first book-length critical study of Yates's work, Kate Charlton-Jones notes for example that the kind of fiction popular in Yates's day "celebrated diversity, instability, change, and above all else, it somehow upheld the notion that anything was possible. It was exciting, experimental and it looked forward, not backward" (4). In contrast, Yates's writing, revisiting as it does many of the scenes of his own childhood and young adult life, keeps looking backward to the 1940s and 50s. As a result, according to Charlton-Jones, it is also "[u]nashamedly WASPish" (4). Furthermore, Yates never tries to open up a world of many possibilities to his readers. Instead, we meet a gallery of ordinary men and women who long to escape the mediocrity that characterizes their lives, but who all ultimately fail due to a mixture of circumstances and individual failings of their own. The narrative world of Yates is thus a dark one with little or no hope; one made all the more painful by the detailed examination of the kinds of shortcomings that we can all uncomfortably recognize in ourselves.

It is undeniable, however, that Yates's stories have also always had the power to move readers that were lucky enough to come across them. Towers, for example, explains how Yates's first short story collection, *Eleven Kind of Loneliness* (1962), although out of print when his second one was published, had somehow reached "cult" status, "the mere mention of its title [being] enough to produce quick, affirmative nods from a whole generation of readers" (1981, par.1). In her acknowledgments, Charlton-Jones also points to the specific grip that Yates's fiction exerts on its readers, remembering how her own introduction to Yates—when a friend handed her a copy of *Revolutionary Road* through her kitchen window—could be seen as a perfect illustration of what Richard Ford has called the "cultural-literary secret handshake among [Yates's] devotees" (Charlton-Jones 2014, xiii; Ford 2000, par. 2). Thanks to the reprinting of all of his works by Vintage at the beginning of the 21st century and the successful film adaptation of *Revolutionary Road* by Sam Mendes in 2008, there will now, hopefully, be a growing number of readers who will have access to and take pleasure in Yates's unique fictional take on the American condition.

The Yates Revival and the Affective Turn

This latest revival of interest that Yates's work has seen in the last decade and a half might not be completely fortuitous, coming as it does in the midst of a change in cultural wisdom and accompanying critical trends that have developed in recent years. From the 1960s, when Yates published his first novel, to the end of the 20th century, playfully metafictional postmodern novels were the kind of literary writing that received most critical accolades, while also attracting the attention and rhetorical acrobatics of deconstructive literary analysis. The realist mode, as the hallmark of a naïve past where people still believed in an objective reality (beyond its representation in arbitrary systems of signification) that could be accurately portrayed, became almost taboo. Yates was well aware of being out of synch with the aesthetic fashion of his days but nonetheless believed in the affective superiority of his own brand of realism compared to much of the then trendy postmodern writing which, according to Charlton-Jones, he felt was "led by intellectual rather than experiential ideas" (2014, 8). In a 1972 interview for *Ploughshares*, he admitted

> I've tried and tried, but I just can't stomach most of what's now being called "The postrealistic fiction." I can't read John Barth with anything but irritation. I can't read Donald Barthelme at all. I can read hardly any of the many other new "postrealists," whatever their ever-increasingly famous names may be. I know it's all very fashionable stuff and I know it provides an endless supply of witty little intellectual puzzles and puns and fun and games for graduate students to play with, but it's emotionally empty. It isn't felt [2011, 221–22].

As though vindicating Yates's artistic judgment, the mood has now shifted and the taste for self-referential stylistic pyrotechnics and deconstructive readings has waned, allowing for a return to the (guilty) pleasures of realistic personal narratives with which readers can identify and in which they can become fully absorbed. Toril Moi makes this "paradigm change" in literary fashion explicit in order to explain the unprecedented interest that Karl Ove Knausgaard's series of autobiographical novels, *My Struggle*, has garnered among readers, not only in Norway but across the world. She admits that trying to account for this phenomenon "has turned out to be a challenge [...] for literary scholars" since "it shows us something that everybody knows but that literary critics have done their best to forget, namely that the author exists, and that he always conveys the world as he sees it based on his own experiences and his own worldview." The "established doctrine that art, style and language at all costs must be perceived as divorced from life" (Moi 2013, 206) has itself become a tired cliché rather than a universal point of critical departure. What matters again is truth to life and experience and with it the much reviled realist mode. What better times can there be for a writer like

Yates for whom "[v]eracity is everything" (Atkinson 2002, par. 11)?[1] What counted as a liability in his own lifetime—his overt reliance on autobiographical experience—might thus also be the key to his newfound success. Indeed, what allows readers to connect on a personal level with Yates's fiction is the reality they see reflected in his individual character portrayals. On opening one of his books, readers are instantly able to identify with the emotions and motives that inform his characters, both the ones they are conscious of but, more importantly, those they try to hide from everyone including themselves. Apart from entering into a fictional world that they find compelling, readers are also invited to confront truths about themselves, making "the act of reading" Yates "one of recognition" (Charlton-Jones 2014, 2).

The paradigmatic shift that the field of literary criticism has been witnessing according to Moi has a correlation in the concomitant "Affective Turn" that has developed within many academic discourses. The focus on language and signs (and their slippery unreliability as a source of meaning and communication) has led to "a perceived impasse in cultural studies," making more and more scholars shift their attention to the world of affects as a more solid and direct guide to understanding human behavior (Hemmings 2005, 549). The turn towards affect also promises to deliver us from the post-structuralist "critical paranoia" characterized by "the search for, and deadening (re)discovery of, prohibition everywhere: prohibition where it appeared there was freedom, prohibition in a space we had not, until now, thought to look" (553). Such a "hermeneutics of suspicion," having disabused us of any generally held "truths" we might harbor, has now come full circle and needs to be replaced by a new discourse that can help us get to the heart of what really moves us.[2] This new scholarly attention to affects has led to highly productive readings of both contemporary social phenomena—using, for example, fear and disgust in order to understand more deeply the post – 9/11 context (Ahmed 2004)—and literature, with shame serving, for example, as a similarly revealing concept in Sedgwick's (2003) and Moi's (2013) interpretation of Henry James and Knausgaard respectively.

In much of the discourse on affects, importance is placed on their being in essence precognitive, thus not "governed by our beliefs, cognitions, and desires" and having "no inherent knowledge of, or relation to, the objects or situations that trigger them" (Leys 2011, 437). As a result, care is taken to differentiate them from feelings which are "personal and biographical," or "emotions [that] are social," affects being instead "pre-personal" (Shouse quoted in Leys 2011, 442). The focus on affects thus promises to give us access to "the residue or excess that is not socially produced" and which "constitutes the very fabric of our being" (Hemmings 2005, 549). Not all affect theorists agree, however, that a strict distinction can be made between the concepts of affects and emotions.[3] Nor would they all accept that affects are "visceral forces" (Leys 2011, 437) independent of the social context in which they manifest themselves and thus "outside social meaning" (Hemmings 2005, 565). In *The Cultural Politics of Emotions* (2004; 2014), for example, Sara Ahmed explains her approach as one that rejects individualized, ahistorical, and acultural tendencies in the study of emotions, arguing instead that "emotions should not be regarded as psychological states, but as social and cultural practices." What her study of contemporary public displays of emotions such as fear, disgust, or shame proposes to do instead is "offer a model of sociality of emotion" (2014, 9). William Ian Miller's full-length study of disgust also stresses how this is an emotion that is often particularly social in both its origin and consequences (1997). Furthermore, Claire Hemmings maintains that affects "might in fact be valuable precisely to the extent that [they are] not autonomous" so that a critical focus on them would greatly enrich our understanding of the texts and contexts in which they are manifested (2005, 565).

This second approach to affects and emotions is the one which can be most fruitful in interpreting the work of Yates. As we have already seen, truth figures foremost as a value that informs Yates's whole artistic project. In order to bring the reader "near enough to life's palpable details" (Ford 2000, par. 22), he felt required to draw his characters with an eye to all the affects and emotions that influence their individual behavior and relations with the people and world around them. Far from disconnecting his characters' feelings from the social context in which they are experienced, Yates provides a profound insight into how they are implicated in the reproduction of social norms, often also sealing the fate of those who already find themselves on the margins. Emotions thus work more as the ties that bind us to the social order rather than as tools that can potentially free us from it. It is fear (of failure) for example that pushes many of his characters towards conformity or, worst of all, a sense of personal inauthenticity.

Another emotion that works in a similarly socially constricting way in Yates's fiction is disgust. Disgust is a negative affect that results from the encounter with an object we find repellent and our innate reaction to it is that of "pulling away" (Tomkins 2008, 356). As Silvan S. Tomkins explains, "Disgust is primarily [...] an act of distancing the self from an object" (357). This aversive reaction is necessary since the object found disgusting has the power to defile and pollute that which comes into contact with it (Tomkins 2008, 416; Miller 1997, 2; Ahmed 2014, 87). While it might seem counterintuitive to investigate the social meaning and consequences of disgust—disgust after all "looks too much like a purely instinctual drive" (Miller 1997, 7), an automatic reaction to what the body inherently finds repellent—Miller argues that disgust has "intensely political significance" in the way it "work[s] to hierarchize our political order" (8). Following Miller, Stephanie Lawler also implicates disgust in the stratification of society and the maintenance of the status quo, claiming that it plays a central role in "the work of drawing distinctions" (2005, 438). My reading of *Cold Spring Harbor*, therefore, will be informed by this understanding of disgust as a way both to establish or perpetuate social boundaries, and to condition the subject experiencing it. Although disgust recurs in much of Yates's fiction, often connected to the same kind of figure, I will focus my attention on this one particular novel since I believe it is here its function is most fully and revealingly explored.

Gloria Drake as Cold Spring Harbor's *Object of Disgust*

As noted previously, affects tend to attach themselves to objects or bodies and, in *Cold Spring Harbor*, disgust is emphatically associated with Gloria Drake, the mother figure who is often a thinly veiled portrayal of Yates's own mother. The moment we enter Gloria's apartment, together with father and son Charles and Evan Shepard, we are told that "her sad living room [...] smelled of cat droppings and cosmetics and recent cooking" (Yates 2008b, 20). Her apartment, if not yet Gloria herself, immediately constitutes an affront to the senses. As Miller explains, disgust is probably the emotion that appeals most to *sensory* images in order to give expression to the offensive nature of the object (1997, 9). The characterization of Gloria as an object of disgust is no exception in this context as the first sense that is activated is that of smell.

As we discover on our next visit to Gloria's apartment, such a repulsive display is not a unique occurrence—a sign of Gloria having been taken off guard by the fact that she generally receives few visitors. Instead, Evan is confronted by "the reek of catshit again, and the grubby upholstery, and the torrentially talking mother" (Yates 2008b, 31). We continue to follow the affect of disgust as it successively impacts upon the sense of smell, sight, and even touch—the adjective "grubby" suggesting, more than the unsightly accumulation of dirt on the sofa, the apprehension at the thought of having to come into contact with it. The third element in Evan's description—"the torrentially talking mother"—invokes yet another sense, that of hearing, in its depiction of his mounting disgust. More importantly, however, this addition works finally to connect the distaste felt about the dirty surroundings in which Gloria allows herself to live to a rejection of Gloria herself, showing how quickly disgusting objects have a tendency to pollute everything in their proximity.

Moreover, the correspondence between the unpleasant sound of Gloria's endless talking and her general physical repugnance is expressed early on: "The Shepards were both ready to believe, this afternoon, that only a long-divorced woman would ever talk as if talking were sustenance, talk until veins the size of earthworms stood out in her temples, talk until little white beads of spit were gathered and working on each other near the corners of her mouth" (Yates 2008b, 23). Quickly, the sense of disgust continues to deepen as the male gaze moves downward from her mouth to her breasts, when, in her attempt to "pantomime 'worry'" about her children coming home late "she made as if to put her hands on her heart, but instead it cupped and clasped her pendulous left breast, as if she was feeling herself up" (23). This awkwardly inappropriate gesture arguably gives cause for more mirth than outright disgust; nonetheless, the movement from mouth to breast, while not quite producing the often disgust-eliciting association between mouth and vagina (Miller 1997, 93–95), adds a sexual component to the taxonomy of repulsive feelings Gloria evokes in her guests. Furthermore, her lack of dignity and decorum does not reside so much in the sexual gesture itself, than in the fact that no one really likes to witness the spectacle of a middle-aged divorcée so publicly "dying for love" (Yates 2008b, 30) since her neediness can no longer arouse romantic fantasies in the two men.

Gloria breaches several norms of propriety in the course of this first afternoon: she gives in to many excesses, talking and drinking too much, and she also fails in a traditional woman's duty to keep herself and her home clean and presentable. Together with her drinking, or the food stains on her clothes—none of her dresses are ever "quite clean" and the one she wears to go out to dinner with Charles evinces a "grease stain left by a fallen slice of sausage on the bodice" (41)—or the putrid smells emanating from both her home and body (64–65; 71), it is also her combination of selfishness and vulnerability that makes people want to keep their distance. In the world Yates depicts where everyone has to work hard to get through life in spite of all the shortcomings they have, only resentment can be felt for someone who clings so desperately to others.

In this context, the reader might be excused for not feeling much sympathy for Gloria. As Charlton-Jones observes, this is symptomatic of the portrayal of older women in the fiction of Richard Yates who tend to be "treated harshly," while often only younger female characters are meant to attract the readers' empathetic response: this is the case for example of April Wheeler in *Revolutionary Road*, or Gloria's daughter Rachel, in *Cold Spring Harbor* (2014, 170). Blake Bailey also points to the uneven treatment of Yates's characters, writing that his "compassion for human weakness, for the flaws that make failure so inevitable, is everywhere in his work"—everywhere, that is, except for "certain characters based on his mother" (2003, 17). Moreover, in painting the picture of Gloria Drake, the most accurate portrayal of his mother according to Yates himself (553), Bailey believes that the author "milk[ed] her repugnant features all the more" (550) seeing "something a little gleeful in the narrator's tabulation of Gloria's defects, most of them expressed in grossly physical terms" (552).

According to Bailey, "one of the essential truths of Yates's childhood—of his whole life, perhaps—is that he loved and admired his mother at least as much as he later claimed to despise her" (8). The biographical correspondence between Gloria and Pookie notwithstanding, Yates's portrayal of Gloria should not be dismissed as simply a form of literary sublimation of his ambiguous feelings towards his mother. In fact, its broader social resonance is revealed through Charles's thoughts at the time of his first visit. His perception of the apartment, quoted previously, is accompanied by his critical appraisal of her social status: "She stepped back to welcome them into her sad living room [...] and Charles had her figured at once as a nice person down on her luck. New York was honeycombed with this kind of wretched gentility" (Yates 2008b, 20). Pity and sympathy often trump disgust in Charles's relation to Gloria; her flaws, after all, can be excused by her marginal position in society, both as a divorced mother raising two children on her own, and as a woman whose class position is somewhat precarious. She is "down on her luck," yet cannot let go of her social aspirations. Ironically, however, the "gentility" Charles assigns her corresponds more to what Gloria aspires to than to where she comes from. She has, very partially, succeeded in projecting the desired image of herself but, nonetheless, it is evident that her performance is more than a little off-key. Gloria, for her part, also misinterprets both Charles's "congeniality" (29) and his residential address in Cold Spring Harbor as signs of "old money" (43). This erroneously leads her to put her hopes of social climbing on her family's connection with his, an association the ultimate disappointment of which is at the dramatic core of the novel.

What Charles takes as a sign of Gloria's social decline is the simultaneous presence and absence of the marks of social status. Consequently, for example, when Gloria announces that her son Phil is enrolled at a prep school, Charles is immediately struck by the fact that "[t]here was nothing about this place, or these people, to suggest the kind of money a preparatory school would cost" (25). He is also surprised to discover that what Gloria means when she says "I live by my wits" is that she "live[s] on alimony" and not, as he thought, that she was resourceful in finding ways of earning a living (23). More than anything, Charles resents the fact that she persists in pretending. Instead of squarely facing up to the situation she is in, Gloria lives in a fantasy where climbing the social ladder always promises to happen thanks to the next encounter she makes, the next apartment she moves into, or any of the other "bold" moves she makes. She might believe in the all–American idea that anyone can make it, but a society where there is "a constant shift in classes" often implies that "great emphasis is put on appearance" (Trilling 2008, 210).[4]

And, as we have seen, Gloria more often makes the wrong rather than the right impression. As a result, her efforts aimed at improving her family's social standing do more damage than good. One such occasion is when "a sad telltale display of cigarette ashes on the oriental rug beside her chair," and a tired look indicating that she "had talked her heart and lungs and brains away" all afternoon, reveal to her son Phil that she has failed to make a good impression on Mrs. Talmage, a new acquaintance on whom Gloria had lately placed her desperate hopes of hobnobbing with "old money" (Yates 2008b, 97).

Significantly, Gloria's failure to uphold the rules of social decorum affects others just as much as herself. This is not only due to her contaminating influence as an object of disgust, but also to the ironic tendency that her attempts at self-aggrandizement have in revealing even more the mediocrity of others. Charles who, for example, puts a lot of emphasis on the value of not appearing other than what you are no matter how insignificant your life might seem, is unable to escape with his dignity unscathed from his association with Gloria. A key moment occurs in the presence of Mrs. Talmage when Gloria's insistence on calling Charles "Captain Shephard" stops simply being foolish and annoying and becomes truly mortifying (145). The rank of Captain which Charles can in fact claim as his own has been earned in the army and not the navy, and thus is a sign not of the proud fulfillment of his military career, but of his low level of professional achievement. Earlier in the novel, Charles tried to explain this delicate point of fact to Gloria telling her, "Let me explain this if I can. If you ever met a man in civilian life called 'Captain,' he's most likely to have been in the navy, don't you see? Rather than the army? Because the naval rank of captain is far more—exalted: it's only one notch below rear admiral; whereas the army's use of the same designation is an entirely different and lesser thing. I'm sure you'll understand" (76). Gloria however chooses to ignore this inconvenient truth since it does not fit in with the romanticized version of the world which she has imagined for herself and since she also fails to see why it might matter to Charles.

This trait of character is one that Gloria shares with other mother figures in Yates's work. In *The Easter Parade*, for example, Pookie also refuses to look reality in the face preferring instead the rose-tinted version she dreams up. This is perhaps best exemplified by her insistence on nicknaming the estate of her in-laws "Great Hedges" (Yates 2008a, 47). The landlord's jocular protest—unheeded by Pookie in the same manner as Gloria's treatment of Charles—that a better name for it would be "Overgrown Hedges" underlines the fact that Pookie's romantic gesture has the unintentional result of bringing the decrepit state of the place into even greater relief.

In instances such as these, Yates's fictional mothers not only make their own but also other people's shortcomings more blatant, reminding them of the knowledge, best repressed, that they themselves have fallen short of what they aspire to be. Their social faux-pas also call attention to the precariousness of personal dignity where slippages can easily occur. This realization brings with it a self-consciousness that, far from leading to a deeper knowledge of oneself, contributes instead to more damaging feelings of shame. Miller sees the two affects of disgust and shame as intimately connected to one another, being in fact opposite sides of an encounter between two objects where one feels shame as a result of being the cause of disgust in others (1997, 24). In the narrative world of *Cold Spring Harbor* no such direct pattern occurs, however. Instead, the person experiencing disgust also ends up being the one affected most by shame. This reversal comes no doubt as a result of the difficulty, especially for Gloria's children, of dissociating themselves from the object of disgust which, after all, is their own mother. It also comes from Gloria's own lack of self-awareness and inability to clearly see the consequences of her behavior—characteristics that Charlton-Jones sees as common to most of the mothers in Yates's work (2014, 55). Gloria's tenuous relation to reality was formed early on in life as she gradually learned the art of lying to herself and others, always taking care to act as though everything was really "just what [she] wanted" (Yates 2008b, 51) no matter how much reality disappointed her expectations. Gloria's predilection for going to the movies at night—"going in the daytime always meant you had to come out into the blinding streets of reality" (86)—is further evidence of her troubled relationship with the real world. This disconnection from reality is what insulates Gloria from feeling shame. This also suggests that she has not fully internalized the norms by which she is judged to be socially deficient.

Disgust as a Strategy of Diversion

The association with Gloria is thus a costly one. But, if her failure to behave adequately according to appropriate social norms leads to social insecurity and embarrassment among those around her, the shared feelings of disgust which Gloria provokes nevertheless manage to achieve a number of other things: it helps forge alliances that bring (temporary) relief, and it also allows people, albeit precariously, to divert blame for their own failure onto her, an external threat that can hopefully be contained.

Disgust, as Ahmed suggests, has the power to bring people together by turning them into "a community of those who are bound together through the shared condemnation of a disgusting object or event" (2014, 94). The first example of this is Charles's and Evan's introduction to Gloria, which gives the two men a rare opportunity to bond through a few jokes made at her expense. This connection is quickly interrupted, however, by Charles's feeling of pity toward Gloria—"there's never been anything funny about a woman dying for love" (Yates 2008b, 30).

More significant, however, are the occasions when Gloria's daughter Rachel allows herself to voice the revulsion she has always felt for her mother. Rachel's modest project in life consists in creating a small space of suburban bliss for herself and her husband Evan, but her fundamental dilemma is that her mother is both the enabler of, and main obstacle to, that domestic project. This inevitably leads to tensions between Rachel and Evan that can only be alleviated through Rachel's transfer of emotional allegiance from Gloria to her husband—something achieved by their sharing of disgust. The first occurrence happens when Rachel tells Evan of Gloria's suggestion that they should all live in the same house together. Embarrassed even to mention this to Evan, Rachel finally reveals an intense physical repulsion for her mother—one that other characters and perhaps the reader as well already feel, but which gains strength by virtue of being articulated by Rachel herself:

> "She's really sort of—crazy, Evan. I mean that. She's always been crazy. Oh, I don't suppose anybody'd want to commit her to an insane asylum or anything, but she's crazy." [...] "...And she doesn't smell very good, either."
> "Doesn't what?"
> "Smell very good. I guess that's a horrible thing to say about one's own mother, but it's true. It may be that she doesn't take baths often enough, or that when she does take a bath she forgets to use the soap, but I've dreaded getting up close to her as long as I can remember. And do you know a funny thing, Evan? I've never told anybody about that until this very minute."
> "Well, good," he said "I like it when we tell each other things" [64–65].

Prior to their acquaintance with the Shepards, the Drake children's relationship with their mother is characterized by an atypical closeness preventing such shocking admissions of disloyalty, even between themselves. However, in a desperate attempt to protect her fragile relationship with her husband, Rachel breaks from the costly and stifling sense of solidarity within the Drake cocoon and instead openly adopts the gaze (and olfactory sensibilities) of strangers. The collective alliance between Rachel and Evan born in the acridity of disgust allows the couple to emotionally lean on one another in a way that they seldom do otherwise. Similarly, emboldened by this first expression of truth, Rachel later imagines how her relation to her brother could also be strengthened by "talk[ing] about such matters as the way [their mother] smelled" (71).

Evan's affectionate reaction to Rachel's admission, which she barely notices at first in the heat of expressing such forbidden thoughts about her mother, suggests that her strategy is initially successful. Ironically however, at this stage, this sharing of disgust has the effect of creating less rather than more distance between themselves and Gloria—disgust shared is disgust halved?—since Evan takes this as a cue to consider and eventually accept the living arrangements proposed by Gloria. Thus Evan fails to accurately register Rachel's distress, which is not so much an attempt to consolidate her relationship with him as an expression of fear of the contamination that Gloria setting up house with them would engender. After all, as already noted, "[a]nything which has had contact with disgusting things itself becomes disgusting" (Tomkins 2008, 358), and the "metonymic slide" effected by disgust "does not move freely: it sticks to that which is near it; it clings" (Ahmed 2014, 87). Rachel is the one who stands most in peril of contamination and her character's trajectory certainly proves this threat to be very real. Rachel's downfall begins when she comes "carefully downstairs one morning, in a dressing gown that wasn't quite clean" (Yates 2008b, 126) and continues with emotional outbursts that are reminiscent of her mother's (156–57). The temporary relief Rachel experiences by giving in to disgust thus ends in failure because of her inability to pull away from the object that causes it. At the end of the novel, a further expression of Rachel's entry into the realm of the disgusting occurs when Evan describes her as "soft as shit" (175), later fantasizing about leaving her by driving to the other side of the country with his ex-wife and their daughter (177).

The treatment of Gloria as an abject member of the community that requires expulsion brings about a third alliance, this time between Charles Shepard and Gloria's ex-husband Curtis Drake. Gloria's growing marginalization comes to a head as the two families are gathered around Rachel's hospital bed after she has given birth to a son. Refusing to take the blame for ruining her children's lives, something Rachel accuses her of, Gloria explodes in an abusive outburst against Curtis, leading him and Charles to react in concert, taking her by the arms and forcibly removing her from the hospital building. After Gloria is "carefully loaded" into a taxi and the driver instructed that "[t]his lady's emotionally disturbed," the scene develops into a brief moment of male solidarity as "the two of them strolled like friends into the shaded, air-conditioned barroom of the Crossroads Restaurant and Lounge" (158). While trivial on the surface, this dramatic episode shows us for the first time Charles failing to support Gloria, choosing instead to bond with another man and, in so doing, asserting his own masculinity, something the male characters in Yates's fiction always tend to find difficult. Obviously, this moment can hardly compensate for the steady unraveling of Charles's masculine aspirations which began when he arrived in France three days after World War I was already over, thereby missing out on the fighting that promised to make him a man (2). However, the kinship he seeks to establish with Curtis, not least in the parallel he draws between the Drake marriage and his own, has the effect of bestowing upon the two men the gratifying status of victims (159). Identifying themselves as the long-suffering husbands of neurotic wives absolves Curtis of culpability for the Drake family situation and gives Charles the opportunity to also avoid blame for the drunken mess that his own wife Grace has slowly turned into.[5]

As can be seen from the two key episodes discussed above, Rachel and Curtis give as the ultimate explanation for their rejection of Gloria not only her physical repugnance, but her alleged mental instability as well. Both Yates's mother and Yates himself suffered from mental illness and Yates may therefore have wanted to give this theme a pronounced place in his writing.[6] What the characterization of Gloria as mad gives the other characters in the novel, however, is another chance of containment: if mad, Gloria is in a sense safely categorized as Other, and the risks of contamination associated with her as an object of disgust are made much less. The kind of ontological difference that the demonization of Gloria as a mad woman establishes between her and themselves also nourishes the hope that their own repeated failures in life can come to an end the moment they finally manage to keep her at a safe social distance.

In *Cold Spring Harbor*, Gloria clearly functions as a psychological scapegoat on which everyone can blame their own limitations and failings. According to Tomkins, "[c]ontempt–disgust is fundamentally a defensive response." It is also a type of response, in which "[i]n contrast to shame, [...] there is least self-consciousness," attention being focused on "the source, the object, rather than to the self or the face" (2008, 356). The turning of Gloria into an object of disgust ensures that the gaze remains squarely focused on her, in a similar way that madness attracts attention to itself. In this context, the alliances forged between the characters against Gloria through this sharing of disgust and their designation of her as a mad Other act as diversion strategies, shifting the focus away from themselves. With everyone pointing the finger at the repulsively unstable Gloria, none of them feel the need to search within themselves for the real source of the disappointment that characterizes their lives.

Central as authenticity was to both the life and work of Richard Yates, it hardly comes as a surprise that it should also be one of the major themes of *Cold Spring Harbor*. Yates, however, shows in this novel that bad faith constantly gets in the way of authenticity. With bad faith, people who fail to act on their dreams and aspirations always try to find excuses elsewhere, blaming their inaction on God, fate, society, or, in this case, a mad (m)other. Letting a seemingly mad mother carry all the blame prevents the characters from acknowledging their own agency and taking responsibility for their own lives. As a result, they go on repeating the same mistakes, never wanting to know why things really went wrong. Evan keeps on following the path that offers the least resistance, requiring the least level of personal commitment, while blaming others when things do not turn out as he had hoped. His wife Rachel duplicates this chronic condition of existential bad faith, lacking both the will and strength to take charge of her own life. Charles continues to convince himself that there is "nothing to be done" (Yates 2008b, 77) for the women around him, which allows him to ignore the fact that he has sacrificed his wife Grace's health and sanity in vain pursuit of trying to measure up as a man.

The reader is not allowed to see how the life of these characters develops after Gloria leaves the house in Cold Spring Harbor, but we are given enough clues to assume that not much will change because, like all the characters in Yates's fiction, "they can't help being the people they are" (Yates 2011, 212). There is, however, no doubt that Yates wanted us to look beyond one single character, in this case Gloria, for the ultimate explanation of his characters' failed lives. In an interview he gave for *Ploughshares* in 1972, he indicates as much:

> I mean, if you can blame everything on one of the characters in the story, then where's the weight of the story? Nothing falls into your own lap. […] I much prefer the kind of story where the reader is left wondering who's to blame until it begins to dawn on him (the reader) that he himself must bear some of the responsibility because he's human and therefore infinitely fallible [2011, 212].

By his own admission, Yates's uncompromising exploration of his characters' least edifying behavior and emotions aims in fact at holding up a mirror to us as readers, the unsparing honesty of his portrayals forcing us to recognize ourselves in his depiction of human fallibility. In many ways, therefore, his stories function as morality tales for our modern world. Thus, as Richard Ford has observed, Yates "invites us to pay attention, have a care, take heed, live life as if it mattered what we do, inasmuch as to do less risks it all" (Ford 2000, last par.). While there is certainly a sense of deterministic pessimism running through Yates's work, his fiction nevertheless offers the possibility to understand the mechanisms at work in the existential condition of bad faith. Showing how our tendency towards inauthenticity and self-delusion can for example masquerade as genuine and legitimate disgust, a novel like *Cold Spring Harbor* forces us to examine our most visceral reactions with a much more self-critical eye.

NOTES

1. Kate Atkinson continues, observing that "even when, at last, all that remains is 'stunted thought and shrivelled hope,' it must be viewed with an unrelenting, truthful eye" (2002, par. 11). In his introduction to *The Collected Stories of Richard Yates*, Richard Russo also sees authenticity as the greatest strength of Yates's writing "The excitement one feels reading these dark stories, I believe, is the exhilaration of encountering, recognizing and embracing the truth" (Russo 2002, xx). Moreover, Rajski (2016) shows, in his insightful reading of *Revolutionary Road*, how authenticity is a prime stylistic as well as thematic concern for Yates, his own prose working to expose the risks that the effectivizing of the forms of communication in the corporate world posed to the honest exchange of feelings in private

relationships. That truth was central to the author's life and work is also evidenced by the fact that Blake Bailey chose to entitle his biography of Yates *A Tragic Honesty*.

2. Hemmings questions, however, the extent to which the affective turn offers a radically new departure (558). She also shows a general wariness towards the tendency that any discourse vying for hegemony has to simplify the one it hopes to replace. The flaws of the "old" are emphasized so that the need for the "new" can be more urgently felt (2005, 555–56).

3. See Leys (2011) in which she points to the many similarities between affect theories on the one hand and the "Basic Emotions paradigm" on the other. She also questions the validity of what she sees as the central premise of both, i.e., that affects/emotions are "inherently independent of meaning and intention" (55C). Since what interests me is the social function and consequences of disgust, I do not find it meaningful to insist on calling it either an affect or an emotion, preferring to use the two concepts interchangeably.

4. See also Charlton-Jones (2014, 21) to whom I am indebted for showing this connection between Trilling and Yates. The aspect of appearance and more specifically performance provides the thematic center of Charlton-Jones's book on Yates.

5. Unlike Gloria, Grace at least knows how to make herself "disattendable," a quality Miller sees as indispensable in order to avoid causing disgust in others (1997, 199). She does not subject the world to embarrassing social displays, only ever rarely leaving her room and house. When she does, however, the risk that she could provoke disgust increases as evidenced by Rachel when she tells Evan that his "mother's pickled[…]. I mean I've seen her drunk before, but this is different: she's embalmed. It's like having to look at a corpse in an armchair" (2008b, 151).

6. Bailey discusses in his biography of Yates the real possibility that Dookie experienced a degree of mental illness (2003, 22). Yates himself suffered from manic depression (22), which turned particularly acute at the time he was working on *Cold Spring Harbor*, the draft of which was partly written using the hospital's "swinging food table as a desk" (Bailey 2003, 54ɔ). In his work, a number of characters show signs of mental instability. This is, for example, the case of both Pookie and her daughter Emily in *The Easter Parade*, John Wilder in *Disturbing the Peace*, or John Givings in *Revolutionary Road*.

BIBLIOGRAPHY

Ahmed, Sara. (2004) 2014. *The Cultural Politics of Emotions*. Edinburgh: Edinburgh University Press.

Atkinson, Kate. 2002. "Cast a Cold Eye." Review of *The Collected Stories of Richard Yates*. *The Guardian*, February 2. https://www.theguardian.com/books/2002/feb/02/ fiction.re views3.

Bailey, Blake. 2003. *A Tragic Honesty: The Life and Work of Richard Yates*. New York: Picador.

Charlton-Jones, Kate. 2014. *Dismembering the American Dream: The Life and Fiction of Richard Yates*. Tuscaloosa: The University of Alabama Press.

Daly, Jennifer. 2014. "'Emily Grimes is me': Anxiety, Feminism, and the Masculinity Crisis in Richard Yates's *The Easter Parade*." *Irish Journal of American Studies* 3. http://ijas. iaas.ie/index.php/emily-grimes-is-me-anxiety-feminism-and-the-masculinity-crisis-in-richard-yatess-the-easter-parade/.

Ford, Richard. 2000. "American Beauty (Circa 1955)." *New York Times*, April 9. https://www. nytimes.com/books/00/04/09/reviews/000409.09fordlt.html.

Hemmings, Clare. 2005. "Invoking Affect: Cultural Theory and the Ontological Turn." *Cultural Studies* 19 (5); 548–567. DOI: 10.1080/09502380500365473.

Leys, Ruth. 2011. "The Turn to Affect: A Critique." *Critical Inquiry* 37 (3): 434–472.

Lawler, Stephanie. 2005. "Disgusted Subjects: The Making of Middle-Class Identities." *The Sociological Review*, 53: 429–446. doi:10.1111/j.1467–954X.2005.00560.x.

Miller, William Ian. 1997. *The Anatomy of Disgust*. Cambridge, MA: Harvard University Press.

Moi, Toril. 2013. "Shame and Openness." *Salmagundi* 177 (Winter): 205–210. http://proquest.

umi.com.ezproxy.ub.gu.se/pqdweb?did=0000002939561321&Fmt=3&cl ientId=43168&
RQT=309&VName=PQD.

O'Nan, Stewart. 1999. "The Lost World of Richard Yates: Why a Great Writer of the Age of
Anxiety Disappeared from Print." *Boston Review*, October 1. http://bostonreview.net/
stewart-onan-the-lost-world-of-richard-yates.

Pei, Lowri. 1986. "The Power of Weakness." Review of *Cold Spring Harbor*, by Richard Yates.
New York Times, October 5. http://www.nytimes.com/1986/10/05/books/the-power-of-
weakness.html.

Rajski, Brian. 2016. "Writing *Systems*: Richard Yates, Remington Rand, and the Univac." *Contemporary Literature* 54 (3): 550–577. https://muse.jhu.edu/article/527195/pdf.

Russo, Richard. (2000) 2002. "Secret Hearts." Introduction to *The Collected Stories of Richard
Yates*. New York: Picador.

Tomkins, Silvan S. 2008. *Affect Imagery Consciousness: The Complete Edition*. New York:
Springer Publishing.

Towers, Robert. 1981. "Richard Yates and His Unhappy People." Review of *Liars in Love*, by
Richard Yates. *New York Times*, November 1. http://www.nytimes.com/1981/11/01/books/
richard-yates-and-his-unhappy-people.html?pagewanted=all.

Trilling, Lionel. (1950) 2008. *The Liberal Imagination*. New York: New York Review of Books.

Venant, Elizabeth. 1989. "A Fresh Twist in the Road: For Novelist Richard Yates, a Specialist
in Grim Irony, Late Fame's a Wicked Return." *Los Angeles Times*, July 9. http://articles.
latimes.com/1989-07-09/news/vw-5311_1_richard-yates.

Yates, Richard. (1976) 2008a. *The Easter Parade*. London: Vintage Books.

_____. (1986) 2008b. *Cold Spring Harbor*. London: Vintage Books.

_____. (1972) 2011. "From the Archive: An Interview with Richard Yates." *Ploughshares* 115
(37): 207–224.

Richard Yates's Autofictions and the Politics of Canonization

Sophie A. Jones

Nobody knows what to do with the traces of Richard Yates's life. Even Yates himself struggled with the matter; in a 1972 interview with *Ploughshares*, he questioned whether he had "earned the right" to transform personal material into fiction, and mused, "Anybody can scribble out a confession or a memoir or a diary or a chronicle of personal experience, but how many writers can *form* that kind of material? How many writers can make it into solid, artistically satisfying fiction?" (Yates 1972)

The autobiographical dimension of Yates's writing has played an awkward role in his posthumous canonization. The 2003 publication of a mass-market biography by Blake Bailey undoubtedly helped to bring Yates's books back into print, but the book, tellingly titled *A Tragic Honesty*, has also been established as a final court of appeal in a way that has constrained interpretations of Yates's work. Bailey presents the novels and short stories as the flesh of the life's skeleton, as though the fiction had been lying in wait for its biographical timeline. While presenting a wealth of new information about Yates's life, Bailey's biographical readings often reinforce the speculations of Yates's contemporaries—including Robert Towers, a reviewer of Yates's final short story collection, *Liars in Love* (1981), who charged the author with remaining trapped in the "prison" of his experience, leaving him to forever circle "the same half-acre of pain" (Towers 1981).

Towers's accusatory tone points to a sense that, in smuggling experience into fiction, Yates has broken the rules: from this perspective, Yates's autobiographical fiction contravenes what Philippe Lejeune (1989) has termed the "pact" between reader, author, and publisher that determines whether a work is read as referential or fictional (Lejeune 1989, 13). For Lejeune, an agreement of this kind conditions the reader's approach to the work: if the pact is referential, the reader might well look for discrepancies between the author's experience and its literary representation; if, as in the case of Yates's fiction, the pact is fictional, the reader is likely to search for resemblances between the life and the writing (14). When such resemblances are found, usually through paratextual investigation, the reader is supposed to have caught the writer out—or, perhaps, discovered them trapped in the "prison" of memory. Lejeune does not pursue the implications of such readerly detective work for his theory of autobiography: surely if the pact is readily broken by the author, its ability to determine literary critical classifications of autobiography is minimal. Nevertheless, the ostensibly illicit nature of Yates's use of his experience—usually framed as a concealment of the autobiographical within the fictional—has often been approached by his critics as a problem to be solved.

Though Bailey's biography has loomed since 2003 as the dominant paratext for readers looking to catch Yates in the act of breaking the rules of fiction, Towers was speculating about Yates's confinement to the personal in 1981, citing only his repetitive treatment of the same themes, plots and characters as evidence. For Towers, Yates's fiction is *compulsively* autobiographical: his life conditions his writing as the walls of the prison condition the experience of the incarcerated. Bailey, somewhat contradictorily, maintains that Yates's best writing transcends the autobiographical, even as he appeals to the fiction as evidence for his account of the author's life. The stakes have been established: Yates's writing either transforms his life into the universal, or it is helplessly mired in personal experience. In this essay I want to multiply the possibilities for interpreting Yates's approach to fictionalizing experience, and pose what I see as more pressing questions for our posthumous readings of Yates: what are the politics of Yates's personal writing, and how have they been negotiated alongside his canonization?[1]

These questions get to the root of the trouble Yates's autobiographical writing has posed for his literary rehabilitation. The novels and short stories have been published, the film has been made, the features have been written, and we have been handed a figure that one of Yates's salesmen would have relished: an outmoded masculinist in an age of women's liberation, a literary realist in an age of postmodernists. The wave of literary criticism on Yates at the beginning of the twenty-first century fueled this caricature: dedicated to "Flaubertian detachment" (Bailey 2004, 183), his work, we have been told, is "free of the metafictionalists' or even the modernists' tricks" (O'Nan 1999). In academic criticism of recent years, a more sophisticated picture of Yates's complex engagement with realism is beginning to emerge. However, the project of canonizing Yates has clung to the biographical image of him as a masculinist traditionalist. This image is haunted by an inconvenient excess: Yates's satires of homosociality and his interest in feminized and racialized labor disrupt the coherence of his hard-won posthumous reputation.

This essay will actively pursue such disruption, operating on the premise that the act of analyzing Yates's writing should be distinguished from the act of selling it. The moments at which the fiction becomes a fractured or distorted mirror of the biography should not be smoothed over to serve the industrial production of a marketable authorial persona. In this spirit, I focus particularly on the works often deemed to be among Yates's weakest: his second and third novels, *A Special Providence* (1969) and *Disturbing the Peace* (1975). The critical dismissal of these books belies their complex engagement with the practice of fictionalizing experience. As we shall see, Yates's reflections on the limitations of autobiography are central to his explorations of labor, gender, race, and sexuality.

Disturbing the Peace begins in 1960, on the eve of its salesman protagonist John Wilder's first psychiatric crisis. Committed to New York's Bellevue mental hospital over Labor Day weekend, Wilder has an abortive encounter with a psychoanalyst upon his release. He subsequently revisits his dream of being a movie producer, spurred on by an affair with a wealthy younger woman named Pamela. To Wilder's protest that he has ' No money; no talent," Pamela replies, "But you said you always wanted to be the man who raised the money and hired the talent" (Yates 1975, 111). In fact, it is Pamela who drives the project: she enlists friends from her *alma mater*, an elite arts college, to write, act and direct a film called *Bellevue*, based on Wilder's account of his hospitalization. But after Wilder experiences a delusional episode on set, during which he becomes convinced he is the second coming of Christ, the director abandons the project and the energy around the film fades.

What follows resembles a Baudrillardian nightmare. Wilder and Pamela take the pitch to Hollywood, where the producer Carl Munchin tells them that to make their Bellevue film idea "a commercially viable property" they "need a man who's *doomed*" (199). Hired writer Jack Haines then proposes an alternative ending for the film. Haines, who has only just met Wilder, does not realize *Bellevue* is autobiographical, but his pitch echoes the plot of *Disturbing the Peace* with uncanny accuracy: he opines that the protagonist should see a quack psychoanalyst when he leaves Bellevue, and then meet a girl. Soon, Haines overtakes Wilder's past and pitches what turns out to be a prophecy:

> He systematically destroys everything that's still bright and promising in his life, including the girl's love, and he sinks into a depression so deep as to be irrevocable. He winds up in an asylum that makes Bellevue look like nothing. And I think you'll see, Carl, when the whole thing's on paper, that there's an inevitability to it. The seeds of self-destruction are there in the man from the start [200].

Wilder leaves the meeting and shouts at Pamela: "Oh, I'm a Dark Character, all right, baby; I'm Doomed; I've got the fucking Seeds of Self-Destruction coming out my *ears*[…]" (202). True to Haines's words, Wilder ends the novel as a decade-long inmate in an institution, baffled by any suggestion that he should ever leave.

In his biography, Bailey stresses the autobiographical nature of Wilder's final breakdown by quoting his daughter: "Monica Yates attests that John Wilder's third, most devastating breakdown in the novel was 'as true as [her father] could write about how [his breakdown in Los Angeles] went,' and what slender evidence exists would seem to confirm as much" (Bailey 2004, 349). But it would be wrong to describe *Disturbing the Peace* as a straightforwardly autobiographical novel, partly because the novel features not one but two Yates avatars: throughout, Wilder is shadowed by the novelist Chester Pratt, an ex-lover of Pamela's who is hired to write the screenplay for *Bellevue* when Haines is dismissed. Pratt's novel, *Burn All Your Cities*, stands in for *Revolutionary Road*, and his work in Hollywood recalls Yates's experience writing the screenplay for William Styron's *Lie Down in Darkness*. Eventually, Pamela leaves Wilder for Pratt, whose experience of time is linear where Wilder's is inverted and uncanny: "The future would take care of itself. He had learned in AA to take things a day at a time" (246). Unlike Wilder, Pratt is able to overcome his alcoholism—coincidentally, with the help of the kindly sponsor Wilder rejects at the beginning of the novel: "All the poison was out of his system now. He was working well, if you could call writing a movie script 'working,' and as soon as this job was over he would get back to his second novel" (245). *Disturbing the Peace* thus invites an autobiographical reading only to split its ostensible subject in two: one character fails and the other thrives. Yates's doubled authorial avatars mean that *Disturbing the Peace* resists categorization as autobiography. Indeed, the novel casts doubt on the very possibility of self-representation with their evocation of Baudrillard's simulacral images that "precede the real to the extent that they invert the causal and logical order of the real and its reproduction" (Baudrillard 2008, 84). Jack Haines's script proposals draw Wilder into the simulacrum, preordaining his downfall. Meanwhile, the character of Chester Pratt appears as a superstitious defense against such temporal inversions: if Yates's experience, like Wilder's, is to be determined by fictional images, then Pratt's fate is at least a desirable one.

Such apparently postmodern impulses might lead to *Disturbing the Peace*'s classification as "metafiction," a term that emerged into literary discourse as Yates was writing the novel. As coined by William H. Gass in "Philosophy and the Form of Fiction" (1970), metafiction describes not just authorial self-reference but also a particular mode of authorial power. Gass writes, "These days, often, the novelist resumes the guise of God; but he is merely one of us now, full of confusion and error, sin and cleverness. He creates as he is able; insists upon his presence and upon his wickedness and fallibility too" (1970, 20). However, *Disturbing the Peace*'s relationship with metafictional tropes is skeptical to say the least. In contrast to Gass's chameleonic author, it is Yates's characters that take on "the guise" of the author, and their attempts to write their lives in advance frequently fail. If Gass's metafictional author is a mischievous demon, distinguishable from the characters that surround him by his ability to move masterfully between the planes of fiction and reality, Yates's author is fractured and confused, dispersed among his characters and insisting upon nothing. In *Disturbing the Peace*, fiction plunders and erodes Wilder's experience. Chester Pratt is saved from this fate because he has kept a safe distance from self-narration: instead, he is engaged in the less risky project of adapting other people's work for film. In Yates, the process of folding the real into the fictional is simply too fraught to allow the author-character the mobility and authority bestowed by Gass.

Indeed, Yates darkly satirizes Gass's model of the "Godlike" author become "one of us" through Wilder's delusion that he is the second coming of Christ. The distressing episode is foreshadowed by two earlier events in the novel: the Bellevue inmates' habit of requesting cigarettes with the slang phrase "save me"—a detail Wilder wants to integrate into the film with a crucifixion sequence described by the director as "cornball" (Yates 1975, 132)—and Pamela's revelation that she and her college friends used to call Nathan Epstein, their philosophy professor, "God" (123). Yates's disdain for much of what was, by the 1970s, being celebrated as postmodern literature has been well documented, but *Disturbing the Peace*'s critique of metafiction is more subtle than Yates's habit of railing against postmodern literary "clowns" might suggest (see Clark and Henry 1972). The novel's intervention is perhaps closer to Michel Foucault's in "What is an author?" (1969; repr. 1998). Foucault notes, "A certain number of notions that are intended to replace the privileged position of the author actually seem to preserve that privilege and suppress the real meaning of his disappearance" (207). Foucault recognized that appeals to "the work" or to "writing" risked simply transposing "the empirical characteristics of the author into a transcendental anonymity" (208). In a similar way, by revealing the author-God as a delusional salesman, *Disturbing the Peace* targets the contradictions of an emergent postmodern literary discourse that wants to both destabilize the author and leave his authority intact.

In his account of the "program era" of institutionalized creative writing, Mark McGurl observes that realism and metafiction share an empiricist injunction to "write what you know," despite their fabled status as the antithetical poles of post–1945 literary culture (McGurl 2009, 81). McGurl states:

Ultimately, this experiential-observational emphasis would contribute both to the dominant position of realism (whether regionalist, ethnic, or domestic) in the postwar creative writing establishment and—as "observation" turns inward to that feature of authorial experience which is the act of writing itself—to the strong presence there of a metafictional aesthetic [95].

Yates is at odds with this veneration of the knowing observer, and thus at odds with both realism and metafiction.[2] Throughout his literary career, Yates was concerned with the slippery, inaccessible nature of experience—with the simultaneous necessity and impossibility of obeying the injunction to "write what you know." Yates's fiction disputes the unspoken part of the dictum: in order to write what you know, you must know your experience, but what happens when experience fails to generate knowledge?

With *Disturbing the Peace*, Yates takes this question to its extreme limit by fictionalizing an episode of psychosis. It is not enough to conclude, as Bailey does, that the evidence points to the "truth" of Wilder's breakdown, because *Disturbing the Peace* continually reminds us that the "truth" of psychosis might well be inaccessible even to he who experienced it. Mood disorders, as Debra Beilke has suggested, pose particular challenges to the autobiographer, for they make "the sense of fragmented, multiple, defective selfhood all the more dramatic" (2008, 30). Yates takes the experience of psychosis as an example of the inherent limitations of both autobiographical realism and postmodern metafiction. Beilke suggests that "the everchanging flux of moods, perceptions, and energies of bipolar illness" can "reinforce, even magnify, postmodern formulations of the unstable self" (31). For Yates, psychosis does not reinforce such formulations; rather, it marks the point at which the pain, distress and uncertainty of the "unstable self" refuses to generate theory, knowledge, or self-reflection.

The problem of generating knowledge from experience is explored, across Yates's body of work, in his use of shifting narrative perspectives. Most of *Disturbing the Peace* is narrated in the third person from John Wilder's point of view. While the plot is structured around his three discrete breakdowns, the transitions from psychological stability to delusion and back again are gradual and indistinct, as are the occasional shifts to other characters' perspectives. During his final psychiatric crisis, from which he never recovers, Wilder is in the grip of a series of delusional convictions: he imagines not only that he is the second coming of Christ, but that he shot JFK (the novel is set at the time of the assassination), killed black people all over Los Angeles, and murdered his wife and son. As he wanders Los Angeles, Wilder suddenly discovers a way of sorting true experience from false:

He walked steadily away from home, going west along Santa Monica with his head down, watching his naked feet tread the pavement. Once he stumbled and went down on one hand, and his thumb picked up a trace of dogshit. He wiped it on his pants but the smell remained, and the smell soon became his sole proof that he was mortal and earthbound—only a man. No second coming of Christ would have dogshit on his thumb.

"...The man is said to be in Los Angeles," Walter Cronkite was saying on television screens all over America, "and is said to be walking the streets alone. Los Angeles police have been cautioned not to be misled by imposters...' [228].

Even as Wilder attempts to root himself to reality by smelling the dogshit, he can hear Walter Cronkite reporting on the coming of the Messiah. Soon, the connection to reality represented by the dogshit becomes an outward sign of his psychiatric crisis as he sits down to listen to a boy playing guitar:

"Don't let me interrupt you," Wilder said; "that sounds nice. You just go on doing what you're doing and I'll do what I'm doing."
"What're you doing?"
"Smelling my thumb."
And the boy got up and walked away [228].

The scene points to the fact that *Disturbing the Peace* is not only a novelization of an experience of mental illness, but a critique of what McGurl calls the "experiential-observational" (95) norm in literary writing. If readers want experience, Yates wryly suggests, they can have the olfactory experience of dogshit: anything more is not so simply grasped—and, indeed, it can easily be lost. At the end of *Disturbing the Peace*, Wilder is living out his life in a state asylum, and he looks "like a middle-aged man to whom nothing had ever happened" (251). Without a fictional form to attach it to, Wilder has lost his only commodity in Hollywood—his experience. If Yates is, as charged, trapped in the prison of his personal history, the conclusion to *Disturbing the Peace* suggests a more chilling alternative: a total eradication of the autobiographical past.

Screening Experience: Yates's Autofictions

The final image of Wilder as a man "to whom nothing had ever happened" points to Yates's interest in the inaccessible dimensions of experience. Eschewing the authority assumed by those who "write what they know," Yates approaches personal experience in a posture of submission, continually referencing its opacity. I want to suggest that Yates's interest in disarticulating knowledge from experience means that autofiction, rather than autobiography, is a more generative descriptive term for his work. Originally coined by the French writer Serge Doubrovsky, in reference to his novel *Fils* (1977), as "fiction of strictly real events and facts" (trans. Ferreira-Meyers, 214), autofiction is a much disputed term. Paul Jay has queried the distinction between autobiographical fiction and autobiography proper, contending that "if by 'fictional' we mean 'made up,' 'created,' or 'imagined' something, that is, which is literary and not 'real'—then we have merely defined the ontological status of any text, autobiographical or not" (Jay 1984, 16). Reflecting on Jay's assertion, Sidonie Smith and Julia Watson suggest that the distinction of autofiction is its use of "textual markers that signal a deliberate, often ironic, interplay between the two modes" (Smith and Watson 2001, 186).

I here follow Karen Ferreira-Meyers in considering autofiction as a hybrid form that not only focuses on the interplay of the fictional and the veridical, but does so in a way that specifically engages traumatic experience. Drawing on Sigmund Freud's theory of screen memories, Ferreira-Meyers (214) notes that autofiction recognizes, with Freud, not only that the psyche might fabricate or alter memories to cover over psychological conflicts, but also that such fabrication constitutes a form of subjective truth. The author Catherine Cusset observes that autofiction provides a mode of narrating trauma for writers such as Christine Angot, whose work explores incestuous abuse. According to Cusset, autofiction "feeds on extreme and painful experiences: death, illness, abandonment, madness and loss" (2012, 6).

Wilder's disastrous encounter with a psychoanalyst testifies to what Leigh Gilmore has termed the "constitutive ambivalence" of trauma studies, where language "is asserted as that which can make trauma real even as it is theorized as that which fails in the face of trauma" (Gilmore 2016, 156). When he sees a psychiatrist after leaving Bellevue, Wilder keeps returning to instances of mis-representation, whether in the movies—"we've all been raised on movies, and we're just now beginning to figure out what frauds most of them are"—or in his father's false claim that Wilder had fought in the Battle of the Bulge (88–89). Wilder ultimately challenges his analyst, Dr. Blomberg: "When the hell are *you* gonna start talking?" (92) In Los Angeles, he turns to psychiatric medication instead, but this, too, fails him: Wilder's psychiatrist, taking no account of his alcoholism, simply orders him to stop drinking while he is on the medication. His inability to do so precipitates his final breakdown. Wilder is failed by both psychoanalytic and biomedical psychiatry: taking Wilder's claims that he has stopped drinking at face value, both approaches presume, erroneously, that he is giving a transparent account of his experience.

At the heart of the novel's representation of psychoanalysis is a critique of the contradiction between the demand for an account of psychic experience and the impossibility of giving such an account. Although Wilder's psychiatrists are uninterested in this contradiction, Freud certainly was. Freud used the term "screen memory" to describe vivid memories of apparently trivial events, which endure in the memory as substitutes for significant experiences that have been repressed.[3] Memories do not simply emerge, Freud insisted; they are formed in moments of psychical intensity, and "a number of motives, with no concern for historical accuracy, had a part in forming them, as well as in the selection of the memories themselves" (Freud 1899, 322). For Freud, the screen memory gestures towards a traumatic experience that cannot be directly represented. If autofiction's distinctiveness compared to fiction and autobiography lies in its ability to address trauma, we can recast this in Freudian terms as autofiction's interest in the process of *screening* trauma.

Freud's broader theory of trauma is relevant here, but I focus on screen memories in particular because the screen is such an important concept in Yates's work. As a spatial phenomenon in his fiction, the screen combines three functions: it conceals, divides, and displays. A further meaning of the word screen establishes its temporal dimension: as investigational delay, as deferral with a purpose. My application of the term "screen" to Yates's work combines all these senses. Yates uses fiction to simultaneously represent and conceal the autobiographical. At the same time, his autofictions situate characters at the intersection of individual and historical traumas. These traumas—whether framed by race, class, sexuality or gender—are repressed, but they resurface obliquely, often as characters' delusions or reveries. Freud's use of the term screen, as Barbara Creed (2004) has observed, reflects the fact that psychoanalysis and cinema both emerged in the late nineteenth century: as Creed notes, "the cinema may well have influenced psychoanalysis" (Creed 2004, 80) In Yates's autofictions, the project of screening the real often makes reference to the cinema: films are a prominent trope not only in *Disturbing the Peace* but in a number of his other works, including *A Special Providence*, to which I now turn.

In the interview quoted at the beginning of this chapter, Yates derided *A Special Providence* as a misjudged "autobiographical blowout": a failed attempt to fictionalize his experience of fighting in World War II (Clark and Henry, 1972). Yet one of the novel's chief concerns—the roles films play in mediating subjective experience—would become an enduring trope in Yates's oeuvre. Robert Prentice, the novel's protagonist, is an eighteen-year-old soldier in the war. He compares his soldierly performance to the movies in a manner that anticipates the temporal inversions of *Disturbing the Peace*:

"Jesus, kid," he said. "You going out *now*?"
"Guess I've got to," Prentice said, beginning to feel very much like the hero of a war movie [Yates 1969, 90].

Like many other Yates protagonists, Prentice anticipates his verbal exchanges like a screenwriter and actor: "God damn it, I didn't fall behind, he silently rehearsed in his mind" (272). Filmic conventions characterize the temporal confusion of war: "Things seemed to happen out of sequence, as in a movie that someone has mindlessly cut and scrambled and spliced together at random" (96). Later, Prentice breaks a pane of glass with his gun "less because he knew it would make for better aim than because it was what gunmen always did behind windows in the movies" (264). Even when Prentice smashes the screen he cannot escape its operation. The multiple meanings that made the term screen so resonant for Freud are all at work here: the film screen reorganizes time and mediates Prentice's experience by simultaneously representing and distorting it.

For Prentice, the movies also screen same-sex relationships, which is to say they simultaneously represent, defer, and conceal them. *A Special Providence* establishes Prentice's obsession with a fellow soldier named Quint as an interplay of sexual desire and emulation. Quint provides a way for Prentice to understand his role in the army after a disastrous beginning: "All he wanted now, beyond a certain basic competence, was to be as intelligent and articulate as Quint, as independent as Quint, as aloof from the Army's indignities as Quint. He very nearly wanted to be Quint, and at the very least he wanted to get to know him" (27).

Prentice's relationship with Quint exists on what Eve Sedgwick has termed the homosocial continuum. Sedgwick's model intends to "draw the 'homosocial' back into the orbit of 'desire,' of the potentially erotic" (Sedgwick 1985, 1). Sedgwick's work is an explicit attempt to read the historical development of male homosexuality as "inextricable from the changing shapes of the institutions by which gender and class inequality are structured" (27). Quint is an alternative to the army's institutional model of masculinity, and becomes a way for Prentice to evaluate his own masculine performance after losing his virginity to a girl he meets in a bar: "Maybe all Quint had done with the other girl, Nancy, was to pay for her beer and put her on the bus for home; maybe that was all you were supposed to do with girls like that, if you had any pride" (52). But during their conversations Quint is also an object of desire who has a feminizing influence on Prentice: "it was all Prentice could do to keep his voice from rising and giggling in pleasure like a girl's" (29). In turn, Prentice evaluates himself as a masculine object of Quint's male gaze: "Prentice did his best to put an easy, old-combat man swing into his walk as he moved away down the street, very much aware that Quint would stand there watching him until he was out of sight" (102). This dynamic is re-invoked in another of Yates's autofictions, the novel *A Good School* (1978), in which the friendships at an all-male prep school frequently take on romantic overtones. William Grove, the protagonist, hopes to share a room with Hugh Britt next year, and "it was a time of subtle pursuit and hurt feelings and last-minute settlings for second best" (Yates 1978, 70).

In his biography, Bailey describes Yates's "frank, utterly unapologetic homophobia," citing as evidence a passage in the novel *Young Hearts Crying* (1984) where his "counterpart" character (a revelatory term of Bailey's) worries that his newborn son will grow up to be gay (506). According to Bailey,

Yates's close personal relationship with his agent Monica McCall, a lesbian, was a "sovereign exception" (506). Other than Yates's published work, the evidence for his homophobia is not cited. I do not propose to re-evaluate whether Yates was, indeed, a homophobe; certainly, I have no evidence to disprove Bailey's conclusions. My appeal is, rather, that we allow for a degree of dissonance between Yates's biography and his fiction—not least because his portrayal of same-sex relationships foregrounds the blurred line between self-fashioning and self-representation.

For Yates, the cinema screen, which both represents and distorts the viewer's self-image, becomes a figure for the interplay of desire and identification in homosocial relationships. Laura Mulvey's 1975 claim that the male cinema-goer identifies with the male protagonist on film in a non-erotic way as a "more powerful ideal ego conceived in the original moment of recognition in front of the mirror" does not quite capture this interplay (Mulvey 1975, 12). Complicating this account, Steve Neale has cited the spectator's "constant work to channel and regulate identification in relation to sexual division, in relation to the orders of gender, sexuality, and social identity and authority marking patriarchal society" (Neale 1993, 11). In Yates, the interplay of desire and identification at work in cinematic spectatorship casts the subject adrift: at one moment he recognizes himself, and at the next the identification fails. This process makes cinematic spectatorship a rich metaphor for the way the homosocial operates in Yates's fiction: Prentice gazes at Quint in the same way he gazes at the cinema screen, experiencing identification and desire at once.

Yates's mentally ill characters often have intense relationships with the cinema, a trope which develops an analogy between the distortions of psychological suffering and the distortions of the movie screen. In *A Good School*, Grove gains hope when Britt observes that his best friend and Grove's rival, John Haskell, is "cracking up." Haskell's escalating mental illness is punctuated by rants about the movies, which he claims "help people hide from reality" (61). Such a view has often been attributed to Yates, who notoriously dismissed the cinema in a late essay with the line, "I almost never go to a movie now, and have been known to explain loftily, if not quite at the top of my lungs, that this is because movies are for children" (Yates 1981). In his novels, however, the movies, as a rhetorical object, become a way of commenting on fiction's own practice of screening reality. The screen's function as both mirror and display make it an apt symbol for the problems of autobiography.

The multifaceted significance of the concept of the screen, and its relation to writing as well as cinema, is most clearly rendered in "Builders," a story originally published in Yates's first short fiction collection, *Eleven Kinds of Loneliness* (1962). In his *Ploughshares* interview, Yates describes "Builders" as an "experimental warm-up" for *A Special Providence*, noting that the protagonists of both works are named Robert Prentice. Admitting that "Builders" is "almost pure personal history," Yates suggests that, unlike his second novel, the story works. He explains, "Somehow, and maybe it was just luck, I managed to avoid both of the two terrible traps that lie in the path of autobiographical fiction—self-pity and self-aggrandizement (Yates 1972)."

"Builders" is a story about autobiography: it tells the tale of writer Bob Prentice's brief spell ghostwriting the memoirs of Bernie Silver, a cab driver. The story takes its title from Bernie's advice on writing. He tells Bob that construction workers and writers must ask themselves the same question: "Where are the windows? That's the question. Where does the light come in? Because do you see what I mean about the light coming in, Bob? I mean the—the philosophy of your story; the truth of it; the—" (Yates 1962, 149). The window, as a representational screen, is a symbol of the writer's ability to access the real—the "truth" of the story. Bob's first-person narration—a rare departure from the third person for Yates—is initially condescending towards Bernie's metaphor: "In the end I built –oh built, schmilt. I put page one and then page two and then page three into the old machine and I *wrote* the son of a bitch" (166). But Bob-as-narrator appropriates the analogy himself in the story's final paragraph: "Maybe the light is just going to have to come in as best it can, through whatever chinks and cracks have been left in the builder's faulty craftsmanship" (173).

Initially introduced as a cliché, the story subsequently deploys the symbol of the window in an ostensibly non-ironic manner. Yates establishes the story's self-reflexivity in the form of an apology in the first line of "Builders": "Writers who write about writers can easily bring about the worst kind of literary miscarriage" (141). But the story is full of writers who write about writers. Bob's day job is as a "rewrite man" with the United Press (141). His out-of-hours fiction writing forges a "tenuous parallel between Hemingway and me" (142). And his ghostwriting for Bernie is a form of collaborative autofiction that blends Bernie's account of himself with Bob's fictionalization of it. In light of this, the first-person narration must avoid assuming the guise of an exposure or confession that would unveil the origin of the work. "Builders" eludes this fate by emphasizing the multiplicity of the screen metaphor.

The heavily symbolic windows are not the only screens in the story. Bob writes behind a "three-fold screen in the corner" of the one-room apartment he shares with his wife Joan (142). This screen-as-partition symbolizes Bob's insistence on the concretion of class divisions in the face of their dissolution. Even as Bob gives his wife a "crisp, impatient briefing on the hopelessness of trying to ignore class barriers," it remains unclear where these barriers are situated (161). Cab driver Bernie's house is "very clean, spacious and cream-colored, full of carpeting and archways" (143). By contrast, Bernie "seemed surprised by the crumbling doorway and dirty stairs" of Bob and Jean's house, "whose rent was probably less than half of what he and Rose were paying uptown" (162). Bob understands class as a matter of intellect: "I guess I had some snobbish notion that it wouldn't do Bernie Silver any harm to learn that people could be smart and poor at the same time" (162). However, the retrospective narration indicates that Bob's "snobbish notion" has changed. Moreover, if the windows metaphor places Bob in the working class role of manual laborer, Bernie is figured as a writer. He persuades Bob to take the ghostwriting job by proffering a check, given to a previous writer, as if it "were a prose work of uncommon merit in its own right" (147). Bob's subsequent analysis of "Bernie's cramped scribbling on the other side" reveals the payment to be for five stories rather than one, as he had initially assumed (153). Bob's observation that he "hadn't really been robbed—conned a little, maybe" is also a comment on what he as a ghostwriter is doing to his readers (153).

The multiplicitous screen in "Builders" is neither wholly transparent nor wholly opaque. Bernie observes passengers "in the rearview mirror of his cab"–another screen that becomes a staple narrative device within Bob's ghostwritten stories (149). The cinematic screen is also evoked when Bernie summons the "shining name of a movie star" (145) former school friend, to persuade Bob of his project's viability. And of course, the windows themselves are not straightforwardly transparent: at night they reflect the author's face. The windows in "Builders" are a symbol of the ambivalence of autofictional screening, showing that self-representation always involves obfuscation and deferral.

Screening Race and Gender

In *The Psychopathology of Everyday Life*, Freud suggests that screen memories "offer a remarkable analogy with the childhood memories that a nation preserves in its store of legends and myths" (1901, 48). According to Freud, the psyche's distortions and displacements of childhood traumas find a parallel in the nation's encoding of historic violence in folk tales, which endure across the generations as screen memories endure throughout a life. In a similar way, the figure of the screen recurs in Yates's autofictions as a symbol of social, as well as individual, trauma. In *A Special Providence*, the cinema screen simultaneously marks and deflects Prentice's acknowledgment of same sex attraction and identification. In "Builders," the class divide is screened: it is both represented and repressed. In *Disturbing the Peace*, the screened trauma is not only John Wilder's psychiatric crisis but the larger political crises of the 1960s: during his final delusional episode, he hallucinates that he is guilty of racist violence against the black psychiatric workers who attend his successive hospitalizations, the assassination of JFK, and domestic violence against his wife and child.

In particular, *Disturbing the Peace* draws a parallel between the racist violence that populates Wilder's delusions and the way individual autobiography can occlude social life. During the filming of *Bellevue*, Wilder has to address a question about his presentation of Charlie, the black nurse who offered him sympathy and kindness during his time on the psychiatric ward. The man in Charlie's role asks Wilder why he is "the only Negro in the cast who speaks what white people call Perfect English" when, as a nurse, he would not have had the same level of education as the actor playing him (119). Wilder's answer accounts for the "real" Charlie's speech too: he tells the actor that Charlie has "been in charge of all these lunatics every day for a good many years, and maybe he's developed that manner of speech as the best way of—you know—maintaining authority (120)." Wilder's answer belies the fact he actually knows very little about Charlie's life and education history, despite having pretensions to the contrary. In fact, Charlie's life story is of little interest to Wilder: it merely serves the fictionalization of Wilder's experience, just as Charlie served Wilder's recuperation in Bellevue.

The early section of the novel set in Bellevue allows another white inmate to comment on the over-representation of African Americans as employees on psychiatric wards:

"Why d'ya think? Because they're so 'gentle' and so 'kind'? Yeah, yeah, they've got a Natural Sense of Rhythm too. They're scared of ghosts and they're just plain crazy about watermelon. What the hell were you, born yesterday? It's because no white man'd *work* here for the kind of money they get. You know what kind of money they get? Even Charlie there? Huh?"

"Excuse me, Mr. Wilder," Charlie said, blocking their path. "Those pajamas of yours don't fit very well, do they?"

"No, I—No, they don't."

"Sometimes the night people are careless. We have Small, Medium, and Large. A man of your size needs Small. I'll see about it" [28].

This early scene represents the racist context of Charlie's job in a psychiatric hospital in 1960, and references the extent to which American society depended on the underpaid labor of African Americans. The passage also aligns the character of Charlie with the longstanding film stereotype that Kwame Anthony Appiah has termed the "black saint (Appiah 1993, 81)." Speculating that this stereotype prevails because it draws on "the tradition of the superior virtue of the oppressed," Appiah criticizes the assumption that "positive" representations of black people are a measure of liberation (83).

Disturbing the Peace embeds the racism of Wilder's film within a longer history of racist filmmaking and "black saint" figures. In an argument with Pamela, Wilder defends the film *Gunga Din* when she makes fun of it for getting "some actor dressed up like Rudyard Kipling" to recite a poem. He states, "you wouldn't have laughed when they showed Sam Jaffe's ghost coming up through the poem, wearing a full-dress British uniform and making a British salute" (106). Wilder's sentimental appreciation of Jaffe's blackface portrayal of Gunga Din foreshadows his portrayal of Charlie, and situates the nurse character within a legacy of "black saint" stereotypes. Significantly, though, this reference to a notoriously racist film does not lay the legacy of colonialism entirely at Hollywood's door: the film *Gunga Din* is, of course, an adaptation of Rudyard Kipling's eponymous poem. For Yates, literature is complicit in the operation of white patriarchal power. By extension, *Disturbing the Peace* is not absolved of *Bellevue*'s sins: it remains complicit, despite its self-critique.

Autobiography has been central to literature's complicity with colonial violence. Sidonie Smith and Julia Watson have noted that "an important historical use—although by no means the only use—of 'autobiography' has been as a master narrative of Western rationality, progress, and superiority" (Smith and Watson 2001, 113). Autobiography, they write, helped to consolidate "the formation of the Western subject as an accomplished and exceptional individual," a process which "was a key means of legitimating the spread of imperialism around the globe" (112–113). Yates stresses the colonial violence of Wilder's autobiographical project by marking its dependence on racialized labor. Wilder survives his spell in Bellevue thanks to Charlie's emotional and material care; subsequently, he fashions himself as an exceptional white man by remaking Charlie as a stereotype in his autobiographical film. The self-representation of the "accomplished and exceptional individual" relies, Yates suggests, on the repression of the racialized labor that props up white self-representation. Just as Freud drew an analogy between historical and individual trauma, so Yates casts Wilder's psychiatric crisis as an encounter with his own role in historically repressed racism. Wilder's delusions of committing racist violence against black care workers represent the racist violence that has been repressed by the white western autobiographical project. At the same time, *Disturbing the Peace* takes Wilder, not Charlie, as its subject: as a white man's story, the novel becomes its own indictment.

Throughout his career, Yates never occupies the perspective of a black character, whether male or female. He does, however, fleetingly adopt the perspectives of his white female characters. Accounts of his gender politics have been constrained by the critical tendency to read Yates in terms of transparent (or transcendent) autobiography, rather than opaque and deflective autofiction. Nick Fraser (2008), writing in the *Guardian* on the occasion of Random House's 2008 reissues of Yates's fiction, asserts that Yates "was an anti-feminist, grandly patronizing women in the old style." Bailey's biography provides much ammunition for such a view, however much it jars with the novels and short stories themselves. Kate Charlton-Jones's recent book on

Yates negotiates this discordance by maintaining an unconvincing "split between Yates's *intellectual* appreciation of how life is peculiarly difficult for women within marriages that constrain or diminish them and his *emotional* distaste for anything that smacks of a political move to address those issues" (2014, 154). Along similar lines, James Wood (2008) writes that Yates's work is "probably most radical in its obsessive treatment of the question of gender," but concludes that "Yates's work is not feminist, partly because it is much more interested in men than in women."

My purpose here is not to rehabilitate Yates as a feminist, but to argue that the apparent contradictions in his treatment of gender can be understood as a formal response to the constraints of a masculine subject position. Considering Yates's works as autofiction institutes a break in the continuum linking Yates's biography, as constructed by Bailey, to his fictional investments. As I have outlined, the category of autofiction stresses the importance of the unacknowledged and unspoken dimensions of experience—that which cannot emerge fully into the domain of veridical representation. Framed in this way, Yates's retreat from the inner lives of his women characters (with the notable exception of *The Easter Parade*) can be most productively understood as a screening of women's experience. Female subjectivity exerts a pressure on Yates's writing even as it cannot be fully represented. What Fraser and others have read as anti-feminism, I interpret as a complex, paradoxical dynamic whereby Yates recognizes patriarchal structures by expressing, on the level of literary form, his complicity with those structures.

Disturbing the Peace begins and ends as Janice Wilder's story. The opening line, "Everything began to go wrong for Janice Wilder in the late summer of 1960," makes John Wilder's narrative subservient to his wife's (1). Wilder is introduced for the first time from Janice's point of view, as he calls on the evening of his first psychiatric crisis to inform her that he is unable to come home because he is afraid he might kill her. Before he reveals his violent impulses, Wilder tells Janice about a "little PR girl" he "screwed five times in the Palmer House" (3). The narration adopts free indirect discourse to reveal Janice's internal response:

> It wasn't the first news of its kind—there had been a good many girls—but it was the first time he'd ever flung it at her this way, like an adolescent braggart trying to shock his mother. She thought of saying What would you *like* me to think? but didn't trust her voice: it might sound wounded, which would be a mistake, or it might sound dry and tolerant and that would be worse. Luckily he didn't wait long for an answer [3].

This passage, which provides access to Janice's perspective for the last time until the novel's closing chapter, contains an admission of failure on behalf of the narrative. Janice's lack of trust in her own voice reflects the novel's distrust of its ability to occupy her point of view, which is mirrored by Wilder's disinterest in his wife's response. In the next passage, her voice abruptly gives way to that of the couple's friend Paul Borg, who finds Wilder and commits him to Bellevue. Paul's perspective then fades into Wilder's, which dominates for the rest of the novel. Janice's point of view only retakes the reigns in the final chapter which is set in 1970, and reveals that she has divorced Wilder and married Paul in the intervening decade.

For the bulk of the novel, the reader encounters Janice only through Wilder's perspective, which recounts their few, strained conversations and his occasional, misogynistic appraisals of her. Occasionally, however, her speech reveals glimpses of her feelings. When Wilder is hospitalized after the film shoot at Pamela's cottage, having told his wife he would be away on a business trip, Janice cuts short his explanation for his extended absence with the admission, "Don't you think Tommy and I have learned not to expect very much of you?" (147). The comment is cutting in its brevity, gesturing towards all the detail the novel does not provide about Janice's emotional life. Later, when Janice tells Wilder that Tommy has been exhibiting "hostile, anti-social behavior" at school, she confides in him: "I've been so lonely, John, and there's never anyone to talk to. I'd be in analysis myself if I thought it would do any good" (163). But Wilder retreats into the domain of masculinity, along with the narrative he commands. Failing to respond to Janice's disclo-sure, Wilder realizes "his balls were rising, right there in the coffee shop" and wonders whether "the reason for a retractable scrotum in all male mammals is to protect the reproductory organs in hazardous or distressful situations" (163–164). This passage satirically acknowledges the novel's complicity with patriarchy—and acknowledging complicity does not, to be sure, deliver abso-lution. Rather, as with the novel's representation of Charlie as both character and cinematic stereotype, it is a form of critical self-indictment. *Disturbing the Peace* highlights its own confinement within Wilder's masculinist subject position in the mode of dramatic irony: the novel is powerless to ameliorate its failures but determined to catalogue them. If both autobiographical realism and postmodern metafiction are presumed, erroneously, to be based in self-knowledge, Yates breaks with both traditions by continually stressing all that lies outside the scope of the novel. Yates cannot represent an individual expe-rience of psychosis because he cannot access the experiences of the gendered and racialized subjects who are so integral to that experience. Positioning psychosis as the endpoint of Wilder's autobiographical project, Yates makes the condition a paradigm for the solipsistic violence of white male self-narration.

The novel's final chapter does not only relinquish Wilder's perspective—it obliterates it. In a repetition of the first chapter, Janice's point of view ref-erences her distrust of her own voice:

She knew her next question would be a difficult one, but she decided to ask it anyway. She might never be in California again; she might never see him again. She had to wait for a swelling in the throat to go down before she could trust her voice. "John," she said, "have you made any plans or—you know—given any thought to what you might do when you leave here?" [253].

Janice's struggle to speak is also, of course, the novel's struggle to speak in Janice's voice. When she finally summons the courage to ask her question, Wilder is nonplussed by her question and simply repeats "Leave here?" (253). The novel leaves its protagonist in a realm of total externality: he looks, as noted above, like a man "to whom nothing had ever happened." The relinquishment of Wilder's perspective is perhaps, in part, Yates's decisive rejection of an autobiographical identification with him. However, its displacement by Janice's point of view positions the loss of Wilder's inner life as a consequence of his absorption in it. A "swelling in the throat" afflicts not only Janice but *Disturbing the Peace*, as Yates grapples with two apparently incompatible options: to give voice to female characters, or to represent his complicity with their social occlusion.

What would it mean to take this "swelling in the throat" as the starting point for our construction of "Yates the author"? To make this critical move would involve displacing the caricature of Yates as an "anti-feminist" with a more complex picture of the way his fiction consistently displays its own failure to represent women's experiences. Janice's "swelling in the throat" recalls the struggle for self-expression waged by Alice Prentice, the protagonist's mother in *A Special Providence*. When Alice realizes she has been abandoned by her partner she "could never afterwards remember how she managed to conclude the conversation" (159), and her inability to understand his actions "made it impossible to cry [...] all she could do was fail and fail and fail to understand" (160). The repetition of "fail" divides, or perhaps multiplies, the blame: Alice's repression of her traumatic experience is a failure that belongs not only to her character but also to Yates's novel, and to the autobiographical tradition itself for throwing the spotlight on the "exceptional man" while repressing those whose labor underwrites his success.

In *Disturbing the Peace*, Wilder acknowledges "his strange compulsion to let people know the worst about himself—this confusion of what was weak and ugly in himself with what was 'interesting'" (126). This line might be a reference to Yates's own self-reflexive comments on his failures to represent subjects other than straight, white men. However, Yates's autofictions do not simply turn in on themselves and their own limitations. Rather, they remind us that the life stories of white American men are valuable not only for what they reveal, but for what, and whom, they leave out. Yates's inauguration into the American literary canon has enlisted his life story but marginalized his life writing. Now, in the wake of his canonization, Yates's politicized approach to autofiction demands attention.

NOTES

1. This chapter returns to and develops research I carried out at the University of Cambridge in 2009. Thanks to Michael Hrebeniak, Mary Jacobus, and my colleagues on the Criticism and Culture MPhil for guidance and advice on approaching the (then) brave new field of Yates studies. I completed the chapter with the support of Sadler funding at the University of Leeds, where Katrina Longhurst provided helpful references on mental illness and literature.

2. My reading thus departs from Leif Bull's characterization of *Disturbing the Peace* as "Yates' most openly metafictional work." Bull argues that Yates's fiction "is at once metafictional and representational." I suggest, on the contrary, that Yates is concerned with the limits of both metafiction and representation. See Bull 2010, 226.

3. Freud initially suggested that screen memories operate retroactively, displacing an event of adolescence or adulthood with a childhood memory. From *The Psychopathology of Everyday Life* onwards, however, he emphasized memories that are "displaced forward," in which an unconscious event in the subject's early life is screened by a more recent memory.

BIBLIOGRAPHY

Appiah, K. Anthony. 1993. "'No Bad Nigger': Blacks as the Ethical Principle in the Movies." In *Media Spectacles*, ed. Marjorie B. Garber, Jann Matlock, and Rebecca L. Walkowitz. 77–90. New York: Routledge.
Bailey, Blake. (2003) 2006. *A Tragic Honesty: The Life and Work of Richard Yates*. London: Methuen.
Baudrillard, Jean. 2008. "The Evil Demon of Images." In *The Jean Baudrillard Reader*, ed. Steve Redhead. 83–98. Edinburgh: Edinburgh University Press.
Beilke, Debra. 2008. "The Language of Madness: Representing Bipolar Disorder in Kay Redfield Jamison's 'An Unquiet Mind' and Kate Millet's 'The Loony Bin Trip.'" In: Clark, Hilary (ed.) *Depression and Narrative: Telling the Dark*. New York: SUNY Press.
Bull, Leif. 2010. "A Thing Made of Words: The Reflexive Realism of Richard Yates." Unpublished Ph.D. thesis. Goldsmiths, University of London.
Charlton-Jones, Kate. 2014. *Dismembering the American Dream: The Life and Fiction of Richard Yates*. Tuscaloosa: University of Alabama Press.
Creed, Barbara. 2004. *Pandora's Box: Essays in Film Theory*. Melbourne: Australian Centre for the Moving Image.
Cusset, Catherine. 2012. "The Limits of Autofiction," at http://www.catherinecusset.co.uk/wp-content/uploads/2013/02/the-limits-of-autofiction.pdf.
Doubrovsky, Serge. 1977. *Fils*. Paris: Galilée.
Ferreira-Meyers, Karen. 2015. "Autobiography and Autofiction: No Need to Fight for a Place in the Limelight, There is Space Enough for Both of these Concepts." In *Writing the Self: Essays on Autobiography and Autofiction*, ed. Kerstin W. Shands, Giulia Grillo Mikrut, Dipti R. Pattanaik and Karen Ferreira-Meyers, 203–218. Flemingsberg: Södertörns högskola.
Foucault, Michel. (1969) 1998. "What is an author?" in *Essential Works of Foucault Vol. 2: Aesthetics, Method, and Epistemology*, 205–222. New York: The New Press.
Fraser, Nick. 2008. "Rebirth of a Dark Genius," *Guardian*, 17 February. https://www.theguardian.com/books/2008/feb/17/biography.fiction.
Freud, Sigmund. 1901. *The Psychopathology of Everyday Life*. In *The Standard Edition of the Complete Psychological Works of Sigmund Freud*, Vol. VI, ed. James Strachey. London: Random House.
_____. 1899. "Screen Memories," in *The Standard Edition of the Complete Psychological Works of Sigmund Freud*, Vol. III, ed. James Strachey. 301–322. London: Random House.
Gass, William H. 1970. "Philosophy and the Form of Fiction," in *Fiction and the Figures of Life*, 3–26. New York: Alfred A. Knopf.
Gilmore, Leigh. 2016. "Limit Cases: Trauma, Self-Representation, and the Jurisdictions of Identity." In *The Routledge Auto/Biography Studies Reader*, eds. Ricia Anne Chansky

and Emily Hipchen. 154–158. New York: Routledge. Originally published in *Biography: An Interdisciplinary Quarterly*. 24.1 (2001). 127–49.

Jay, Paul. 1984. *Being in the Text: Self-Representation from Wordsworth to Roland Barthes*. Ithaca, NY: Cornell University Press.

Lejeune, Philippe. 1989. "The Autobiographical Pact." In *On Autobiography*, ed. Paul John Eakin, trans. Katherine Leary. 3–30. Minneapolis: University of Minnesota Press.

McGurl, Mark. 2009. *The Program Era: Postwar Fiction and the Rise of Creative Writing*. Cambridge, MA: Harvard University Press.

Mulvey, Laura. 1975. "Visual Pleasure and Narrative Cinema." *Screen* 16.3: 6–18.

Neale, Steve. 1993. "Masculinity as Spectacle." In *Screening the Male: Exploring Masculinities in Hollywood Cinema*, ed. Steven Cohan and Ina Rae Hark. 9–19. London: Routledge.

O'Nan, Stewart. 1999. "The Lost World of Richard Yates." *Boston Review*, October. https://bostonreview.net/stewart-onan-the-lost-world-of-richard-yates.

Sedgwick, Eve. 1985. *Between Men: English Literature and Male Homosocial Desire*. New York: Columbia University Press.

Smith, Sidonie, and Julia Watson. 2001. *Reading Autobiography: A Guide for Interpreting Life Narratives*. Minneapolis: University of Minnesota Press.

Towers, Robert. 1981. "Richard Yates and His Unhappy People." *New York Times*, 1 November. http://www.nytimes.com/1981/11/01/books/richard-yates-and-his-unhappy-people.html?pagewanted=all.

Wood, James. 2008. "Like Men Betrayed." *The New Yorker*. 15 December. http://www.newyorker.com/arts/critics/books/2008/12/15/081215crbo_books_wood?currentPage=1.

Yates, Richard. (1975) 2008. *Disturbing the Peace*. London: Vintage.

_____. (1978) 2007. *A Good School*. London: Vintage.

_____. (1961) 2007. *Revolutionary Road*. London: Vintage.

_____. 1981. "Some Very Good Masters." *New York Times Book Review*, 19 April.

_____. (1969) 2008. *A Special Providence*. London: Vintage.

_____. 1972. DeWitt Henry and Geoffrey Clark. "An Interview with Richard Yates," *Ploughshares*, 1.3. https://www.pshares.org/issues/fall-2011/archive-interview-richard-yates.

Richard Yates and Marriage
The Failed Idea of America
and the Legacy of F. Scott Fitzgerald

HELEN TURNER

In a 1972 interview with DeWitt Henry and Geoffrey Clark, Richard Yates suggested that an aspect of Alfred Kazin's response to the manuscript of *Revolutionary Road* had led to a consistent misinterpretation of the novel. When asked by the interviewer to clarify whether the book was an attack on marriage, Yates responded emphatically:

> Oh, of course not. That's another false interpretation too many people put on the book. [...] Kazin [...] said in part—only in part—"This novel locates the American tragedy squarely on the field of marriage." So the publishers grabbed up that one quote out of context and [...] I let them do it [...] I've regretted it ever since[....] After all, who but a maniac or a God damn fool would sit down and write a novel attacking marriage? And who'd want to read such a novel? [Yates 1972, 66].

While acknowledging the position that Yates takes with regards to the manner in which his novels have been misrepresented as being opposed to marriage, his treatment of the institution does suggest that he uses it metaphorically to explore the frustrations of American life in the middle decades of the twentieth century. This essay will suggest that in the fiction of Richard Yates, marriage is used as a microcosm of a burgeoning way of life, which championed financial success and consumerism as the pinnacle of success. Simultaneously, the compromise that lies at the heart of any marriage is used symbolically to represent the compromise made by individuals in their pursuit of social acceptance, in defiance of the founding principle of America. This individualism, so tied to the idea of America however, is not fully relinquished by Yate's protagonists and is frequently manifested in the pursuit of an artistic vocation. This combination of a desire for both social acceptance and individual fulfillment results in the frustration and disappointment that is present throughout Yates's fictional world.

The America of the postwar years with its growing economy, increasing consumerism, and expanding suburbs is the world that Yates's characters inhabit. It is in stark contrast to the world on the other side of the Atlantic as Europe struggled to rebuild after the destruction of the 1930s and 40s. America, particularly as it was depicted and exported in its popular culture of music, films, and magazines was a land of endless possibilities, security, and prosperity to those trapped in a Europe of food rations and decimated cities. Yates's characters may prosper financially, but few flourish in this supposed Promised Land that equates the American Dream with financial and social success. In his depiction of what lies at the core of the overused, but ill-defined, concept of the American Dream, he is closely allied with F. Scott Fitzgerald, the writer—along with Gustave Flaubert—he most admired. In contrast to Fitzgerald's characters, who are seduced by the trappings of the American experiment (wealth, the pursuit of social standing) at the cost of their individuated identities, Yates's characters consciously try—frequently by taking on the role of the artist—but ultimately fail to escape them.

Underneath the surface of an apparently functioning world depicted in the expanding suburbs and their new build homes is its mirror image: the houses are not as solid and well-built as they appear, and neither are the people who inhabit them nor the marriages and relationships that they have with other people. The mantle of the artist, however, appears to reject the dishonesty that lies at the heart of this clinging to a rather shabby sense of security, whilst simultaneously not fully relinquishing it. This concurrent acceptance and rejection of modern American life can be explored through the depiction of marriage, a microcosm of the society of which it is the cornerstone. The contradictory nature of American life is evident in the breakdown of relationships in Yates's fiction. At the heart of these failed relationships is the conflict between security and predictability and the revolutionary founding principle of America as articulated by Yates in his *Ploughshares* interview regarding *Revolutionary Road*: "Because during the fifties there was a [...] blind desperate clinging to safety and security at any price [...] a great many Americans [...] felt it to be an outright betrayal of our best and bravest revolutionary spirit..." (Yates 1972, 66). Although the conflict is most explicitly exposed in this novel, it is evident in the author's fiction more generally. The question being posed is as much about the nation as it is about the individual. What should America be? And as Americans, what should we value most highly: the security and acceptance that comes with the embracing of societal expectations, or the risk that comes with the attempt at self-realization? This exploration of the conflict between two versions of America once again draws parallels to Yates's literary hero, Fitzgerald, albeit with some telling and significant differences. Fitzgerald's fiction also asks these questions of America, his readers, and himself, but the protagonists that he creates to explore these issues are greatly at odds with Yates's.

The nature of Yates's devotion to Fitzgerald was complex, straddling both artistic and personal sympathies. He cited *The Great Gatsby* in his 1981 essay "Some Very Good Masters" as both 'a miracle of talent" and, perhaps more importantly for the apprentice writer, "a triumph of technique" (Yates 1981). Alongside Fitzgerald's technical mastery, Yates identified with the former's subject matter: the loss of both love and dreams, and the gradual shift from hope and optimism to an all pervading disappointment. Yates was not as fixated with the lives of the wealthy as Fitzgerald, but both writers repeatedly explored failure in love and vocation whilst avoiding the re-assurance of identifying the reason for that failure. To return to Yates's 1981 essay, he applauds *The Great Gatsby* and *Madame Bovary* for the refusal of both novels to identify a villain: "The force of evil is felt in these novels but is never personified—neither novelist is willing to let us off that easy" (Yates 1981).[1] Steven Goldleaf correctly suggests that "Avoiding blame, or at least avoiding blaming villains, became a characteristic of Yates's gloomy vision, which lacked even the dubious satisfaction of identifying a clear cause of the tragedies he described" (Goldleaf 2015, 221). This characteristic of his fiction was one that he shared with—indeed, by his own admission, learned from—his literary mentors.

The second aspect of Yates's sympathy with Fitzgerald is connected to obvious biographical parallels between the two writers, including alcoholism and financial worries.[2] They shared a tendency to draw on their own experiences as source material for their fiction while carefully avoiding openly confessional writing. For Fitzgerald, the use of his own life in his work frequently focused on his complex marriage to Zelda Sayre. As much of a reflection on the troubled—indeed at times tormented—relationship with his wife, Fitzgerald also contemplates marriage as an institution that can interrupt a vocational calling. Marriage is presented as placing limitations on individuals that result in the sense of disappointment that pervades much of his work. While the focus is on men, marriage is not depicted as a particularly happy experience for women either. He articulates this idea in a 1938 letter to his daughter, Scottie, as he reflects on his relationship with her mother:

When I was your age I lived with a great dream. The dream grew and I learned how to speak of it and make people listen. Then the dream divided one day when I decided to marry your mother[....] I was sorry immediately I had married her[....] I was a man divided—she wanted me to work too much for her and not enough for my dream [Fitzgerald 1994, 363].

In Fitzgerald's fiction, as in the author's life, there is a consistent conflict between the possibilities of the individual and the lure of social acceptance and values. Fitzgerald locates his protagonists at the site of this conflict and, as with Yates, marriage and the relationship between the genders is a productive area to explore the conflicts evident in twentieth century America. In Jay Gatsby, Fitzgerald presents a man who is elevated by Nick Carraway to a shining light of the hope and optimism that epitomizes the New World, an "intricate machine that registers earthquakes ten thousand miles away" with "an extraordinary gift for hope," and "a romantic readiness such as I have never found in any other person and which it is not likely I shall ever find again" (Fitzgerald 1991, 6). However, if we read past Nick's reflective narration written in the aftermath of the appalling summer of 1922, a different Jay Gatsby can be identified. By marrying his dream of himself to Daisy Buchanan, he very consciously surrenders his pioneering spirit that was previously summed up in his abandonment of St. Olaf's College in southern Minnesota because of its "ferocious indifference to the drums of his destiny, to destiny itself" (77).

However, both writers mark the moment of marriage as a moment of optimism. Within the first ten pages of *Young Hearts Crying*, Michael Davenport has met and married Lucy Blaine. In the aftermath of his wartime experience as a waist gunner on a B-17, Michael attends Harvard University. After the cynicism that the experience of war has created, his attitudes begin to soften as he progresses through his college career, and are then transformed when he meets his future wife: "Then one spring afternoon in his junior year—all bitterness gone, all cynicism drowned—he wholly succumbed to the myth and the legend of the lovely Radcliffe girl who could come along at any moment and change your life" (Yates 2008b, 5).

The suggestion that the meeting of a woman—so often referred to as a "girl" in the early stages of these fictional relationships—is not dissimilar to Jay Gatsby's reflection after his first sexual encounter with Daisy Fay during World War I that he "knew Daisy was extraordinary but he didn't realize just how extraordinary a 'nice' girl could be" (Fitzgerald 1991, 117). Indeed this sentiment is echoed again by Davenport after *his* first sexual encounter with Lucy: he "hadn't even guessed at what a boundless, extraordinary new world a girl could be" (Yates 2008b, 7). Both characters project ideas about who they want to be on to the women that they are pursuing. The conquest of these women is a symbolic representation of their belief in their future selves as social and financial examples of successful masculinity who will be proved worthy of, in Fitzgerald's words, "the golden girl" who represents that success (Fitzgerald 1991, 94). Davenport's marriage and his vocation as a writer, a vocation which is chosen rather than something which evolves, allows him to be open to the possibilities that postwar American life has to offer. It is only after his marriage to Lucy that she reveals to him that she is worth millions of dollars. His rejection of her substantial wealth is an attempt to remain committed to the work ethic that he considers is his birth right and, indeed, the widely perceived cornerstone of the American nation. It is also an attempt to stave off the indolence that he fears may overtake him if he permits himself to live off of his wife's fortune:

> he had always assumed he would make something of himself on his own. Could he really be expected to abandon that lifelong habit of thought overnight? Living off her fortune might only bleed away his ambition, and might even rob him of the very energy he needed to work at all; that would be an unthinkable price to pay [Yates 2008b, 13].

Lucy's attitude is markedly different, echoing the attitude of Fitzgerald's most complex and most wealthy heroine, *Tender Is the Night*'s Nicole Warren Diver. At the center of both marriages is a conflict between vast wealth and the need to fulfill a vocational calling. In both partnerships it is the wife who brings the money. Yates and Fitzgerald highlight the unease this generates in their respective protagonists of Michael Davenport and Dick Diver, and illustrate how financial independence in their wives is emasculating for both men. A position that is the result of solidly middle-class backgrounds, it would seem unlikely that *The Great Gatsby*'s Tom Buchanan would be so squeamish about the wealth of his wife. What separates the two women is that Lucy complies with her husband's request not to live off of her income whereas, after an initial attempt, Nicole rejects such a position. Initially however, Lucy also urges her husband to take advantage of the freedom that money can offer. Lucy believes

> that money had never meant anything to her; why, then, should it mean anything to him beyond an extraordinary opportunity for time and freedom in his work? They could live anywhere in the world. They could travel, if they felt like it, until they found the right setting for a full and productive life. Wasn't that the kind of thing that most writers dreamed of? [Yates 2008b, 12].

When Nicole discusses her financial affairs with her sister, Baby Warren, at the time of her marriage to Dick Diver, she initially takes on board her husband's position with regards to her extraordinary wealth, declaring that "We're going to live very quietly in Zurich for two years and Dick has enough to take care of us" (Fitzgerald 2001, 183). She goes so far as to state that, "Dick refuses to have anything whatever to do with it" (183). It is made evident that the reason for Diver's initial rejection of his wife's money equates with Michael Davenport's concern that it would interfere with his ambition and commitment to work. Throughout the passages detailing his courtship with Nicole, numerous references are made to Dick's work as being the primary focus of his attention. When Nicole lists, rather self-consciously, her list of accomplishments that vie for her attention, Dick responds: "I envy you. At present I don't seem to be interested in anything except my work" (165).

This vocational dedication is, through the course of Book Two in the novel, consistently undermined until it has all but disappeared in Fitzgerald's portrayal of Diver in Book One, the events of which occur chronologically after those of Book Two. The shift from doctor to party host is presented rapidly through Nicole's stream of consciousness from the point of her marriage to the moment she is seen on the beach by Rosemary Hoyt at the opening of the novel. In the space of a mere four pages, the reader sees the trajectory of Dr. Diver change. In the course of his studies, he has written and published a book entitled *Psychology for Psychiatrists*. However, his position as a serious psychiatrist who is respected amongst his peers begins to wane. At the beginning of her internal monologue Nicole reflects her husband's standing by noting that his publishers want the aforementioned book "published in six languages" (183). In the next paragraph despite Nicole's previous agreement to live within the financial means of her husband and support his work, she asserts, "[t]hat seems unreasonable, Dick—we have every reason for taking the bigger apartment. Why should we penalize ourselves just because there's more Warren money than Diver money?" (183–184). The metamorphosis of Diver is completed by Nicole challenging the manner in which he signed a hotel register: "Dick, why did you register Mr. and Mrs. Diver instead of Doctor and Mrs. Diver? [...] You've taught me that work is everything and I believed you. You used to say a man knows things and when he stops knowing things he's like anybody else, and the thing is to get power before he stops knowing things" (186).

It is Dick Diver, however, who surrenders his power—which is located in his vocation—by this rejection of his title, an advertisement of his learning and expertise. Despite references throughout the novel to the Warren family's sapping of Dick's vitality, this act of surrender, which is challenged by Nicole, is evidence of Diver's own role in his descent into unproductivity and alcoholism, leading to eventual social and professional obscurity.

Unlike Fitzgerald's Dick Diver, Michael Davenport succeeds in resisting the temptation of his wife's money. Dick Diver's failure to do so is first demonstrated by his agreement to move to a larger apartment that in turn would become the Villa Diana in the South of France. This use of property as a motif for attitudes towards money is also used by Yates in *Young Hearts Crying*. Michael Davenport resists the luxury that his wife's money can provide in terms of locale. Instead the couple falls into a pattern of middle-class predictability, firstly, in a New York apartment, which is followed by a predictable move to the suburbs and the daily, monotonous commute back to the city. Jessica Mayhew, in her essay "Pantomimes of Death within Suburbia: Abject Boredom in Yates' *Revolutionary Road*, Lynch's *Blue Velvet*, and Bowen's *Attractive Modern Homes*," explores boredom as a modern phenomenon, arguing that "boredom itself cannot be perceived as a state" and is only recognized when an event disrupts it (Mayhew 2015, 617). It is certainly the case that the word or concept of boredom is not specifically referenced in Yates's work, but it is evident in the physicality of the suburban world he describes. Mayhew draws attention specifically to Yates's depiction of the suburban environment:

> In *Revolutionary Road* Frank and April Wheeler view their prospective suburban house and ask, "who could be frightened in as wide and bright, as clean and quiet a house as this?" The frightening aspect of this environment is difficult to articulate because it is concealed in blandness[....] They can sense the capacity within themselves to be "frightened" here [...] the house resists their tentative attempts at imposing their own "homeliness" on the enforced suburban domesticity [618].

The uniformity and conformity that is implied by the resistance of the personified house to be altered indicates the expectation that all who live in the suburbs share the same values, seek the same experiences, and identify the same markers of success. Yates's indication of the Wheelers' underlying fear as they move into the suburbs indicates the all-consuming nature of the environment if one allows oneself to be absorbed by it. Despite Frank Wheeler's criticism of the suburbs at the beginning of the novel—"[i]t's as if everybody'd made this tacit agreement to live in a total state of self-deception. The hell with reality!" (Yates 2000, 65)—he, too, will eventually be consumed by the way of life which he originally dismissed. This shift in attitude will precipitate the disaster that befalls the Wheelers and ends in April's death. Frank Wheeler's self-deception makes April's self-awareness sharpen in focus. It was their previous shared self-awareness that protected them from the suburban nightmare that they originally feared. Frank's growing self-deception isolates April and her desire for escape, leading inexorably to her annihilation. Yates, in his interview with DeWitt Henry, insists that the suburbs are not the reason for the failure of Frank and April Wheeler or their marriage despite their suggestion that it is. Yates states "that was *their* delusion, *their* problem" (Yates 1972, 66). Their retreat to the suburbs is perhaps unsurprising. However, Blake Bailey suggests that in postwar America the "temptation was particularly keen to accept the easy rewards of suburban comfort, an undemanding job, and to fill the emptiness that followed with dreams of potential greatness or adventure" (Bailey 2003, 232). This locating of themselves in the suburbs is a decision, even if not a fully conscious one, that marks compromise but is not the cause of it as the process has already begun.

Conversation in Yates's writing is often about miscommunication and misunderstanding. Characters, such as Frank and April Wheeler, talk at each other, failing to engage with and understand the other party, highlighting the sense of isolation that is apparent even in relationships that outwardly appear to be functional. This constant miscommunication is made apparent by Yates's shifting narrative point of view. The reader does not see the fictional world through either Frank or April's eyes but is moved from one to the other, not only creating sympathy for both parties but also, as Blake Bailey suggests, the technique maintains "a certain judgmental detachment" (233). This narrative technique ensures that the reader is ever conscious of the inability of Frank and April to communicate effectively with one another despite their constant discussions and arguments. Interestingly, this roaming point of view narrative style is also used by Fitzgerald in *Tender Is the Night*, providing complexity in the form of a double narrative which illustrates Dick and Nicole's differing interpretations of the events of their marriage, and provokes in the reader sympathy and distaste for both parties.

Marital miscommunication and suburban self-deception is also evident at the opening of *Disturbing the Peace*. Although she lives in the city, Janice Wilder shares the values and expectations of the suburban housewife. The novel opens with the lines, "Everything began to go wrong for Janice Wilder in the late Summer of 1960. And the worst part, she always said afterwards, the awful part, was that it seemed to happen without warning" (Yates 2008a, 1). The suggestion that John Wilder's descent into alcoholism and mental illness, resulting in a stint in the Bellevue Psychiatric Hospital, occurred without warning is fanciful and evident of Janice's self-deception articulated in the use of the word "seemed." It "seemed to happen without warning" but it did not. Her husband's growing instability is ignored, or not recognized, by Janice Wilder because she too is swept along by the practices of the growing consumerist middle-class who equate achievement with purchasing power. This focus on how an individual's identity becomes increasingly tied to what he or she owns is demonstrated by the types of occupations that many of Yates's central characters undertake. Michael Davenport initially looks for a job in advertising before settling on a role in publishing; John Wilder sells advertising space for a magazine; Frank Wheeler is also employed in sales. The mid-twentieth century was the point at which advertising came into its own. It could be argued that one of its central purposes is selling what is not needed, what is surplus to requirements but can define an individual's aspirations and illustrate their purchasing power. This in turn is evident of money and, by definition, success. At the heart of these jobs, however, is a kernel of meaninglessness. John Wilder, for example, does not advertise anything, nor does he sell anything. Instead he sells empty space to advertise, and it is this emptiness that he attempts to fill through alcohol and an extramarital affair, despite the plethora of 'things' that surround him courtesy of his ability to make money, a skill so admired by the consumerist society in which he lives. This growing focus on the purchasing power that money provides rather than the freedom it gives to pursue an individual's passions or fund philanthropic pursuits, is also evident in Fitzgerald's writing. Alongside the demonstrations of wealth in *The Great Gatsby*, there is also conspicuous consumption in *Tender*

Is the Night, most famously in the lengthy list of absurd purchases bought by Nicole Diver in Paris when she is accompanied by Rosemary Hoyt on a shopping expedition: "Everything she liked that she couldn't possibly use herself, she bought as a present for a friend" (Fitzgerald 2001, 65). The objects, however, are frivolous and certainly have little use despite Nicole's justification for buying them for others. Among the items she buys are artificial flowers, a guest bed, and a rubber alligator. She also purchases some new cloth "the color of prawns" that has, of yet, not been fashioned into anything that can be used at all (65). The shopping expedition also demonstrates the difference between inherited and earned money. Rosemary may aspire to be just like Nicole Diver, but her attitude to income and its uses are markedly different. Rosemary sees Nicole's attractiveness through what she refers to as "her mother's middle-class mind" and was "associated with her attitude about money" (65). Rosemary spends money she has earned whereas Nicole spends money that she has not. Fitzgerald articulates this difference by recounting Rosemary's near death experience filming a movie to generate her income. In contrast, Nicole is described as being "the product of much ingenuity and toil" (65). Not only is the Warren family income the product of work so is the figure, both literal and metaphorical, of Nicole Warren Diver. The toil, it would seem and, more significantly, the ingenuity of her forebears has resulted in a banal and worthless process of buying and consuming goods that are, at times, not only frivolous but utterly without meaning.

Marriage forms part of a shared notion of success demonstrated in 1950s America by mod-cons, new homes, cars, and keeping up with the proverbial Joneses. The emptiness that this constant need for consumption attempts to alleviate is certainly part of the "modern phenomenon of boredom" that Mayhew articulates, evident only when it is disrupted by an event. April Wheeler and John Wilder are examples of this disruption, but they only create ripples on the surface of the suburban version of the American Dream and with their removal life returns very much to normal. Indeed John Wilder's mental breakdown can only be absorbed and fully recognized by those around him and the wider community when it is transformed into a work of art, limiting his distress and frustration into a linear narrative that has a beginning, a middle and, most importantly, an end.

For many of Yates's characters the role of the artist provides some defense against the encroaching all-consuming world of suburbia and its baggage. In fact, they choose the identity of artist as a means of resisting the all-consuming nature of the tightly-knit communities in which they live. Michael Davenport spends the whole of *Young Hearts Crying* trying to develop seriously as a poet, but only ever achieves minor status. The novel also depicts his wife and then ex-wife, Lucy Blaine's excruciating search for an artistic role, flirting with acting, writing, and painting as a means of establishing a sense of self. John Wilder turns to the film industry. Frank and April Wheeler long to head to Paris, a place they see as a center of creativity to finally begin a life which has some meaning. What is interesting about this pursuit of the role of the artist is that it is an identity that can be clearly defined and appears to reject the conventions of the consumerist middle-classes, but it is still identifiable and admirable to that class. Whilst being able to define it, however, many in the wider community would be mystified by it believing that it can only be truly understood by the initiated few. This double sided attitude towards the arts is illustrated in Frank Wheeler's dismissive rants aimed at his neighbors because of their apparent lack of engagement with the arts. However, it is these same individuals who go and watch April's play. Appreciation of the arts is used as a means of demonstrating superiority but also illustrates, in the character of Frank Wheeler, an inferiority complex. He wants to be the only man in his neighborhood who can recognize and appreciate the value of art.

Within these groups of characters who identify themselves as artists or writers, similar pressures relating to success and status are also found within the suburban communities that they so readily dismiss. In the early pages of *Young Hearts Crying*, the artist Paul Maitland is dismissive of the more financially successful Tom Nelson, whom he feels, by virtue of his popularity and success, is short-changing the true vocation of the artist. He suggests to Michael Davenport that Nelson is "a good illustrator" (Yates 2008b, 77). He then continues by stating "if a picture's any good it's self-sufficient; it needs no text. Otherwise all you're getting is something clever, something ephemeral, something of the moment" (77). Financial and commercial success, it is believed, are at odds with true artistic endeavor. During the argument that will mark the end of their marriage, the Davenports fight bitterly over the subject when a psychiatrist produces a best seller entitled *How to Love*. Lucy suggests that Michael believes everything that makes the best seller list is trash; Michael qualifies her statement by declaring that most of it is, to which Lucy responds:

> "I don't think that's true at all. If a man can write something that appeals to a great many people; if his ideas and his way of expressing them turn out to be what a great many people want or need—isn't that a substantial achievement?"
> "Oh come on, Lucy, you know better than that. It's never been a question of what people 'want' or 'need'—it's a question of what they are willing to put *up* with. It's the same rotten little commercial principle that determines what we get in the movies and on television. It's the manipulation of public taste by virtue of the lowest common denominator. Oh Jesus, I *know* you know what I mean" [115].

While dismissing commercial success as an indication of inferior work, Davenport desperately seeks it. The reader is repeatedly told of the play that is not quite finished, and there is reference to an on-going anxiety that when it is finally written it might not "turn out to *be* my big-assed breakthrough? Or the next play either?" (101). Underneath these anxieties is the fear that he will be consumed by what he is so desperately trying to reject. The failure to finish his play is as much an act of procrastination in an attempt to delay the expected moment of failing as it is about any artistic concerns. It perfectly mirrors Dick Diver's ever-present manuscript that sits on his desk unfinished and, as a result, remains an unacknowledged failure rather than a proven one. The clinging to their vocation in the form of unfinished work is indicative of the failed compromise that lies at the heart of their marriages, and symbolically lies at the center of twentieth century American life. Dick Diver cannot finish his manuscript as he has become absorbed in the distracting, glamorous lifestyle that his wife's vast wealth can afford. In *Young Hearts Crying*, there is a clear suggestion that Michael Davenport lacks true artistic ability, which would result in work of genuine merit; however, there is also an evident compromise that diminishes Davenport's artistic output. Although he may have rejected the lavish lifestyle that his wife can afford and which is the root of Dick Diver's problems, Davenport is compromised by his need to provide a suburban lifestyle which reflects success even if it is not the success that he truly seeks. His employment in the city is as much a distraction as Diver's hosting on the French Riviera. Michael Davenport's fear that his working life will take over any other ambition permeates the novel. He does not want to be white collar management and dismisses colleagues such as Harold Smith out of hand, particularly after the latter's suggestion, "Wouldn't it be a little nicer to write your poems and your plays on fifty thousand a year?" (101). He also doesn't want to be a university English teacher, something he makes abundantly clear in response to Lucy's suggestion that when he has published a couple more well-received collections of poems he will be approached by colleges across the country. Davenport's response is as dismissive of academia as it is of middle management: "[i]f I ever become a college English teacher I can guarantee you'll be bored shitless with me inside of two years" (102). The statement could be seen as almost prophetic. Lucy is bored of him (although it doesn't take Davenport's predicted two years) and by the end of the novel he is a college English teacher. At the heart of the portrayal of Michael Davenport is the awful, and irresolvable, problem of wanting to achieve more than he is capable of and an equal inability to accept his limitations. At the end of their marriage it is Lucy who articulates this, not to Michael, but only to herself: "And I'll tell you something else," she whispered fiercely at the wall. "A poet is someone like Dylan Thomas. And a playwright—oh, God!—a playwright is someone like Tennessee Williams" (117).

Despite Michael's protestations about success being the result of appealing to the lowest common denominator, Lucy, by identifying Thomas and

Williams, illustrates the manner in which such an argument is used to justify not only a commercial lack of performance but also artistic failure. Similarly, Paul Maitland's attitude towards the relationship between commercial success and artistic credibility has changed by the end of the novel. Maitland has settled into a domesticity that is at odds with his earlier incarnation, and he has formed a friendship with Nelson who now admires his success where previously he had dismissed it. When telling Michael that he regrets not having got to know Nelson earlier, Michael responds by trying to reassure him: "I could understand how you felt [...] [a]nybody who makes it big in a commercial way at twenty-six or -seven is bound to be a little intimidating to strangers (380). Maitland, however, overlooks most of what Davenport says but picks up on his use of the word "commercialism" in relation to Tom Nelson:

> "Well, but the word 'commercialism' isn't really appropriate to Tom," Paul objected. "It may apply to a flukey kind of luck like Morin's, but that's an entirely different thing. Tom's a professional. He found his line early and he's stayed with it. You have to admire that."
>   "Well, I guess you have to respect it: I'm not sure it's something you necessarily have to admire" [380].

Michael Davenport has constructed the role of the artist for a particular purpose. It is an identity that, like many of Yates's characters, is chosen by Davenport, and was decided upon in a peculiarly clinical fashion because of what it is permitted to represent. This identification with artistic endeavor is located in the idea of escape. The role of the artist, even more than art itself, represents escape—or at least the possibility of escape—from the tedium of a nine to five job, escape from the narrow-minded perspective of suburban lives and, on a more grandiose scale, the prospect of transcending life through artistic immortality. This need for transcendence is something that is almost palpable in Yates's fictional world because of the tedium and meaninglessness that characters are always trying to keep at bay. In Yates's 1972 interview with DeWitt Henry and Geoffrey Clark, the author articulates the desire for conformity that emerged in postwar America and the need to reject it. Speaking of *Revolutionary Road* he states:

> I think I meant it more as an indictment of American life in the nineteen-fifties. Because during the fifties there was a general lust for conformity all over the country, by no means only in the suburbs—a kind of blind desperate clinging to safety and security at any price [...] a great many Americans were deeply disturbed by all of that—felt it to be an outright betrayal of our best and bravest revolutionary spirit [Yates 1972, 66].

Although Yates does not limit this drive for security to the suburbs exclusively, it is this environment which is used so effectively by the author to demonstrate the frustrations that such a clinging to a sense of security can create. The physicality of the suburban world is used to articulate the facades and masks that are in constant operation in Yates's fictional world: "Nothing had ever worked in this makeshift kitchen; nothing had ever been right in the whole of this makeshift house or in the secondhand, second-rate piece of real estate around it" (Yates 2008b, 117). Similarly, Gatsby's mansion is "a factual imitation of some Hotel de Ville in Normandy," but it is not what it purports to be (Fitzgerald 1991, 8). At the heart of Gatsby is phoniness. In his attempt to recapture Daisy he abandons his fundamental, true self—Dan Cody's adventurous protégé—and attempts to transform into an individual who can attain and maintain the approval of men like Tom Buchanan. His love for Daisy, in this respect, is an act of self-betrayal. At the point when he first kisses Daisy, he pauses as he realizes the significance of investing his idea of himself into this woman: "He knew that when he kissed this girl, and forever wed his unutterable visions to her perishable breath, his mind would never romp again like the mind of God. So he waited, listening for a moment longer to the tuning fork that had struck upon a star Then he kissed her" (Fitzgerald 1991, 86–87).

This self-consciousness marks a shift from the pursuit of the pioneering individual, so evident in the schedule that is written into his copy of *Hopalong Cassidy*, with its focus on self-improvement, and moves towards a desire for social acceptance and admiration which can be achieved through marriage. Daisy Fay is a prize that is awarded to the individual who best demonstrates successful masculinity according to the codes of the wealthy upper-classes, perfectly represented by Tom Buchanan. In pursuing Daisy, Gatsby is seeking the approval of other men. His contemplation of marriage to Daisy is as much a consideration of the social ramifications as it is a contemplation of personal fulfillment. He tells Nick that once Daisy is divorced from Tom they were "to go back to Louisville and be married from her house—just as if it were five years ago" (86). This is more than Gatsby's oft quoted desire to "repeat the past" (86), but is deeply tied to his need for social acceptance:

> He demands and needs the social recognition that marriage to Daisy has within patriarchal culture that sees women as something that men symbolically bestow upon each other as recognition of their socially valid manhood. Hence, Gatsby's adamant demand that they marry from her house in Louisville. The significance is not that it is Daisy's house but that it is Daisy's father's house and therefore represents patriarchal acknowledgement and acceptance [Turner 2015, 162–163].

Of course, it is an acceptance that can never come. The rigid social codes that have, to a large extent been imported wholesale from the Old World, will not allow the likes of Jay Gatsby to replace the Tom Buchanans. In the moments before his death at the hands of George Wilson, it is suggested that that realization has come: "he must have felt that he had lost the old warm world, paid a high price for living too long with a single dream. He must have looked up at an unfamiliar sky through frightening leaves and shivered as he found what a grotesque thing a rose is and how raw the sunlight was upon the scarcely created grass" (Fitzgerald 1991, 126).

It is the moment of realization that the true self has been sacrificed in order to attempt to conform to the expectations of society. In this regard, Fitzgerald's hero equates with the frustrated lives of Yates's protagonists; at their core is self-betrayal and self-deception as they chase an imagined identity, be it Jay Gatsby and his multiple personas created by himself and others, or Michael Davenport and his hopeless pursuit of the identity of artist. In the closing pages of *Young Hearts Crying*, as Michael and Lucy meet once again, many years after their divorce, Lucy articulates the pretenses evident in Michael throughout the course of the novel: "Fuck art," she said. "I mean really, Michael. Fuck art, okay? Isn't it funny how we've gone chasing after it all our lives? Dying to be close to anyone who seemed to understand it, as if that could possibly help; never stopping to wonder if it might be hopelessly beyond us anyway" (Yates 2008b, 419). Lucy identifies the marker of this self-deception, the self-conscious pursuit of something rather than the creative act that seeks neither the approval nor disapproval of its imagined audience. Similarly, Tom Buchanan is acutely aware of the persona that Jay Gatsby is trying to present to the world and points out the self-conscious aspects of Gatsby's behavior and clothing as proof that he is failing.

Marriage in the work of both Richard Yates and F. Scott Fitzgerald is presented as a microcosm of modern American life, a means of exploring the compromises and disappointments that are demanded of the novels' protagonists as they seek out an identity that can be perceived *by others* to be successful. Marriage becomes a means of exploring questions about what America should be. Should it conform to old world values and ideals? Or should it strive for greatness in the form of fully individuated selves embracing the pioneering spirit? In the final evaluation, however, marriage is not blamed for the failures of individuals, and neither is the suffocating suburban sprawl that Yates creates nor the distracting glamour of Fitzgerald's fictional world. These become symbolic of the compromise that individual characters have already made as they trade individual fulfillment for the appearance of social success in an attempt to have both. Yates and Fitzgerald suggest that an individual cannot pursue a social identity that conforms to social expectations symbolized in their fictional worlds as marriage and still remain true to their individual identity and ambitions, which is evident in the elevation of the idea of vocation. Marriage, therefore, is not the cause of their failure but it would appear to be a symbol of it. The glaring difference between Yates's protagonists and Fitzgerald's heroes is that the latter are capable of greatness before they allow themselves to be compromised. They could have, indeed should have, embraced the pioneering spirit that so encapsulates the idea of

America but are distracted by the trappings of social and monetary success represented in marriage to Fitzgerald's famed "golden girl" (Fitzgerald 1991, 94). Yates's protagonists are different. Their tragedy is, perhaps, even greater in that despite their desire to embrace that same pioneering spirit, they do not have the talent, the energy or vitality to do so.

NOTES

1. Yates continues "Tom and Daisy might have been blamed for Jay Gatsby's death, but Fitzgerald prevents us from seeing it that way by having Nick say, in his own final judgment, that they were simply 'careless people.'"

2. Steven Goldleaf in "Master and Model: F. Scott Fitzgerald's Role in Richard Yates's 'Saying Goodbye to Sally,'" sums up these parallels in the essay's opening paragraph: "An American writer of realistic fiction, of an ancestry that derived both from recent immigrant forebears and from colonial ancestors (including one eminent historical figure still widely read—or sung—in the twenty-first century); a young and undistinguished soldier during the final months of a world war, from which he emerged with a mild case of tuberculosis that lingered through his lifetime; a losing battler against the lure of alcohol which, combined with the financial pressures of his final years, resulted in a nervous breakdown, a horrific experience he recounted in print, where he revealed personal details that his critics felt were self-flagellating" (219).

BIBLIOGRAPHY

Bailey, Blake. 2003. "Richard Yates on the Edge of Success." *New England Review* (1990) 24 (3):6–31.
_____. (2003) 2004. *A Tragic Honesty: The Life and Work of Richard Yates.* London: Methuen.
Fitzgerald, F. Scott. (1925) 1991. *The Great Gatsby.* Edited by Matthew J. Bruccoli, *The Cambridge Edition of the Works of F Scott Fitzgerald.* New York: Cambridge University Press.
_____. (1934) 2001. *Tender Is the Night.* Edited by James L.W. West III, *The Cambridge Edition of the Works of F. Scott Fitzgerald.* New York: Cambridge University Press.
_____. 1994. *A Life in Letters.* Edited by Matthew Bruccoli and Judith Baughman. New York: Scribner.
Goldleaf, Steven. 2015. "Master and Model: F. Scott Fitzgerald's Role in Richard Yates's 'Saying Goodbye to Sally.'" *The F. Scott Fitzgerald Review* 13 (1): 219–235.
Henry, DeWitt. Review of *Disturbing the Peace. Ploughshares* 3 (1): 159–165
Mayhew, Jessica. 2015. "Pantomimes of Death within Suburbia: Abject Boredom in Yates' *Revolutionary Road*, Lynch's *Blue Velvet*, and Bowen's 'Attractive Modern Homes.'" *Interdisciplinary Literary Studies* 17 (4):617–634.
Naparsteck, Martin. 2001. "Drinking with Dick Yates." *The North American Review* 286 (3/4):75–79.
Turner, Helen. 2015. "Gender, Madness and the Search for Identity in Selected works of F. Scott Fitzgerald." Ph.D., Department of Literature, Film and Theatre Studies, University of Essex.
Yates, Richard. 1981. "Some Very Good Masters." *New York Times Book Review* 19.
_____. (1961) 2000. *Revolutionary Road.* New York: Vintage.
_____. (1986) 2005. *Cold Spring Harbor.* London: Methuen.
_____. (1975) 2008a. *Disturbing the Peace.* London: Vintage.
_____. (1984) 2008b. *Young Hearts Crying.* London: Vintage.
_____. 1972. DeWitt Henry and Geoffrey Clark. "An Interview with Richard Yates." *Ploughshares* 1 (3): 65–78.

What About the Children?

KATE CHARLTON-JONES

> "They're so busy hating each other now, and so busy being in love with their new people, that I've sort of come to despise them both. And the worst of it is they feel so guilty about me."
>
> —Yates *YHC* 2005, 269

The world Richard Yates observes as a writer is also one he recoils from. There are many reasons for this: the performative nature of almost all relationships; narcissism, that seems to be the chief engine driving human endeavor; dependence on the false gods of film, television, and advertising as role models for behavior; a growing reliance on psychiatry and psychology which Yates feels threatens the viability of friendships, relationships, and open communication; and the way in which children are consistently marginalized in the face of their parents' attenuated marriages. The impoverishment of children is not solely financial, Yates suggests, but is primarily the result of poor parenting: this is highlighted by a lack of robust communication between parents and their children and an apparent inattentiveness to the needs of those children. The typical Yatesian family home is always found wanting by this writer since it provides little or no haven for the children who inhabit it: for Phil Drake in *Cold Spring Harbor*, Jennifer and Michael in *Revolutionary Road*, Laura in *Young Hearts Crying*, Tommy Wilder in *Disturbing the Peace*, Emily Grimes in *The Easter Parade*, and for many children in his short stories, home is a bewildering place. They live in houses either dominated by the fractured relationships of their parents or infected by their divorced mother's self-interested decisions. Yates makes it clear that cramped space and financial difficulty may add to their troubles, but for the children it is lack of disinterested love and honest communication that damages them.

There is no perfect family paradigm in Yates's work and very few scenes depicting family harmony. This is not just the result of Yates's own personal experience growing up in a family riven by divorce but is borne out of his horror of sentimentality and inauthenticity. To create an image of domestic bliss—a father shaking pre-dinner cocktails while the mother looks adoringly at him from her chair, their bathed and pajama-clad children (a boy and a girl) playing quietly at her feet—would be to succumb to "the great sentimental lie of the suburbs" (Yates 2001, 112) disseminated by television, film, and advertising hoardings. Yates's fiction is emphatic: this family does not exist. Imperfection is the best to be hoped for but how those imperfections are revealed and addressed suggests much about the strength or weakness of the family lives he fictionalizes. The picture of childhood he paints is invariably bleak: the children are lonely, disenfranchised, loved in a remote, partial way, poorly cared for and inadequately educated.[1] They are at the mercy of their parents' failing marriages and subject to the vagaries, sometimes violence, of their moods.

In all his fiction Yates attempts a depiction of the truth of life as he experienced it, as an adult and as a child, as a parent and a writer. By examining Yates's presentation of children across his œuvre it is possible to deepen our understanding of how people in mid-twentieth century America lived their lives. Noting the details of his writing as it is relevant to the children of his fiction (and that inevitably involves some attention to their parents) adds depth and texture to our appreciation of that world and in particular to its inconsistencies. Whilst government, religious and civic officials placed great store on the encouragement of procreation and the family unit after World War II, Yates suggests that the reality of life for children was that they were more tolerated than celebrated; highlighted as a blessing and a political necessity after the turmoil and instability of war, they were, in Yates's view, marginalized in the domestic sphere. Louisa Randall Church wrote about the new responsibilities for parents in a post–Hiroshima world: "The new philosophy of child guidance makes of parenthood not a dull, monotonous routine job, but an absorbing, creative profession—a career second to none" (quoted in May 1988, 135). Building on this, Tyler May suggests that more than duty was involved: "the joys of raising children would compensate for the thwarted expectations in other areas of their lives" (May 1988, 135). It was believed that "parenthood was the route to happiness" (137). Concurring with this view, Marilyn Irvin Holt writes that, "[postwar] American society pictured itself as caring about children and regarded its families as child-centered." However, she goes on to write that this "self-image was fixed, but it was also rife with contradictions" (Holt 2014, 149). It is those discrepancies between the public and political view of life within families and the reality of life as he observed it that Yates sought to portray in his fiction.

Yates is always interested in the disenfranchised. Throughout his stories figures appear with the kind of disabilities or physical imperfections that ensure they remain outsiders, either on society's margins or at the margins of their own social confidence. Alcoholism is a dominant and pervasive sickness for both Yates's male and female characters, but mental illness and consequent hospitalization are equally part of his landscape. Physical disabilities or impairments, such as the polio that chemistry teacher Jack Draper copes with (*A Good School*), or Keith Smith's cerebral palsy (*Young Hearts Crying*), or episodes of impotence (*The Easter Parade* and *Young Hearts Crying*), are a strikingly unusual aspect of his fiction. What Yates suggests in his work is that being young and poor in a society that pays scant attention to its youth is a disabling factor not routinely noticed. His fictional children are nearly always the poorest amongst their peer group, and the friends that they make never understand what lack of money means. As Blake Bailey describes throughout *A Tragic Honesty* (2004), Yates himself went through this all his life. The world of the 1950s and 1960s that Yates's work predominantly describes is aspirational and places a high value on material goods, appearance, and social status. His aim is to reveal the underbelly of such a society and to create a sense of what growing up as a poor, white child of divorced parents feels like. Yates often uses narrative shifts to mirror the differing perspectives of his adults' self-interest and manipulative tendencies. Although he sometimes employs this technique when writing about children (most notably in prolonged descriptions of Phil Drake's perspective in *Cold Spring Harbor* or Richard Groves's experiences in *A Good School*), he restrains its use to descriptions of children who are a primary focus of the narrative. Where children are seen as 'incidental' to the main storyline (and, as I will argue, they are never incidental to how we receive the story), Yates's narrator observes them rather than mimics them. It is as if Yates wants his presentation of children to suggest their inviolability; they are as they appear. This is the exact opposite of what he strives for in his presentation of adults, young or old, who have lost innocence, authenticity, and truthfulness. His use of the dual narrative for adults allows him to show their deceptions, and in effect, undercut their presentation of self.

In order to develop a sense of integrity in his depiction of children, Yates is very particular about his descriptions of their comments and behavior. Our attention is drawn to their actions, their words, and their silences. In work that consistently presents adults as immature, child-like and ill-educated, it is often the children, perhaps only glimpsed in the background, who add depth to the readers' understanding of Yates's purpose. Frequently alerting his readers to the fact that the physical space children occupy is proscribed, the writer's keener focus is on the very limited emotional engagement they have with their parents. Their directness and innocent honesty is, more often than not, in strong contrast to the adults' wavering moral compass, their indulgent performances, and their self-deluding perspectives. This does not mean Yates indulges in a "bath of sentimentality" when describing children (Yates 2001, 66). He does not shrink from describing their meanness and deceptions, their competitiveness and, at times, aggressive behavior. However, the authorial position he adopts and the moral coloring he presents is inclined, always, in favor of children. I have previously argued that, "Yates obfuscates rather than asserts a moral position" (Charlton-Jones 2014, 59). This is true in relation to his adult characters, but that obfuscation is less apparent with regard to his depiction of young children who have no control over their lives, and are seen to be at the mercy of adults who make decisions based on their own best interests.

The loneliness of the children Yates writes about is striking. In marriages that are failing, where communication with them is limited, they are left to muddle through, gleaning what information they can, trying to guess what might be going on around them. Yates describes Laura Davenport, for example, as a shy six-year-old, bewildered by seeing her house packed into boxes, put into the back of the car "for a very long time," attempting to make sense of her parents' conversation: [she was] "trying to overhear and understand as much as possible of what her parents were saying to each other up in the front" (Yates *YHC* 2005, 68). The phrasing is deliberately awkward so that the reader is guided to place emphasis on "to each other." Furthermore, Yates makes "up in the front" sound like a very great distance as he indicates Laura's bewilderment. Few images of confused isolation can be more striking than that of Jennifer in *Revolutionary Road*. After annoying her mother who is busy making plans for Paris, she slips away to her bedroom. A while later her parents go to find her: "there she was, lying down and staring at nothing, with her thumb in her mouth" (Yates 2001, 178). The "nothing" she is staring at is indicative of her reduced role, given no responsibility and only marginally included in their discussion of what is happening. Not encouraged to speak, Jennifer stops her mouth, literally, with her thumb.

The pattern of loneliness for children that is endemic in Yates's failing marriages is only compounded once divorce has occurred. This is particularly evident in the depictions of Kicker and Nancy in two of his short stories, "Saying Goodbye to Sally" and "Trying out for the Race" respectively. In both stories, the reader is struck by the *careless*ness of the mothers, and further struck by how their children become victims of their mothers' self-absorbed behavior. These women discard their responsibilities casually in favor of romance, fun, and alcohol-fueled evenings with their own friends, noticing little, if anything, of their children's poor adjustment to the instability their decisions give rise to. It is worth noting that material wealth is no protection against such emotional deprivation. In "Saying Goodbye to Sally," for instance, Jill Jarvis and her son Alan "Kicker" Jarvis live in an opulently furnished

"vast white mansion" in Beverly Hills (Yates 1981, 219). Jack Fields, the protagonist of the story, enters the house with his new girlfriend, Sally Baldwin,
and takes in his surroundings: "An arrangement of leather-padded wrought-
iron benches was built out around the hearth, and on one of the benches sat
a pale, sad boy of about thirteen, facing away from the fire and holding his
clasped hands between his thighs, looking as though he had come to sit here
because there was nothing else to do" (219). This graphic image is one the
reader cannot forget: as the tale unfolds and the reader, through Jack Fields's
eyes, is witness to the degree of Kicker's abandonment, it becomes clear how
and why he is "a pale, sad boy" without visible friends of his own age, care-
lessly robbed of attachments he does make, and without parents who claim
him.

In "Trying Out for the Race" Yates also depicts life for a child whose
mother is so wrapped up in her own ambitions that she has to "pretend to
take pleasure in her child" (Yates 1981, 66). Yates was all too aware of the
many difficulties for women who were trying to raise children alone in postwar America. After his parents' divorce, his experience of life with his mother
had instructed him about the difficulties single women experienced running
a home on limited finances. He was also attuned to women's loneliness and
their dependence on female friends with whom they could share their romantic conquests, or with whom they could cry when those relationships failed.
However, hurt, perhaps, by his own perception that his mother had neglected
him and his sister, his portraits of these women are often negative and disturbing. Jill Jarvis, Kicker's mother, barely notices her child; Elizabeth Hogan
Baker does, but only when it suits her. Her daughter, Nancy, replies to questions about whether she's worried over her mother's sudden disappearance
without warning or subsequent communication: "No.... I know she'll come
back. She always does" (78). This stoic response from the mouth of a nine-
year-old child, suggests a pattern of neglect that reaches far beyond the immediate circumstances. It is more disquieting to witness a child being so
sanguine about her mother's disappearance in pursuit of a man than if she
had been throwing a tantrum, thus it is to that quiet response that Yates draws
our attention. In stark contrast, only a few paragraphs later, her mother Elizabeth's subsequent foot-stamping demand to her friend Lucy sounds petulant:
"Lucy, I need my child" (79). The emphasis falls on the words "I need" for it
is always her needs that are foregrounded.

For all that children appear to be neglected by the parent or parents
with whom they live, it is clear that those parents are not negligent out of
ignorance. Yates's fiction shows many examples of parents self-interestedly
invoking the needs of their children in a way that he clearly feels is both cyn-
ical and deplorable. It is not that adults do this in a deliberately manipulative
way, but that they lack enough self-awareness, Yates suggests, to examine

critically their own narcissistic aims. In this vein, when Lucy Davenport says, "I felt pretty sure she'd like the house—she might even think it's sort of 'cozy'" (Yates *YHC* 2005, 66), the reader is well aware that her own views are being super-imposed on her young daughter because it suits her to appear attentive to Laura at this moment; in effect, Laura provides her with leverage. When Lucy, who has been more than negligent as a mother, loses her patience with fifteen-year-old Laura, she does so by reminding Laura that she is a child: "*That* might give you some idea of what a child you are" (252). The reader cannot fail to notice that Laura's young age has been forgotten while it has suited her mother. In the same vein, Frank Wheeler, trying to find reasons to remove himself from the plan to go to Paris, says, "It's just that this does seem a pretty inconsiderate thing to be doing, when you think about it, from the kids' point of view" (Yates 2001, 180). It is convenient for him at this point to think about how such a move will affect their children since he wants to end all talk of going to Paris, but there has been very little evidence of such empathy before now. When he later attempts to keep the peace and "enthusiastically romped with the children" (219), the reader is left in no doubt that this is all part of a performance in which the children are mere accessories.

The fact that the motives of parents are often shown to be self-interested is particularly ironic since during the course of different stories many of the protagonists bemoan details of their own upbringing. Yates strongly suggests a circular pattern of poor parenting across generations that goes beyond details of impecunious circumstances, dull jobs, and thwarted ideals: it is the values and aspirations of his fictional parents that he holds up for criticism while remaining empathetic towards the difficulties of their circumstances. April Wheeler felt abandoned by her parents and yet abandons her own children although, tellingly, it is their voices that she must finally shut out before her final act (310). Frank Wheeler has a vivid memory of being shouted at by his father when he was young (36) and then lashes out at his even younger son, terrifying him in the process (52). Michael Davenport, considering Sarah's desire for a baby, thinks that a new child will give him the "chance to atone for all the aching mistakes he'd made over the years with Laura" (Yates *YHC* 2005, 354). The reader is fully aware that the pattern will continue and that atonement is unlikely. As Landis and Landis observe, "The presence or absence of children will not transform maladjusted individuals into happy husbands and wives" (1968, 460).

The most striking example of the circularity of poor parenting comes in *Cold Spring Harbor* with the maternal aspirations voiced by Rachel Shepard. Yates highlights the fact that she desires to be a good mother, protecting her son yet encouraging his independence: "And we're never going to neglect him in any way ... but we won't sort of impose ourselves on him either— we'll never let our problems be *his* problems" (Yates *CSH* 2005, 156). She concludes, "we'll never let him feel he doesn't have a home" (157). It is clear to the reader that she is implicitly striving against all the strictures of her own upbringing; driven by her excited aspirations to be a good, loving, happily-married parent, she ploughs breathlessly on, seemingly unaware of the implications of her speech. However, by the end of the novel, unsure of her husband's whereabouts or even if he'll come home, bruised physically and mentally by their last fight, Rachel's words to her tiny son ensure that the reader knows she will be exactly the same kind of mother as Gloria Drake: "You're a miracle. Because do you know what you're going to be? You're going to be a man" (178). Her words grimly echo those of April Wheeler massaging the ego of her husband Frank in order to manipulate and guide him to her point of view: "You're the most valuable and wonderful thing in the world. You're a man" (Yates 2001, 115). So it is that Rachel will guide and control her son. In contrast to her previous language (with its repeated emphasis on "we") focusing on her restrained hopes for this child and on the freedom she will give him to be who and what he wants, her idiom has become over-inflated, sentimental, and directional. With characteristic pessimism, Yates's ending is bleak.

When John Givings visits the Wheelers for the second time, he asks with his usual peremptory manner, "Hey, by the way, where do you people keep your kids? Old Helen keeps telling me about your kids, and I never see 'em" (Yates 2001, 228). This is a reasonable question in the context of the whole narrative given that the two children are so rarely glimpsed, although it is perfectly clear why they are not there then, and clear to Givings too. It is not that Yates marginalizes the children but that the families he describes usually do. Ushered away from the important business of adult interaction, the children are disenfranchised within the families he describes. Their presence in Yates's white, middle-class homes is not celebrated or encouraged. He places emphasis on the importance of children's bedtime with a significance that might strike the twenty-first century reader as disturbing: "But the day didn't really begin until later still, when the children were in bed with their door firmly shut for the night" (126). In this novel, the children's door is often closed, firmly. Recurring moments of children shut in their rooms, sent off to play outside, or anesthetized by the new babysitter television, are a troubling but recognizable feature of life in America of the '50s and '60s.

It is striking that in the homes Yates depicts television is a new and welcome presence for children often left alone, especially considering that "By the 1950s, televisions were selling at a rate of over five million a year" (May 1988, 172). Marilyn Holt describes the general response to this new phenomenon in the 1960s: "Television brought families and friends together when everyone gathered round the set for an evening of viewing" (Holt 2014, 29). However, Yates's fiction quietly suggests that television weakens the thin thread of communication between children and their parents for it allows parents to ignore their offspring. For Jennifer and Michael Wheeler, watching cartoons is a necessary form of entertainment while their parents discuss issues only poorly understood by them; they are a barely visible presence as they are "silenced by the television" (Yates 2001, 126). Silencing the children always seems important to Yates's parents. In view of the fact that *Revolutionary Road* was published in 1961 when television was still a relatively new and much-celebrated phenomenon, his disquiet about its possible negative effect on communication within the home is prescient.

That children welcome the privacy and calm of their private space is not a surprise when set against the toxicity of the adult world around them. Mimicking the idiom of six-year-old Laura Davenport, Yates's descriptions are distinct: "But she loved the house in Larchmont: her bedroom there was the only truly private, secret place in the world and her backyard offered daily excursions into hazardous adventure" (Yates *YHC* 2005, 69). However, maintaining that space is not in her control; very soon she is uprooted from here to a new home in Tonapac. Yates describes Laura watching the removal men at work, bravely trying to reassure herself all will be well. Her safe haven is now reduced to the inside of their family car: "Laura Davenport and her father and mother would always be safe in the shelter of their own car [...] [which] might come to serve, if necessary, as a small but adequate new home for the three of them" (68). If this is an attempt to mimic her thoughts, I do not find it entirely successful; Laura is six and a half years old but given the world view of someone twice her age. However, I would argue that this is deliberate. As with this example, when Yates *does* employ mimesis of children's thoughts or speech he does so with far less accuracy or commitment to the task than when he uses the same technique for adult speech and thought patterns. In this way, he suggests children remain a little beyond the reach of our understanding, independent of thought and mind and hard to pin down.

As much as children are dismissed by their parents who want to get down to the hard business of drinking or arguing, children also learn to escape. Playing outside in the yard or in their rooms may be one form of escape open to them but Yates draws attention to the necessary and enriching use of the imagination. In "Oh, Joseph, I'm so Tired" the narrator recalls that he and his older sister "found things to do in the courtyard every day, for all of the two years we lived there, but that was only because Edith was an imaginative child" (Yates 1981, 6). This older sister is more than just a companion to her little brother; she provides stability and guidance clearly missing from their mother. Despite their cramped quarters and impecunious state, Edith enhances Bill's experience of childhood immeasurably when she teaches him to develop his imaginative capacity and listen for "the sound of the city" (18).

Listening to "the beyond," to the "faint, faint sound of millions" (33), helps the young boy to accept and adjust to every new change in his life, as is made clear at the end of the story. Yates suggests that with a vivid imagination young children can find comfort, even in bleak circumstances; the creation of more palatable worlds in their heads has the added benefit of being inviolable. In *Young Hearts Crying*, Laura invents her own sister and "would often spend hours in whispered conversation with the phantom child" (Yates *YHC* 2005, 117). Yates's mimetic narrative—and this is one of very few moments where he attempts to imitate the idiom of a child's thoughts—carefully constructs the ebb and flow of a conversation between Laura and her imagined younger sister, Melissa. In this imagining, Laura is helpful, brave and, crucially, appreciated by Melissa. Laura even relishes an imaginary spat with her "sister." In a fictive world fights can be easily and calmly resolved: "Let's not fight anymore" (118). Sadly, the reality of Laura's loneliness eventually intrudes on her consciousness so that "she couldn't help knowing, with more than a touch of shame, that she was talking to herself" (119).

If the loneliness of Yates's fictional children is striking, so too is the lack of information they have to work with when adults rarely address them about what is happening. When Tommy Wilder is faced with a change of plans, he is told what to think, but this telling is dressed-up as a question:

> "Daddy and I have decided to go home tomorrow. You won't mind that very much, will you?"
> And Tommy said he didn't know; he didn't care [Yates 2007, 62].

Silence, or mumbled assent, is often the child's best refuge when the adults around them have no interest in their response. Wrestling to make sense of partial information handed out to them by their parents, Yates powerfully depicts Jennifer and Michael Wheeler's bafflement when they are told they are no longer moving to Paris: "The total neutrality of expression on both children's faces" (Yates 2001, 234) signals much to the reader but apparently little to Frank who demands more reaction. More powerful still is the way in which Yates later shows Jennifer sifting through the small particles of information she has gleaned and is trying hard to comprehend: "Why was it 'better not to just now'? And why had her mother looked so funny and sad when she said 'That's about right'?" (235).

In Yates's fiction, once marriages have broken down, and the parents have divorced, the children stay with their mothers.[2] This was normal procedure until the late 1960s when it first began to be questioned. As Furstenberg and Cherlin state, "Mothers were deemed more fit to care for children because of their supposedly superior moral and spiritual qualities" (1991, 30). This seems ironic set against Yates's portraits of mothers and, clearly, does not reflect his experience. The mothers of his fictional children are generally desperate figures, often dependent on alcohol, and wrapped up in their own personal struggles. The fathers may be less uniformly self-absorbed but parents of both genders are criticized for the poor quality of their childcare in his work. John Wilder, Frank Wheeler, and Michael Davenport are occasionally seen to interact with their children but are poor fathers at best.

At rare moments we glimpse instances of fatherly wisdom as well as compassion and empathy in Yates's portraits of men; if intelligence is imparted of a practical or moral nature (there is nothing approaching spiritual guidance in his fiction), it always comes from the father. Yates draws attention to Walter Grimes's level-headedness, for instance, at the time of the older daughter Sarah's engagement: "It was Walter Grimes, to whom the engagement was presented as an accomplished fact, who asked all the questions. Who exactly *was* this Donald Clellon?" (Yates *EP* 2004, 19). This moment of intervention leads to the exposure of Clellon but cannot prevent Sarah from rushing into marriage with another unsuitable man. Similarly practical, it is Charles Shepard who diffuses Gloria Drake's fussing about Evan and Rachel's plans to marry by stating: "They're both old enough to do as they please, aren't they" (Yates *CSH* 2005, 45). Viewed alongside the many descriptions of Gloria Drake's self-interested histrionics, the reader can only admire the respect Shepard's question implies for the young people's independence even if the reader is also struck by their youth. In *A Good School*, Steve MacKenzie remembers the sage advice his father, Jock, gave him about talking: "the important thing is knowing when to stop. Never say anything that doesn't improve on silence" (Yates *AGS* 2006, 86). However, avoiding all sentimentality, these are not idealized fathers. Young Steve MacKenzie reflects that his father's "anger could be terrible" (85) and Curtis Drake's character is undercut for the reader when he informs his young son that in the near future he must take sole responsibility for his mother, despite being fully aware of how difficult and demanding Gloria Drake is.

In several of the stories in *Liars in Love*, Yates looks at fathers, or father figures, more closely. Woody Starr, though not Kicker's father, has developed a close and loving relationship with the boy and is energetically receptive to his perceptions, his enthusiasms and his need for attention. He talks to him, he plays with him and he camps out with him (and this closeness is felt all the more since it is in stark contrast to Jill Jarvis's neglect of her son). The only time we see Kicker energized is when he is around this man: "Kicker came hurrying in from the pool terrace for an intense, animated discussion with Woody Starr about a broken bicycle" (Yates 1981, 230). After three years of living in this dysfunctional house, and implicitly three years of relative stability for Kicker, Starr is summarily dismissed so that Jill Jarvis can accommodate her new lover. Yates's description of his parting embrace with Kicker leaves the reader in no doubt that father-substitutes can have profound and affecting relationships worthy of respect: "They saw Woody Starr put both arms around the boy and gather him up into an abrupt, tight, clinging embrace" (266).

Yates is specific about the pain and grief some divorced fathers experience at being parted from their children, and effectively disenfranchised from any say in their lives. They often notice pain and bewilderment in the eyes of their children but feel powerless to affect any change, since all their rights, bar that of visitation, seem to have been severed by divorce. Furstenberg and Cherlin, writing about divorce and its effects in the mid-twentieth century, see this as a general pattern:

> Divorce establishes a destructive dynamic between men and women that leads many fathers to retreat from parenthood. When these men stop living with their wives and children, they no longer see themselves (or are seen by their former wives) as full-fledged fathers. It is as if their license for parenthood were revoked when their marriage ended [1991, 34].

In "Oh, Joseph, I'm So Tired" the two young children, Edith and Bill, have been out for the day with their father and Bill, now adult, narrates the story. He recalls that their father has said goodbye and is leaving without handing over the stamps he bought for them that afternoon. They run after him: "He stopped and turned around, and that was when we saw he was crying. He tried to hide it [...] but there is no way to disguise the awful bloat and pucker of a face in tears" (Yates 1981, 8). Unable to lose sight of the integrity of the character whose emotions he is evoking, Yates depicts his narrator, the boy as an adult, reflecting on their childish awkwardness and ineptitude: "It would be good to report that we stayed and talked to him—that we hugged him again—but we were too embarrassed for that. We took the stamps and ran home without looking back" (8). It is clear that the children, though alarmed, are too young to know how to respond to his vulnerability. From a writer whose entire oeuvre exposes artificiality and performance (Charlton-Jones 2014), it is clear that this is not a description of a performance of grief but grief itself. Reading this story in the twenty-first century, one is struck by the implicit attention Yates gives to fathers' rights which were not on the national political agenda in 1978 when the story was first published by *Atlantic* (Bailey 2004, 486).[3] As well as highlighting the father's grief at separation, Yates appears to question the efficacy and justice of placing children with a dysfunctional, deluded mother who lives beyond her means and drains her ex-husband of money in order to pay her debts (these are dominant characteristics of almost all his maternal figures). Furthermore, it is hard not to link the early deaths of several of the fathers in Yates's novels with the strain of providing for such women and with the profound loneliness of lives lived apart from their children; Walter Grimes and Vincent Grove both die in their early fifties.

Longing for more time with his absent children was at the heart of Yates's own experience. The fathers of his fiction sometimes reflect that yearning but surprisingly often they don't. Yates could not abide sentimentalism and knew that describing paternal relationships after divorce was dangerous territory for him. He is clear that being empathetic enough to notice their children's pain, and being saddened by their lack of contact does not of itself make fathers laudable individuals. Sometimes fathers, such as the one in "Oh, Joseph, I'm So Tired" are bewildered, rather shy figures, unable to protect their offspring from the exigencies of life as their children experience it and as they observe it from a distance. These fathers—Curtis Drake (*Cold Spring Harbor*), Walter Grimes (*The Easter Parade*), and Vincent "Mike" Grove (*A Good School*) included—may be marginal characters in their stories but the reader is struck by their authenticity, reliability, and honesty and by the small pieces of wisdom they impart in sharp distinction to the shallow nonsense and flirtatious chattering of their ex-wives. Yates appears to be suggesting that their diminished presence all but removes a necessary counter-balance in their children's lives—lives otherwise dominated by ill-educated, unstable women. However, Yates depicts flawed human beings, probing their intentions with one narrative voice and presenting their actions with another; fathers are not generally spared from his criticisms even if his presentation of their predicaments seems more sympathetic. His description of Evan Shepard taking his young daughter Kathleen out for the day is carefully, deliberately realistic: "He would have to come through with something substantial and serious for her soon, or her laughter might fade into the blank, lost, bewildered look that he never knew how to interpret" (Yates *CSH* 2005, 114). Shepard might notice her "blank, lost, bewildered look" but lacks the imagination or empathy to decipher it. In this way, Yates allows Shepard to reveal his own weakness; he depicts the child's depth of feeling while maintaining the consistency of his characterization of Shepard. Using a dual narrative to explain both Shepard's interior thoughts and what he says, Yates shows him mismanaging his advice and time with Kathleen. If the reader judges him at this point, some empathy towards him is restored when Yates writes that, "There was always a great sadness on these homeward drives; sometimes too there were feelings of inadequacy [...] and of failure. Oh, Jesus, divorce could sure as hell leave a lot to be desired" (117).

Intermittent contact clearly does not foster good communication and Yates shows the truth of this throughout his work. After months away, John Wilder self-consciously attempts to spend time with his son Tommy and takes him to ball games: "(wasn't that the kind of thing responsible fathers did?)" (Yates 2007, 167). His attempts at conversation are stilted and awkward and sound more like the probing of a distant but kindly uncle: "How's summer school going, Tom?" With Tommy's indeterminate answer, "I don't know; all right, I guess" (167), Yates also suggests you have to earn the right to penetrate your child's thoughts, especially if there has been a pattern of disappointment in the past. Performing the role of a good parent is not the same as *being* a good parent and Yates indicates that the children can sense the difference.

In *Young Hearts Crying*, Lucy Davenport, attempts to put the care of her daughter first. However, Yates is unequivocal that this is a performance she occasionally perfects rather than one that naturally emerges from the guiding force of deeply felt maternal wisdom. A short time after her divorce from Michael, Lucy recognizes the importance of routine and stability for her daughter, though there is a whiff of *Woman's Home Journal* about the realization that, "It seemed very important these days to have everything nice in the kitchen when Laura came home from school" (Yates *YHC* 2005, 127). The feeling that her actions are guided by a manual is compounded by this description: "A freshly made peanut-butter-and-jelly sandwich had to be set out on the flawlessly clean kitchen counter, with a glass of cold milk beside the plate, and Lucy had to be waiting there too, nicely dressed and groomed, as if the whole of her life were at Laura's disposal" (127).

The emphasis is all on presentation. The repeated "had to be" cements the notion that this is learned advice and that the correct performance is achieved by attention to these details. The reader is attuned to the irony that Lucy aims to appear "as if" she is a devoted mother when the novel makes it clear that her own needs come first. She is described as behaving in such a way "to prove she was still a conscientious mother" (238) but seems unable to sustain her commitment to that role for more than short bursts. Again, Yates allows his protagonist to give herself away. Using a mimetic narrative, he writes of her desire to go back to her studio and paint as her troubled relationship with Carl Traynor comes to an end: "Except for her house, where her daughter lived, there was only one place now where Lucy Davenport belonged" (243). The use of "where her daughter lived" is staggering since it suggests Laura is mature and independent; the reader is aware that she has recently turned thirteen. Yates implies a cool acceptance of a distance between mother and daughter effected by Lucy's changing needs.

Children are threatened by adults' anger, even if it is not directed at them. Unable to process the emotions behind that anger, children are reduced and fragmented by its appearance. In "Trying Out for the Race" Lucy Towers admonishes young Nancy at length for her behavior towards Russell, her son. Without any knowledge of the circumstances of Nancy's act of revenge, she continues her verbal assault until Nancy is broken:

> All through the upbraiding Nancy had sat silent, with a rigid face and downcast eyes.... There were telltale twitches of the lips, increasingly difficult to control; then [her mouth] came open and was locked in a shape of despair around two partly chewed green peas, and she was crying wretchedly but making no sound [Yates 1981, 90].

Mirroring the action of a zoom lens, the narrative focus moves ever closer as Yates highlights first Nancy's face, then her eyes and finally from eyes to mouth and lips. The effect is both powerful and disquieting.

Occasionally in Yates's fiction we see verbal anger shift towards physical abuse. Yates is unequivocal that it is always unjust, and always reflects badly on the parent for it is never the result of anxiety about the child's safety even if the adult sometimes justifies it this way. The Wheeler children who excitedly try to help their father build the garden path have no idea why he suddenly turns on them. They cannot know that he is rehearsing in his mind the details of the argument he had with their mother the night before in addition to brooding on all that has gone wrong in their marriage. The children become the outlet for his anger and he snaps: "the next thing he knew he had grabbed [Michael] by the belt and spun him around and hit him hard on the buttocks with the flat of his hand, twice, surprised at the stunning vigor of the blows and at the roar of his own voice" (Yates 2001, 52). Yates is equally unambiguous about the intensity of feeling behind Michael's response: "Michael found his need to cry so sudden and so deep that for several seconds after the first shocked squeal no sound could break from him" (52). Michael is four. The narrative glances over the idea that Frank Wheeler "might" have apologized to his children but Yates was writing about America in the 1950s; few parents apologized to their children for their failings then, even if Yates implicitly suggests the efficacy of such an idea.

In "Evening on the Côte d'Azur" Yates depicts two women in southern France looking after their children while their husbands are at sea. In the background of the story the narrative picks out the way the children of those women suffer for their mothers' desperation to assert control over their lives. One mother chases her child Bobby down the beach: "Finally she caught him and gave him a couple of good hard smacks. He set up an awful howl but he came along nicely enough, once she had a grip on his wrist" (Yates *CSS* 2004, 403). Her neighbor is no better: "She came in all dressed up, as usual, dragging Brenda, her six-year-old" (405). When Brenda says she'll tell her father about her mother's boyfriend the mother's reaction is swift: "In two, quick high-heeled steps she bore down on the little girl and hit her so hard the sailboat fell on the floor" (406). The narrative does not comment on these acts but they sit within the story waiting for the reader to consider them. As with all the incidents involving children, they add color and depth to the way in which we receive the adults.

Yates's fiction places the moral compass in favor of the children in their relationships with adults in order to highlight the self-serving nature of adult behavior. However, this does not mean he sentimentalizes childhood or children's conduct. Where we see children alone with other children, there are many instances of their meanness and vindictiveness. Yates includes such incidents firstly to adhere to the truth of children's behavior, and secondly to counter-balance the dominant impression of their innocence; in effect, he wants to remove any impression the reader might have that his presentation of them is saccharine. Most of the incidents described in his fiction may be judged minor or petty but Yates is clear that in the life of the child each event has a negative and powerful impact. In "Trying Out for the Race" Russell Towers is taunted insistently by his friend Harry for the childishness of his toys: "You like stuff like this? You play with stuff like this?" (Yates 1981, 81). In order to distract him, Russell leads his friend to Nancy's room where she is quietly organizing her theater programs. They get her to tell them about *The Mikado* which she saw with her father (and in the context of her circumstances this is a significant factor). Before long she is singing the libretto until she is abruptly disturbed by their mockery: "Harry Snyder distorted his face and made a slow, loud retching sound, as if this were the worst and most nauseating song he had ever heard, and to stimulate vomiting he spilled all the theater programs onto the floor with a splat. That won him a tense little laugh of complicity from Russell, and then there was silence in the room" (83). This incident is an understated but pivotal moment in the story of the children's relationships and in how we receive the story as a whole. The reader refers back to it mentally when assessing the adult's conduct and decisions.

In *A Good School*, Yates describes an altogether more disturbing event when a group of boys are left unsupervised. While the protagonist is pinned down, one of them sits on his face and proceeds to masturbate him. The event is then repeated with a different victim later in the story. In a modern reading, we would regard this incident as a troubling form of sexualized bullying and it is clear to the reader that Yates concurs with this view. However, in the all-male surrounds of a boys' boarding school in wartime America, it passes for what one teacher describes as "a dumb little thing that happens in prep schools" (Yates *AGS* 2006, 144). That reassurance is given to the second victim, the same teacher's son. The reader knows that no amount of reassurance in the vein of, "Don't let it make you worry about yourself, will you promise me that? Do you understand me, son?" (144) will prevent young Bobby Driscoll from internalizing the trauma of the event. Yates knows that and wants the reader to feel it.

The story of "Doctor Jack-o'-Lantern" describes the difficulties for a boy at a new school. His classmates act as one in judging him and laughing at him because he has an odd appearance, speaks in a strange way, and makes elementary mistakes. These facts alone suggest that the story might become very sentimental. Yates never allows that to happen, carefully balancing reader response between being attuned to his dislikable character and being aware of his predicament. The moral compass remains with Vincent Sabella by the end of the story due to the inadequacy of the class teacher, Miss Price. Her failing is to idealize the children's situation, especially that of Sabella. The children's attention is on his appearance ("the roots of his teeth were green") and on the peculiarities of his "unintelligible croak" (Yates *ELK* 2006, 3) of a voice, whereas her focus is on his social background; Yates ensures the reader has both perspectives. Miss Price wants to mold and shape the class's reactions to this boy in order to prove something to herself about her own benevolence and power to influence. What she can't understand is that children run from such inauthenticity. They respect Sabella only when they believe he has joined them in league against Miss Price, and has been beaten by her. Ultimately they turn on Sabella and taunt him when they discover he's lied about the beating: "Jeez, you lie about *everything*, don'tcha, Sabella? You lie about *everything*!" (18).

Children insist, where they can, on accuracy because the truth is one thing they yearn for, feel they can rely on, and often sense. Unable to abide the inauthenticity of her sister's posturing, Emily Grimes, "a stickler for accuracy," insists on describing their father's job with precision: "He's only a copy-desk man" (Yates *EP* 2004, 7). Similarly, Phil Drake cannot listen to his sister's affectations without becoming exasperated and correcting her: "Rachel, will you cut this out? Touch football is about the worst example you could've thought of. I *played* at playing it" (Yates *CSH* 2005, 109). Even if the truth undermines them, these children who are bright and perceptive, will not allow posturing, affectation, or dishonesty to pass uncorrected. Parents seem unprepared for this veracity. Tommy Wilder questions his father, newly returned from Bellevue, and shocks his parents out of their complacent manipulation of him with lies: "Well then, how come your suitcase's been in Mom's closet ever since a week ago last Saturday?" (Yates 2007, 70). It is not just the observation that the suitcase has been there (and not with Wilder on a trip to Chicago) but the specificity of the timing that arrests Wilder and the reader. Often seen moving from one home to another, with all the difficulties for friendship that that suggests, and exposed to the complexity of the adult relationships their parents engage in, children, Yates suggests, look for stability in words. However, Yates makes a further point about how adults fail to communicate with their children when he draws attention to the fact that often they do not have the words with which to work; in all his fiction, children are told very little. Often ignored, or left to glean what is happening from snippets of overheard conversations or arguments, children have to make sense of the world with few facts at their disposal.

Children in Yates's fiction accept love from their family in whatever form as is clear at the ending of "Oh, Joseph, I'm So Tired": "But our mother was ours; we were hers" (Yates 1981, 33). This is happiness in a minor key. However, where possible, children also want their parents to reunite. The older narrator in this story is unequivocal that Edith's main preoccupation—with little understanding of the complexity of relationships—is working out how to get their parents back together. One day, he recalls, Edith tells their father that their mother is going to sculpt President Roosevelt's head. The now adult male narrator observes, "Edith often told one of our parents about the other's more virtuous activities; it was part of her long, hopeless effort to bring them back together" (6). The children in this story are desperate for time to heal a rift the reader knows cannot be healed; they want their version of normal back. Similarly, in *The Easter Parade*, Emily has a brief hope that her father was not leaving for good but had "gone back to the city to get his belongings, but that hope evaporated in the days and weeks that followed" (Yates *EP* 2004, 13). There is no information from her mother or father to clarify the situation and, crucially, Yates writes, Emily "could never find the words to ask her mother about it" (13). Emily is ten.

It is axiomatic that for marriages to be successful there needs to be a profound degree of communication between partners which is never there in a Yates story. Furthermore, there needs to be within each partner a degree of self-awareness and self-knowledge not usually seen, with the exception, perhaps, of Shep Campbell at the end of *Revolutionary Road*. Such self-knowledge provides a platform of strength within a person from which they can give to the 'other' in a disinterested way. If, as in Yates, adults predominantly lack such knowledge of self and are dependent females or selfish males, they are usually immature and always self-interested so that the marriage is likely to fail. The addition of children to this mix of clashing egos adds shockingly little to the strength of the relationship between the parents because their needs are overlooked or constructed to further the ideas of one parent over the other.

At first glance, the reader of Yates's fiction might adjudge that he was not remotely interested in the plight of children so barely visible are they in his novels but this is not the case at all. He is so sensitive to the reduction of their lives, by neglect, by divorce, by self-interested parents, by the alcohol these parents often depend on or by the dreams for a better life that blinds them to the responsibilities before them, that their very absence—or reduced presence—is his strongest comment. As I have observed, where he does write about children he does so in ways that add depth to the manner in which the reader receives the stories about adult relationships. That is not to say Yates uses children simply as a vehicle for commentary; he is fascinated by children, applauds their honesty and is unsentimental about their weaknesses. The real poverty that he suggests children experience is that of poor parenting: lack of communication between adults and their children, combined with parents unwilling to prioritize the needs of their children, create loneliness and confusion. Dissatisfaction, therefore, is a dominant feature of his homes where children are lost to their parents' failing dreams. However, Yates suggests that with keen imaginations, children can develop an interior world which will help enrich their otherwise difficult lives.

NOTES

1. I wrote extensively about children's poor education and in particular about their lack of sex education in *Dismembering the American Dream: the Life and Fiction of Richard Yates* (2014) and will not reexamine that topic here.

2. In Yates's work there is one exception to this pattern. In "A Compassionate Leave" (1981) the children are split between their parents.

3. In mid-twentieth century America there was no national group protecting fathers' rights despite the growth of many local organizations as the divorce rate increased through the '60s and '70s. To this day, there is still no national organization (unlike Fathers-4-Justice in the UK) but only a loose affiliation of connected groups.

BIBLIOGRAPHY

Bailey, Blake. (2003) 2004. *A Tragic Honesty: The Life and Work of Richard Yates.* London: Methuen.

Charlton-Jones, Kate. 2014. *Dismembering the American Dream: The Life and Fiction of Richard Yates.* Tuscaloosa: University of Alabama Press.

Cherlin, Andrew J. 1981. *Marriage, Divorce, Remarriage.* Cambridge, MA: Harvard University Press.

Church, Louisa Randall. November 1946. "Parents: Architects of Peace," *American Home,* pp. 18–19, quoted in May, Elaine Tyler 1988.

Furstenberg Frank F., Jr., and Andrew J. Cherlin. 1991. *Divided Families: What Happens to Children When Parents Part.* Cambridge, MA: Harvard University Press.

Holt, Marilyn Irvin. 2014. *Cold War Kids: Politics and Childhood in Postwar America, 1945–1960.* Lawrence: University Press of Kansas.

Landis, Judson T., and Mary G. Landis. 1968 *Building a Successful Marriage.* Englewood Cliffs, NJ: Prentice-Hall.

May, Elaine Tyler. 1988. *Homeward Bound: American Families in the Cold War Era.* New York: Basic Books.

Yates, Richard. (1986) 2005. *Cold Spring Harbor.* London: Methuen.

_____. (2001) 2004. *The Collected Stories of Richard Yates.* London: Methuen.

_____. (1975) 2007. *Disturbing the Peace.* London: Methuen.

_____. (1976) 2004. *The Easter Parade.* London: Methuen.

_____. (1962) 2006. *Eleven Kinds of Loneliness.* London: Methuen.

_____. (1978) 2006. *A Good School.* London: Methuen.

_____. 1981. *Liars in Love.* New York: Delacorte Press/Seymour Lawrence.

_____. (1961) 2001. *Revolutionary Road.* London: Methuen.

_____. 1969. *A Special Providence.* New York: Picador,.

_____. (1984) 1986. *Young Hearts Crying.* London: Methuen.

Performing Masculinity, Masculinity as Performance

Faking It as Men in the
Short Fiction of Richard Yates

KARL WOOD

"Talent," Robert Blaine said, in his slow, invalid's voice, "is simply a matter of knowing how to handle yourself" (Yates 2001, 417). This early inkling of the importance of performance in the work of Richard Yates opens his 1952 story "Thieves." The entire story revolves around the premise that talent is not the product of knowledge, but rather of knowing how to carry oneself, an ability to project confidence; both are important facets of a particular kind of masculine performance in which it might seem that the sense of manhood resides. Indeed, much of Richard Yates's work can be characterized broadly as being about performances, "examining the self-conscious way in which roles are adopted to create a particular effect" (Charlton-Jones 2014, 9–10). His characters act out roles guided by their own dreams and fantasies, to be sure, but also equally or more by illusions, self-deceptions and, to no small extent, socially conditioned expectations. These often relate to gender roles, and in particular, the frames of mid-twentieth century masculinity. While quite apparent in his novels, this aspect of the performative nature of Yates's characters is developed across a range of male characters in his short stories. Whether as men seeking to find (or lose) themselves in a group identity, fathers, husbands or lovers, the men of Yates's short stories reveal the internally unstable construct of their masculinity. They shift between performances with varying degrees of self-consciousness, sometimes quite aware of striking different masculine poses and guises, but more often than not painfully unaware of the (self-) deceptive roles they may play.

In "Thieves," Yates casts light on the complexity of masculine performance of different roles, the conflicting values of masculinity in the 1950s, and a common man who fails at each of them. Three ill and, to varying degrees, broken men argue about the meaning of talent, and enter into a contest swapping stories about their past exploits. Blaine, the "abrasive sage" of the tuberculosis ward (Bailey 2003, 127), illustrates his point with a story of being treated in a posh Manhattan haberdashery like a man of means who could be trusted to settle his bill later by check simply by carrying himself as one. Admiring, and ultimately removing the tags from, an exquisitely expensive coat, all while making confident and charming chatter with the store clerk, he nonchalantly heads for the door, only to be asked before he leaves to provide an address to send the bill; he then departs, of course, wearing the coat. As the younger men understand the point as one about having the courage to shoplift, swapping tales of small-time theft with juvenile enthusiasm, Blaine derides their simplicity and raises the ante. Seeking to prove himself their better, he tells a larger tale of his time in New York, when simply through knowing how to handle himself, he "stole damn near everything" (Yates 2001, 425)—a wealthy man's money, and, most importantly, Irene, his beautiful wife.

The men of "Thieves" are transparently trying to outdo each other in a game of masculine posturing. As such, we cannot know how much of the men's stories are truth, half-truth, or outright fabrications, although Yates does lead us to believe that there is some element of truth to Blaine's tale. The complexity comes out only at the very end of the story when Blaine, perhaps inadvertently, reveals the kernel of his tale, which is not one of bravura, but of loss. He did, in fact, live extravagantly with Irene, who "thought I had everything. Thought I was a genius. [...] Probably still does" (425). It seems to have been a brief romance, however, because after six months the money was gone and it appears the relationship ended. What also becomes clear is that Blaine had lost his own wife and child as well, apparently to run off with Irene. Completing his story, Blaine breaks down emotionally and physically, quivering, unable to speak and hardly breathing.

Blaine is trying, at least in his storytelling, if not necessarily in his life, to demonstrate his handling of himself in competing and conflicting male roles. He acts the part of the "dutiful husband and father" (425), but also at the same time, the player. While this could all be a tall tale told as simple posturing to prove his manliness to the others, Blaine's breakdown suggests the deep pain of loss. While he wished to believe himself to have been a dedicated family man, his adulterous adventures tell otherwise. Yet he failed as a confident ladies' man as well. "Knowing how to handle yourself" may have gotten Blaine a coat and the girl, for a time, but it ultimately leaves him alone and frail in a VA hospital.

The dual nature of Blaine's failures is characteristic of representations of men in this period during which Yates honed his skills writing short stories. Many of Yates's twenty-seven published short stories were written in the 1950s or early 1960s, published previously (with or without revisions) in magazines, and collected in *Eleven Kinds of Loneliness* in 1962. His second collection, *Liars in Love*, contains stories written in subsequent years and collected in 1981, most of which are also often set in the 1950s and early 1960s. Clearly, this was both a fertile and important time for Yates the author. Significantly, it was also a period that produced the beginnings of substantial upheaval and change in American society, including in interpretations and portrayals of masculinity.

The popular understanding of 1950s masculinity in the United States is generally one of the stifling conformity of the suburban drone in the grey flannel suit, at once the oppressor of others and oppressed by his own world. There is no denying that there is some truth to this image; in particular, white middle-class America was undergoing the upheavals of suburbanization and its concomitant shifts in cultural and social practices. Often considered the apogee of male privilege and monolithic hegemonic masculinity, the postwar era saw popular culture images of John Wayne style manliness and the masculinity of Westerns as compensations for the lives of men trapped in dull office jobs and ticky-tacky suburban developments. The reality of the period, however, was much more complex.

As Bryce Traister writes, "[t]he history of American men as men now not only proceeds as a historiography of masculine crisis but collectively writes itself as an actual history of American masculinity *as* crisis" (2000, 287). This notion of the inherent instability and perpetual crisis of masculinity is a rather contentious one, particularly in discussions of the purported "masculinity crisis" of the 1950s and 1960s (Blayac et al. 2011, 5–11). It is beyond the scope of this chapter to discuss in detail, but Traister's remark is apt in that it identifies the notion of crisis as a historiographical one. Rather than necessarily an experience lived and shared by countless (white, heterosexual) men of the 1950s and 1960s, this narrative of crisis itself is perhaps a product of an involved public discourse. As Jennifer Daly (2016) argues, it is a myth rooted more deeply in the contours of American culture than in the reality of the period, convenient and instrumental for the maintenance of the centrality of the white middle-class heterosexual male narrative, and one "eminently ripe for disruption" (220).

There was, no doubt, a considerable public sense of anxiety about masculinity in public discourse in the 1950s, beginning in particular with the publication of David Riesman's *The Lonely Crowd* in 1950. This was magnified and turned into crisis proportions in subsequent publications such as Sloan Wilson's *The Man in the Grey Flannel Suit* (1955), William H. Whyte's *The Organization Man* (1956), and Arthur Schlesinger's "The Crisis of American

Masculinity" (1958) to name just a few of the most salient examples. This led many to believe that "men are more and more conscious of maleness not as fact but as a problem" (quoted in Cuordilecne 2012, 15). The core fear was a "crisis [that] had its distant origins in late nineteenth century fears of the feminization of American society" (Cuordileone 2012, x), a past ideal promoted by the likes of Theodore Roosevelt and more broadly encompassing an entire generation of idealized "Sons of Leatherstocking" (Smith 1950, 49), and including a preoccupation with, and deep-set fear of, homosexuality. Men, in this narrative, were losing their marhood to the "Organization Man" mentality of office work focusing on teamwork and relationships rather than individualism and creativity. This was further complicated by the growing numbers of women in the workplace, and the impact of suburbanization with the attendant concept of "Momism," which referred to the purported nefarious female influence of the all-controlling domestic realm with far-reaching consequences, producing the loudly decried crisis of masculinity.

This discourse was predominant in the 1950s, and became even more so in shaping subsequent collective memory about the period, meant here as the dominant manner, accurate or not, in which a society recalls historical events or periods. These "places of memory," as Hutton calls them, are assigned various meanings, depending "on the traditions to which they appeal, for each will present the past in a different way" (1993, 160). In this case, the prevailing collective memory of the 1950s period has come to be dominated by Organization Men in grey flannel suits, in crisis about their threatened sense of real-man masculinity as they commuted to and from their suburban homes where their wives lived desperately limited and restricted lives.

James Gilbert, in his magisterial archival study of public discourses surrounding mainstream masculinity in the 1950s *Men in the Middle*, observes that "[t]his was never entirely John Wayne's world any more than it ever belonged to Liberace" (2005, 8). Rather than a single hegemonic white heterosexual middle-class masculinity in crisis facing a threat from, as proponents of the narrative would claim, consumerism and "the controlling influence of modern woman" (89), Gilbert finds instead in American culture "other strong voices that rejected the notion of crisis, even as they grappled with the immense changes of the decade" (30). These voices embodied and embraced facets of a changing masculinity, including those of fathers and companionate husbands who enjoyed the suburban life, domesticity, and emotional closeness that doomsayers so resoundingly condemned as the worst elements of the presumed crisis. The decade that produced suburban Organization Men in grey flannel suits was also simultaneously inhabited by Alfred Kinsey, the Rev. Billy Graham, Ozzie Nelson, and the high-culture and soft porn blending of *Playboy*.

As Richard Russo writes in his introduction to *The Collected Stories of Richard Yates*, "Yates has been called the voice of his generation" while simultaneously transcending it and challenging American culture of his day and beyond (2001, xviii–xix). In his short stories, we can see how the characters exhibit a range of different masculine performances, trying to fill differing roles that they are never entirely sure of. Many of these supposed ideals came from the movies or from television. Gilbert argues that the "heroic, self-confident masculinity [could] only exist as a figment of the imagination [...] only the movies got it right" (2005, 31), while devoting a chapter to the popular comedy of *Ozzie and Harriet*. A humorous representation of the rise of companionate domestic husbands and fathers, Gilbert points out that the joke here is when paternalism tries to reassert itself but always fails, with Ozzie learning a lesson in modern family life, until, at least, the next episode (135–163). Yates was well aware of the insidious seductiveness of such idealized images, and sought to "expose the superficial posturing" (Charlton-Jones 2014, 10) they encouraged in people's behaviors. Yet the dichotomy between an idealized fantasy world and mundane quotidian reality was not necessarily a "crisis" creating men filled with existential angst over their inadequacy, but rather men who somehow muddled through these contradictions nonetheless.

An examination of the men in Yates's short stories shows how they grapple with the confusion that surrounded them in this era of transition. This sense of performance goes beyond the clear-cut case of Walter Henderson, the "they got me" performer of victimhood in "A Glutton for Punishment," who is largely a wash-up by most contemporary measures of a man, but relishes his success at self-consciously theatrical failure. Men in Yates's other stories fail too, but they are often less conscious of their performances, trying to be (or pose as) "good men" while never being fully successful in the effort.

Given the importance of the experience of time spent in the service to men of his generation, it is not at all surprising that military life figures strongly in Yates's stories, both in-service and as veterans. Yates himself had served in the army between 1944 and 1946, earning his combat infantry badge for service on the Western Front in 1945. His time in the military both shaped his life—it was while in the army that he contracted the lung ailment that would later lead to his extended hospitalization—and provided a well of material to draw on for his fiction. For the reader, it also provides a fine opportunity to observe the performances of men for other men, trying to appear manly in the eyes of their peers and, by comparison, to themselves. As Kiesling observes, "performing masculine practices for the social gaze (whether real or imagined)" is a key element of masculinity, a strategy for fulfilling the socially learned construct for dominance (2007, 658). Masculinity, for Yates's men, is an act of "precarious manhood," a status not conferred, but rather earned through performance, and one in need of constant reassertion and re-qualification, often through the approbation of other men (Vandello et al. 2008). In the episodes that appear in Yates's short stories, what is of particular interest is not the military experiences themselves, but rather the way that the men perform their masculinity through them. In some, they seek to emphasize their heroism or toughness as veterans in recalling and retelling their stories, to present themselves as "real" men to others and, self-deceptively, to themselves. In other stories, this individual hero mask falls, and we see men feebly seeking to find their identity within the homosocial group of their comrades. Each of the stories with a military or veteran theme evinces "a deep skepticism towards popular discourses of war, with their gendered catchwords like heroism and camaraderie" (Bull 2010, 140).

Failed military heroes appear several times in Yates's short stories, perhaps owing to some anxiety over his own characterization as a "fuckup," as he would often say when recalling his time in the service (Bailey 2003, 77). This is perhaps most visible in his story "The Canal," which apparently drew directly on Yates's own experience of combat. Rather than a straightforward rendition of an episode in war, however, the story instead takes place in the realm of memory and the dance of a dialogue between two posturing men. The protagonist, Lew Miller, a former rifleman, reluctant to talk about the war, is drawn by his wife Betty into swapping war stories with a fellow veteran at a cocktail party. His interlocutor, a pointedly manly-named Tom Brace, turns out to have been involved in the same combat action as a lieutenant in a nearby outfit. This is potentially a source of embarrassment for Miller, who knows he was no hero, and so he resorts to evasiveness. As Brace eagerly presses Miller for details, seeking opportunities to boast of his own exploits with just enough false modesty, Yates skillfully renders the interplay between Miller's laconic answers and his memories. These return to him despite his own wish to forget them, and he certainly does not wish to share them with Brace. Concealing that he was confused, frightened, and separated from his unit while struggling to carry a reel of communications wire, he reveals to Brace just enough to have him appreciate that he, too, had experienced a rough time—"artillery fire [...] plenty of that. Eighty eights" (Yates 2001, 369), ending with complete exhaustion and sleep when the ordeal was over. It is Brace, however, who dominates the discussion in his initial pointed interrogation of Miller, but his primary concern is in serving his own interest. In this he is aided by Betty, who had been trying to draw out her own husband's exploits. When Brace's wife Nancy returns from getting more martinis, and having missed much of the conversation, Betty fills her in summarizing her husband's war story as, "It seems my husband went to sleep for twenty-four straight hours (376)." She then turns the spotlight pointedly to Brace: "But what happened to you at that canal, Tom?" (376). Seizing the opportunity,

Brace then tells with cinematic clarity the tale of his own heroism in single-handedly taking out a German machine-gun nest, advancing his unit's position and no doubt, saving many of his comrades lives. The conversation then comes to a point, and to an end:

> "Wasn't that the time they gave you the Silver Star, darling?" Nancy Brace asked.
> Brace laughed, winking at Miller. "Isn't that just like a woman?" he said. "That's the only part of the story she cares about."
> "My God," Betty said, "it sounds to me as though you should have gotten several Silver Stars" [377].

The party then breaks up, and Betty begins to complain of how annoying "those damn conceited Brace people" were and wondering how her husband can let them "eclipse you so in a conversation?" (379). The final line of the story has Miller snapping at his surprised and hurt wife: "Betty [...] [w]ill you please do me a favor? [...] Will you shut up? Will you please for God's sake shut up?" (379).

At one level, one could read this story led by the final lines, which would seem to imply that Betty was instrumental in her husband's humiliation. She knew there was not much to tell of his war record, and yet she did press him to enter the conversation, perhaps hoping for something more. In the end, she does not seem to be aware of her role—she expresses her impatience and aggravation, not her apparent (whether sincere or insincere) admiration for Brace. Yet it would be too easy to simply blame Betty, and this would miss the greater part of the story. It is, in fact, Brace who is guiding the conversation throughout, setting up the situation in which he can then brag about his exploits, seeking the position of alpha male when the esteem of women in a social setting was at stake. Of course, the reader knows from Yates's narration what Miller is withholding, and while he is posing and trying to position himself in such a way as to retain his masculine honor, he does not sacrifice at least one key bit of his dignity: he does not lie or exaggerate to make himself look better. While reticent, he remains sincere. With Brace, on the other hand, we have no idea how much of the story of his exploits is true, how much is embellished, and how much sheer fabrication. What is clear is how he relishes the starring role of an apparent hero, the reward of his successful verbal swagger, calculatedly played with Miller shunted into the supporting role of the honest but bumbling counterpoint of a lesser manliness.

In Yates's stories, the experience of military service during the war can serve as a source of consolation or anxiety—and is deployed, in particular, as a pose when in the company of women—depending on how successfully the role is played in the effort to reassert one's manliness. John Fallon, the protagonist of "The B.A.R. Man," lives a confined existence as a gas-blue suit wearing New York office clerk in an unhappy marriage to a woman who earns more than he. Lacking in either external or internal sources of esteem or status as a family man or as a provider, he seeks solace in boasting of his service as a B.A.R. man in an infantry squad, a tough and heavy weapon requiring the kind of solid man that Yates in his own life clearly admired; apparently, when drunk, he would sometimes falsely claim to have been a B.A.R. man himself (Bailey 2003, 82). Fallon, however, is anything but solid and his experience of combat was negligible—less, even, than Miller's. Caught out in his (self-?) deception when he is challenged by a "mere" Navy veteran about just how much action he saw, Fallon grows bellicose, and spends the night alone on the town after a verbally abusive fight with his wife. He careens about town, finding the company of two soldiers in uniform, young peacetime privates whom he can impress with the mention of his having been a B.A.R. man in the war. The night turns into one of escalating violence as he fails to seduce a lovely woman in a club, tracing a vivid mind's eye view of Fallon's fantasy turning from seduction into rape. He finally wanders alone through the city, fuming, the night ending with a police officer's billy club heading toward his head as he assaults a man, a left-wing intellectual. As Fallon watches the terror on his victim's face, he finds a cathartic "sense of absolute fulfillment and relief" (Yates 2001, 106). Whether this arises from the assault, or having a policeman crack his skull, remains ambiguous; it is, perhaps, both.

In the case of Fallon, the lack of fulfillment as either a family man, a professional man, or as a soldier-hero results in a dangerous combination of frustration and rage that would seem to validate the "crisis of masculinity" thesis—a man in crisis he certainly is. He failed in every attempt to assert his manliness by any of the prevailing standards of the day and the result is a brutally violent one. Yet Fallon is an isolated, albeit a starkly vivid character in Yates's stories. Other men have different relations to their military past in their current lives. For example, in "Regards at Home" Bill Grove, in a moment of insecurity in his male rivalry with his friend Dan, seeks to bolster the sense of his own manliness with a silent glare, thinking "Hadn't I been a rifleman in the Army? [...] how else did he think I had won this stunning girl from whom he seemed almost wholly unable to take his eyes?" (310). Here, Grove seeks reassurance by asserting his manliness through his infantry background, and, implicitly linked to that, his ability to get the girl.

Where the military experience in the masculine performances of Bill Grove, Lew Miller, Tom Brace and John Fallon serve (or fail) to underscore their position as men in relation to, and in rivalry for, women, other Army-related stories show men adopting roles and poses when within the company of other men. Some are set in the Army itself—for example "Jody Rolled the Bones" and "A Compassionate Leave"—while others portray groups of veterans in the military-like setting of a Veterans' Administration hospital tuberculosis ward, a surrogate for the barracks, with the adoption of different roles and poses being most visible in "Out with the Old." Seeking, perhaps, to dispel the movie-style myths of army life, but most likely at the same time trying to represent honestly what he observed in these settings, Yates creates an image not of individual heroes in the making, nor of a chummy ésprit de corps, but rather one of men playing their part in an often sophomoric group dynamic.

In the opening of "A Compassionate Leave," for example, we see a group of grumbling, unhappy soldiers of the "luckless 57th" wishing to be sent to Germany as part of the Army of Occupation, where there were supposedly "an extraordinary number of unattached girls" (273). Instead, they are sent into a sort of limbo, working in a demobilization camp in France, and yet not being sent home themselves (mirroring Yates's own duty). Wondering "if this was their punishment for having been indifferent soldiers" (273), morale is understandably low. Phelps, an older man and coal miner in civilian life recently promoted to buck sergeant, chides his men for their puerile longings, saying that they would only gorge themselves on liquor, "getting laid and getting the clap[....] Right? [...] Well, if you ask me, this here is a whole lot better. We got fresh air, we got shelter, we got food, we got discipline. This is a *man's* life" (274). Needless to say, Phelps's articulation of an orthodox vision of a rugged masculinity, an evocation of the frontiersman legacy that Schlesinger lamented was in decline, is met with outright derision from the men: "Jee-sus *Christ*, Phelps, 'a man's life.' [...] Phelps, you're an asshole. You've always *been* an asshole" (275).

We can inquire into Phelps's motivation in his short remarks. It could be that he was simply foolish enough to express honestly his feelings that outdoor army camp life was preferable and better for a man—an adult life— than the adolescent boy fantasy of drinking oneself silly and engaging in promiscuous sex. Yet his speech is also a conscious pose—as Yates tells us, "He folded one arm under his head to suggest a world of peace, using the other to gesture lazily with the cigar" (274)—the image of a man perhaps seeking to bolster his position as a benevolent new sergeant sharing his wisdom with his young comrades. Phelps's pose, however, is disastrous. The performance fails and, to his enormous regret, he becomes the laughingstock of the platoon. An assertion of the outdoorsy, rugged vision of manhood does nothing to bolster Phelps's position with the other men, and instead makes him the source of ridicule, not a role model.

Later in the story, we see the model of rugged masculinity further undermined. When the protagonist Colby is on leave in Paris, he has the chance to fulfill all the wishes that the men stuck back at camp cannot. The young, virginal Colby has emotional issues that prevent him from engaging sexually, but goaded on by the burden of expectations, that does not stop him from feeling the need to try. Lacking any idea whatsoever how to go about this, he insecurely seeks role models he can follow. On leaving the base, he first watches to see how many condoms his buddy, Mueller, would take from a dispenser before taking the same number himself—an optimistic six for a three-day pass. Once in Paris, he looks to a paragon of rugged masculinity for advice. Remembering how Hemingway had shown in *The Sun Also Rises* that "the Left Bank was where everything nice was most likely to happen" (283), Colby wants to head there. Mueller, better informed about the current situation, had listened to what guys at the camp had said and preferred the Place Pigalle as more promising.

After seeing the utter lack of prospects on the Left Bank, they head to the decidedly seedy Place Pigalle where, with Colby's eyes on him seeking hints for success, Mueller heads off with a woman he meets in a café. Colby, after rejecting in his mind the idea of hiring a prostitute, seeks and fails to pick up a woman—any woman—for a tryst. He ends up spending the evening in the company of other soldiers in an American-style bar, drinking bourbon and singing "Roll Me Over"—a popular ribald wartime song of ten verses, clearly about libidinous sex. This, once he comes to understand the irony, along with spending the night in the company of other soldiers at the Red Cross club, was the worst thing that could happen to a man on leave in Paris. The comments of the men back at camp are not difficult to imagine. This role, however, is one Colby knows how to perform: being with other soldiers, singing, drinking, and dreaming about sex.

In "Jody Rolled the Bones," we see another group of immature young men, recruits at basic training camp in 1944. They are a motley platoon of skeptical New Yorkers, and have an attitude toward the entire business of soldiering much like the men of Colby's 57th. Their nemesis is, of course, their drill sergeant, the crisp Tennessean Reece, a man whose entire demeanor exudes Regular Army (as opposed to the reluctant conscripts he commands). He would easily be at least as despised as Phelps, were it not for his authenticity in his role. Reece seems to be a man who genuinely loves Army life, and could almost be cut from the same cloth as a Hollywood drill sergeant, but for his utter lack of any endearing qualities or personal connection with his men. A turning point comes, however, when their unofficial leader and spokesman, D'Alessandro, articulates an appreciation of "soldiering" (39) (Reece's favorite word) that they have all begun to feel. The men begin to perform the role of soldiers with enthusiasm, turning gradually into a group of well-disciplined young men. Yates, however, is not content to leave us with this idyllic view of the soldierly life. Reece falls foul of a jealous and weak lieutenant, and is transferred to a different section and away from what he does best: leading by example and inspiring young men. In the final days before his transfer, Reece destroys the respect he had earned from his men with pointless bullying, no doubt the product of his frustration, and leaves the men with the almost tender admonition to not let anyone push them around. He is replaced by "a Good Joe" (44) who plays a role more typical of a buddy in an army of conscripts, obsequiously and duplicitously licking the ineffectual lieutenant's boots with a wink to his men. Consequently, D'Alessandro and the others quickly fall back into the role of unenthusiastic draftees they were at the beginning of the story.

What is interesting here is how Yates undermines the idea of soldierly camaraderie as forged among disciplined men with a shared purpose and experience. His soldiers are unruly and immature, primarily concerned with seeking carnal pleasures. More pointed is how the ideal of rugged, soldierly masculinity is ridiculed. While Reece is held up as an icon of this kind of masculinity, he appears to lack any existence outside of his crisp uniform in his role as drill sergeant through which he reasserted his rugged manliness daily. When leading his men, he could inspire them by his example. Removed from his direct role leading recruits—in essence, punished for doing his job well—his influence dissipates almost immediately as another leader sets a lax tone that makes him immediately popular, but not respected. Here are not the bold men of Schlesinger's dreams with their "sense of individual spontaneity" (1958, 301), but rather the prototype of conformist followers, not clad in grey flannel but in olive drab, men happy just to go along and get along.

Getting along is what the men of the tuberculosis ward of "Out With the Old" do. They are long-term patients who see themselves as men doing time, hoping for escape someday. Yet their life, as Yates describes it, still bears some resemblance to army life. Again, similar to the "unlucky 57th," the men of the TB ward are misfits of the hospital, not considered to be real veterans like those maimed in the war, whom they resent as "those paraplegic bastards think they own the goddamn place" (Yates 2001, 125). In order to cope with the boredom as well as the grim reality that some of their number would die either of slow decline or of a surprise sudden hemorrhage, the men resort to antics such as smuggling in prohibited whiskey and beer, and generally being obnoxious. In the episode related in the story, a plan for silly theatrics to celebrate New Year's Eve is hatched by the baby-like Tiny Kovacs, the clown of the ward. In the hospital, he plays the immature entertainer, even going to the end of literally embodying his infantilization as a patient, dressing his broad, six-foot-six frame up as a diaper-wearing baby for New Year's Eve. What is embodied as theater for the celebration is in fact an act which Tiny plays the whole time for the men on the ward, and significantly, for himself. Although Tiny's humor has long since worn thin for most of the men, they generally tolerate him. The one man most unwilling to go along with Tiny is McIntyre. A character with certain similarities to Blaine of "Thieves," Mac is the older man who keeps his distance from what he sees as the shenanigans of the ward, using a mask of sarcasm to hint at his being above it all. At the center of the story are the roles that both Mac and Tiny perform on the ward in order to come to terms with situations neither of them wishes, and the transformations in these roles when they return, told in flashback in the story, to their apparent real selves and lives over a rare holiday furlough.

The transformation in Tiny is striking. All of the men undergo some form of transformation as they prepare to leave for the holiday, changing their faded yellow pajama-uniforms for their civvies—sudden visible reminders of their individuality that they have when on the outside. To emphasize the homogeneity of the group of patients when in the hospital, Yates observes how the African American patients lose their membership as part of the gang as "several of the Negroes became Negroes again, instead of ordinary men [...] and they even seemed embarrassed to be talking to the white men on the old familiar terms" (129). Yates portrays the change in Tiny, however, as even greater still. Surprising the men of the ward, Tiny becomes a man in fine clothing with striking dignity, gravitas and confidence, such that the men of the ward were astounded at this figure of a man to be reckoned with. Yet the surprise lies not so much in his stature and transformation from clown into a man of confidence, a man who knows how to handle himself, as in what kind of man he is when at home There, in the circle of his family, "it was real [...] he was Harold, a gentle son, a quiet hero to many round-eyed children" (129). Not a distant, idolized lion of a man valiantly fighting disease, but rather a man admired for his tender religious sensibility and humility. In an unusually sentimental scene, we hear how Harold's niece in her prayers "tells Jesus please to bless Uncle Harold and make him get well again soon" (129). He corrects her, offering praise but also suggesting that "you shunt *tell* Him. You should *ask* Him" before embracing her, hiding from her the gentle tears filling his eyes (129–130). In the safety of a loving home, Tiny can play the role of an entirely different man altogether: a kind and religious Uncle Harold, who should be an inspiration for the children, emotional and yet still concealing his genuine tears just as a man, even a gentle man, was expected to.

McIntyre's transformation, however, heads in the opposite direction. On leaving the hospital, Mac becomes a man diminished: unable to play his onward role as the sarcastic wit, but returning to being a "surprisingly humble" (128) accountant. More significant, though, is what he sees as the change in his home. It is soon apparent that something is amiss in his family, some awkward secret regarding his daughter that he is being sheltered from in an attempt to maintain the façade of a happy holiday family reunion. He attempts to elicit from his eighteen-year-old daughter, Jean, what the problem is, uncertainly seeking to sound like the caring and trusted father he believes himself to once have been. Drama ensues, and his wife, tired of the charade, blurts out to him: "All right, you asked for it. We all done our best to give you a nice Christmas, but if you're gonna come home and snoop around and drive everybody crazy with your questions, all right—it's your funeral. She's four months pregnant—there, now are you satisfied? Now willya please quit bothering everyone?" (133).

Not that McIntyre is satisfied. Still clinging to his caring father role, he continues to press to know who the father is, and when his son insinuates that she might not even know, he snaps, striking him repeatedly out of his own desperate helplessness more than to defend his daughter's honor, destroying any remaining illusion of family harmony and returning to the hospital within hours.

Yet McIntyre's attempts to play the part of a kind and caring father have not yet come to a close. He spends the next week trying in vain to draft a letter, reaching out to his daughter and trying to create, or in his mind reconstruct, a relationship of trust with his daughter. Experimenting with attempts at intimacy and showing understanding, on page three of his letter he falls into the role of the wise adviser:

> (p.3)
>   with you now. Your old dad may not be good for much any more but he does know
> a thing or two about life and especially one important thing, and that is
>   That was as far as the letter went [134].

This exact phrasing appears in each of McIntyre's repeated attempts, but they all end in helpless failure at that very point, when "the pen lay dead in his cramped fingers. It was if all the letters of the alphabet, all the combination of letters into words, all the infinite possibilities of handwritten language had ceased to exist" (136). Finally, looking into the darkness outside his window and being enveloped instead by the reflection of the ward, he surrenders, embracing his role of the decrepit old man of the outgoing year with a long beard in Tiny's play. The story ends, after a successful performance, including of course the entire ward singing "Auld Lang Syne" together, with "Tiny's laughter roaring in his ear and Tiny's heavy arm around his neck" (140).

In "Out with the Old," we see two men playing the roles of very different men depending on where they find themselves, but with very different outcomes. Tiny, in a sense, is the more adaptable. He seems able to perform both of his roles comfortably, taking only a short while on returning to the hospital to adapt and to put on his clown mask again, only occasionally wearing a magnificent bathrobe to remind himself of his dignity, reclaiming for a moment a reminder of the beloved and sensitive Harold he is when in the embrace of his family. The role of Tiny is Harold's way of living with the helplessness of being confined to the hospital.

Mac, however, has much greater difficulty in reconciling his two roles.

On the ward, he clings to sarcasm to maintain his distance as long as he continues to believe in his role as father and husband, his home self. But unlike Tiny, who seems to be grounded by his home that he longs for, McIntyre's longing may well be for an illusion, and this leads him into trouble. It is for a past that he believes he remembers, a time when he could be a kind and sensitive loving father and, presumably, a devoted husband. Just as in the case of Brace's manly tales of heroism in "The Canal," we cannot be sure just how reliable this story Mac tells himself is. Whether it was the passage of time and his children growing into troubled teens without him that rendered him unable to perform this role, or simply that he never really could, is not clear. His recall of a happy past is unreliable, based more on the collective memory of the role of a father figure that he came to believe he had been, or needed to believe. That all his efforts fail and his "snooping around" is not welcome does make one question if he ever really was that father. Mac's longing is not for his home as it is, but for his role there being what he would wish it to be, a dream he is helpless to bring about.

McIntyre is not the only failure in the domestic sphere in Yates's stories. One will in fact search in vain for an unmitigated success. Take, for example, the hopelessly immature Ralph in "The Best of Everything" who, on the night before his wedding, prefers a bachelor party with the fellas over his bride-to-be's attempt to seduce him; or the insincere Warren having an extended and dishonest affair, cheating on his wife before returning to her after receiving a letter in which she takes the blame for all their problems in "Liars in Love"; or the violent and abusive Fallon of "The B.A.R. Man." There is no shortage of men in Yates's fictional world for whom a harmonious domestic life is a challenge, to say the least. Yet the theme is recurring and important, and in some of Yates's stories there is a glimmer of hope for some fulfillment, in men who can adapt to the changing roles of the mid–twentieth century.

To find one such example, we need to return to Bill Grove in "Regards at Home." As the story comes to its close, we see that the ultimate reassurance in the story comes not from his war record or his strong manliness, but from his friend. As Bill and his wife and daughter prepare to sail for France (an echo of Yates's own life and, of course, the unfulfilled plan in *Revolutionary Road*) Dan says to Bill in parting:

> "So okay," he said as we shook hands. "Keep in touch. Only, listen: do me a favor.... Don't piss it all away."
>
> I didn't know what he meant, even he'd winked to show me he was mostly kidding, until it occurred to me that I had everything he must ever have wanted—everything he'd resigned himself, since his father's death, never to wish for again. I had luck, time, opportunity, a young girl for a wife, and a child of my own [319].

Grove's luck to escape to France and a life pursuing his writing dreams are classic Yates themes, but this does not seem in this scene to be the key to his sense of masculine fulfillment. Although in moments of insecurity he seeks solace in his soldierly past, in the end he finds greater solace in the prospect for a happy domestic life and a comfortable, if not passionate marriage. His friend and rival, Dan, ends the story moving to—of all places—Levittown to live with his widowed mother, undermining with irony the popular conventional path to domestic bliss in the suburbs.

Yet for Yates's characters, just as for many men of his generation, it is not just that the right road does not lead through the suburbs. There is not any particularly clear path, but rather uncharted terrain through which they must try to negotiate their way. Of course, we never learn here if Grove and his wife will succeed as a couple, or if things will fall apart as they did in Yates's own life. The way that this theme appears in "Regards at Home," full of promise and hope while simultaneously subverting the suburban ideal, may be a sign of a more mature story written later in Yates's career. But the themes appear in an earlier work in prototypical form, suggesting that they were not a new concept, either to Yates or to American men, when *Liars in Love* was published.

In "A Convalescent Ego," written in 1952, Yates writes revealingly of the inner feelings of a man trying, in his mind, to live up to the ideal he believes a husband should be. Recalling James Gilbert's observation that when it came to masculine roles "only the movies got it right" (2005, 31), in a series of imagined sequences—a movie of the mind—Yates plays with this idea and finds that "right" will fail when confronted with reality. Frail and recovering from tuberculosis at home after having been recently released from a long hospital stay, Bill seems to be singularly inept domestically, and yet, he tries. He accidentally breaks a teacup his wife had just bought, which on their limited budget had been quite expensive. Here the real story begins as the reader is shown a variety of comic scenarios in his mind's eye of how the scene will unfold when his wife returns. Shrugging it off with nonchalance, he imagines, would end up in a fight in which he would indignantly want to show her "once and for all who *did* wear the pants in this family, bathrobe or no bathrobe" (Yates 2001, 464). A non starter, evidently he rejects the resort to patriarchal power as a poor idea. Seeking another pillar of manliness, he thinks to just pull himself together, to get dressed, go out and replace the cup and throw in roses and champagne for a romantic flourish. But this illusion, too, begins to crack once he realizes she would ask about the cost. The fantasy continues, including going back to work to earn the money, but he realizes that all the celebration of his miraculous recovery by simply pulling himself together would be met with his wife's sober assessment of the reality of the situation. His final desperate attempt involves going to work right away. He even goes so far as to get dressed for work, all the while imagining dialogues of how a man has to work to support and provide for his family, chatting chummily with his colleagues at work over how well he feels now, and that his wife only exaggerates things. This reverie, too, ends when he realizes that it would be yet another recipe for disaster, as she would again get the best of him in confronting him with reality. Finally, seeking man's last solace, dressed and heading out the door in search of a drink, he meets his wife and young son at the door. He tries to storm out, unaware that his suspenders were hanging limp around his thighs, exposing, somewhat symbolically, his frailty. This time the real-time fight ensues, one likely to go on for two or three days (foreshadowing the kind later developed in *Revolutionary Road*), and as they stew in separate rooms, it dawns on him that he could, perhaps, try saying "I'm sorry, darling" (472) now, rather than after some days. It is then, only as he prepares to drop his manly attempts to dominate the situation, that quite miraculously and rather unbelievably, his wife approaches him and apologizes for being beastly, and they melt into a romantic and loving kiss.

This ending, though written as if in real-time, seems here an extension of the fantasy sequence, a happy ending most unlikely to happen in real life (or in Yates's stories, for that matter, although a similar ending appears in a more developed form in "Liars in Love" written many years later). Even though the story is not the best example of Yates's skill (it was an early effort, after all), it is interesting for the way in which the protagonist muddles his way through all the possibilities in his mind, seeking to "fix everything" with solutions. And yet, every stereotypically masculine response in the narrator's mind will end in disaster. One could embrace the conventional "crisis of masculinity" narrative of the 1950s and read this as being the result of an overbearing wife who crushes his masculinity at every turn, but this would be a superficial reading lacking in subtlety. What frustrates the narrator's attempts to play out the role of a "real" man (even in fantasy) is not his wife's overbearing or controlling nature, but rather her clearheaded assessment of the facts: he is ill, and trying to make romantic gestures or return to work by "manning up" are nothing but counterproductive bravado that she will not put up with. It is the supposedly rational man who gives himself over to emotion-filled wishful thinking, who when frustrated, even in his fantasy sequence, gives into childish outbursts like "she always won" and "she exaggerates everything" (468). While the ending is highly improbable and comes across as perhaps the author's own wishful thinking, it does hint at something he had "overlooked completely" (472) in all his deliberations: the possibility for reconciliation through understanding, an emotional meeting in weakness rather than striking a manly pose.

This brief examination of the men in Richard Yates's short stories reveals a range of men exhibiting a range of contingent masculine performances. When in the company of other men, one can certainly discern a jockeying for position much like the three men in "Thieves." But just as Blaine grows frustrated with his interlocutors' facile understanding of "knowing how to handle oneself," the roles and poses Yates's men fall into are much more complex than a simple trying to outdo one another as "the better man." In the most homosocial environments, where the attention of women is not involved, we in fact see the greatest skepticism, even scorn for the role of the rugged, outdoorsy type of latter-day Leatherstockings. Even the performances most strongly based on an assertion of martial heroism are questionable in their reliability, and, in the case of the most disturbed character, John Fallon, nearly entirely false. But, characteristically for Yates, many of the roles that the men in these stories play are based on shaky narratives. Where Miller seems to want to forget much of his war memories as they do little to support a particular model of manhood, McIntyre, like Blaine, seems to want to remember his role as husband and father as much better than it in fact was. Memories cannot be entirely trusted, as they seem to serve more to try and prop up a role, a kind of narrative that the man can live with.

And yet we see little evidence of a "crisis of masculinity" as the dominant discourse of the decade would have had it. Although Schlesinger wrote that men had come to see their masculinity as a problem, we see little evidence of crisis awareness in the men of Yates's short stories, or of measuring themselves up to any one set pattern and falling short, falling into a sense of anxiety or crisis over their failings. Instead we see men muddling through in an era with a range of possibilities of how to "do" masculinity, contingent and shifting based on the social circumstances. It's never quite right, but such is the nature of performance.

Bibliography

Bailey, Blake. 2003. *A Tragic Honesty. The Life and Work of Richard Yates*. New York: Picador.

Blayac, Ariane, Claire Conilleau, Claire Delahayte and Hélène Quanquin. 2011. "Critical Masculinities." *Culture, Society & Masculinities* 3: 3–12. doi: 10.3149/csm.0301.3.

Bull, Leif. 2010. *A Thing Made of Words: The Reflexive Realism of Richard Yates*. Diss., Goldsmiths, University of London. http://research.gold.ac.uk/4760/.

Daly, Jennifer. 2016. *Why Is Your Brand Crisis? Challenging the Representation of Masculinity in the Work of Richard Yates, Richard Ford, and Jonathan Franzen*. Diss., Trinity College, University of Dublin.

Cuordileone, K.A. 2012. *Manhood and American Political Culture in the Cold War*. New York: Routledge.

Charlton-Jones, Kate. 2014. *Dismembering the American Dream: The Life and Fiction of Richard Yates*. Tuscaloosa: University of Alabama Press.

Gilbert, James. 2005. *Men in the Middle. Searching for Masculinity in the 1950s*. Chicago: University of Chicago Press.

Hutton, Patrick H. 1993. *History as an Art of Memory*. Hanover, VT: University Press of New England.

Kiesling, Scott. 2007. "Men, Masculinities and Language." *Language and Linguistics Compass* 1/6, 653–673. doi: 10.1111/j.1749–818X.2007.00035.x.

Russo, Richard. 2001. "Introduction." *The Collected Stories of Richard Yates*. New York: Picador.

Schlesinger Arthur M., Jr. 1958. "The Crisis of American Masculinity." *Esquire* (November 1958, 63–65); reprinted in *The Politics of Hope and The Bitter Heritage. American Liberalism in the 1960s* (Princeton and Oxford: Princeton University Press, 2008) 292–303.

Smith, Henry Nash. 1950. *Virgin Land. The American West as Symbol and Myth.* Cambridge: Harvard University Press. UVA Hypertext edition, ed. Eric J. Gislason, 1996. http://xroads.virginia.edu/~HYPER/HNS/home.htm.

Traister, Bryce. 2000. "Academic Viagra: The Rise of American Masculinity Studies." *American Quarterly* 52: 274–304. doi: 10.1353/aq.2000.0C25.

Vandello, Joseph A., Jennifer K. Bosson, Dov Cohen, Rochelle M. Burnaford, Jonathan R. Weaver. 2008. "Precarious Manhood." *Journal of Personality and Social Psychology*, 95(6): 1325–1339. http://dx.doi.org/10.1037/a0012453.

Yates, Richard. 2001. *The Collected Stories of Richard Yates.* New York: Picador.

Antifeminist
or Antipatriarchal?
Richard Yates's Critique of Hegemonic
Masculinity in Young Hearts Crying

Rubén Cenamor

Since the emergence of Masculinity Studies in the late 1970s and early 1980s, scholars have tried to deconstruct the hegemonic model of masculinity in an attempt to pave the way towards more gender-egalitarian societies. However, as James D. Riemer argues, to achieve this goal it is not sufficient to be critical of the normative model of masculinity (Riemer 1987, 298) since men who may want to change do not know how they can—if at all (Carabí and Armengol 2014). Thus, what is needed is "a recognition and reinforcement of positive alternatives to traditional masculine ideals and behaviors" (Riemer 1987, 298). Following on from this, Carabí and Armengol explored non-hegemonic practices of masculinity—what they call "alternative masculinities"—which can encourage new, more flexible ways of being a man, and these, in turn, may lead to more gender-egalitarian societies (2014, 1). Carabí and Armengol focus their analysis on male literary characters since they believe that literature becomes a particularly interesting field for reimagining and recreating masculinity (6). Accordingly, throughout their book, they examine different male characters who provide alternative models of being a man in different situations, including masculinity beyond capitalism and the role of the provider, non-violent masculinities, and models of caring fatherhood, among many others.

Considering how some scholars have analyzed Richard Yates's relationship with feminism, it might come as shocking news that his works could in any way portray these alternative masculinities. Yates has been accused of being a misogynist (Bailey 2009) and a "patronize[er] [...] in the old style"

(Fraser 2008). Some of this criticism comes from Yates's allegedly "cheap shots at feminism," and the way he mocks the feminist movement in *The Easter Parade* (Pane 2009). However, what has led most scholars to label Yates's work as antifeminist is his male protagonists' patriarchal attitude, and their compulsive need to prove their manliness so that they are regarded by other men as supremely and genuinely manly. This is no surprise considering that most—if not all—of his stories are mainly set in the 1950s (Charlton-Jones 2014). Consequently, their male characters embody the prevailing normative masculinity, becoming "types of their time" (Ford 2000), as Yates "render[s] in brilliant detail" the culture of the 1950s (Giardina 2007). The main victims of this obsession are their wives, who are abused psychologically and even physically by their bigoted, patriarchal, misogynistic partners. To name but a few: Frank Wheeler (*Revolutionary Road*), jaded from the constant need to prove his manliness, mistreats April psychologically and physically; Evan (*Cold Spring Harbor*) and Fallon ("The B.A.R. Man,") insult and humiliate their wives; and John Wilder (*Disturbing the Peace*) threatens to kill his wife and his son. However, these male characters also suffer the consequences of their acts and often end up isolated, depressed, and looked down upon by their fellow men, which is the exact opposite of what they were looking for. As a result, they become, as Frank Wheeler in *Revolutionary Road*, "walking, talking, smiling, lifeless" men (453).

These depressing endings have led some scholars to reconsider whether Yates is truly a misogynist and antifeminist, or whether he is actually attacking the very roots of patriarchy. In this line, recent studies have claimed that Richard Yates can actually "write sympathetically about women" (Daly 2014), that his oeuvre is surprisingly critical of 1950s gender roles (Cenamor 2013), and that it denounces the subdued situation of women in the fifties and sixties (García-Avello 2011; also 2013), advancing, to some extent, Betty Friedan's *The Feminine Mystique* (Cenamor 2015).

My aim in this essay is to engage with this debate and argue that his stigmatization of America's patriarchal society moves Yates beyond the dichotomy of feminist/antifeminist. It places him in a third-space in which he viciously attacks hegemonic masculinity and advocates for alternative models, in a similar way to what feminism does, but without completely engaging with it. To support my claim, I will examine the sociocultural context of the 1950s and how normative masculinity was constructed and imposed on society. I will then explore how Yates criticizes the three main traits of normative manhood—namely the role of the breadwinner (and its embedded competitiveness), male violence, and the sexual conquest—and, conversely, advocates practices of caring fatherhood as a possible model of alternative masculinity which can bring about happiness and a sense of transcendence for men. This type of criticism, as Bannon and Correia argue, can potentially lead to the creation of more gender-egalitarian societies (2006) hence, the reason why re-reading Yates's work in this light can actually help feminism in its fight against patriarchy.

The 1950s, the Red Scare Campaign, Maturity and Traditional Gender Roles

In terms of the economy, after World War II the United States entered a period of unparalleled prosperity. Between 1950 and 1960 the gross national product (GNP) almost doubled, going from $285 billion to $500 billion (Young and Young 2004, 3). Most of it stemmed from the changing demographics of the nation. Indeed, the population grew from 139.9 million in 1945 to 180.6 million in 1960 (7). The 1950s were also the era of the Baby Boom and so it showed in the percentage of population under 14 years old, which grew from 24 percent in 1945 to 31 percent in 1960 (Bremmer and Reichard 1982). This massive growth led America into a consumerist frenzy which *Life* magazine described in 1954 as the highest in the history of the United States. The economic difficulties of the Great Depression and the rationing of World War II seemed to be gone, apparently never to come back. Indeed, the prevailing idea in the 1950s was that thrift was no longer a virtue, as advertisements urged people to "buy, buy, buy" (Young and Young, ix–x). This brought about a renewed positivism unwitnessed since the Roaring Twenties. For the first time in decades, people's "(d)aily lives resonated with the expectation that at last the American Dream could become reality (xii). Beyond the U.S.'s borders, America became the center of the world's economy (Cohan 1997, ix) becoming by 1946 "the workshop, the bakery, and the banker of the postwar world" (McCormick 1989, 47). It should come as no surprise, therefore, that some regard the decade as "the Fabulous Fifties" (Young and Young xiv), the "Golden Fifties" (Brandt 2007, 11), or even the best decade in the history of America (Oakley 1987).

This splendor had an effect in the political sphere. The United States hurried to enhance and perpetuate their hegemony over global politics by setting itself up as the "epitome of [world] democracy" (Cuenca 2010, 111, my own translation), and tried to be in charge of the integration of Europe and Japan into North Atlantic and North Pacific markets and political communities (McCormick 1989, 238). The type of democracy the U.S. tried to establish world-wide was based on a strongly heterosexist capitalism (Cuenca, 111). Consequently, their main enemy in achieving this goal became the USSR, which the U.S. tried to isolate and vilify throughout the Cold War. This was accomplished, in part, thanks to Joseph McCarthy's infamous Red Scare campaign and its ensuing pressure regarding gender roles.

In February 1950, Senator Joseph McCarthy claimed that Communism had infiltrated the United States and had reached the State Department, which allegedly had employed up to 205 active communist agents. McCarthy intended to track down and punish all who favored Communist ideologies, or who simply thought differently than him, infamously stating that anyone who was against him was either a "Communist or a cocksucker" (quoted in Cuordileone 2000, 521). These accusations triggered the Red Scare campaign, in which he encouraged Americans to inform authorities of any subversive or suspicious acts carried out by fellow men and women. To make sure citizens did not take it lightly, the government created propagandistic documentaries and movies such as *The Hoaxters* (1952) and *My Son John* (1952) to show how dangerous Communism and its followers were for the American way of life. Those who were suspected of allegiance to Communism, regardless of whether it was based on false accusations, became blacklisted, ostracized, and had serious difficulties from then on in finding work in any public institution. Thus, in practical terms, the Red Scare campaign became nothing but a media and social witch-hunt, as criticized in Robert Anderson's *Tea and Sympathy* (1953), Arthur Miller's *The Crucible* (1953), Jack Finney's *The Body Snatchers* (1955), and Philip K. Dick's short story "The Father-Thing" (1959).

Conservatives took advantage of McCarthy's words and the reigning paranoia to try to further deteriorate homosexuals' image and emphasize their possible link with Communism. GOP party chairman Guy Gabrielson proclaimed that homosexuals had "infiltrated our government" and were "perhaps as dangerous as the actual Communists" (cited in Cuordileone, 532). Likewise, the Republican leader in the Senate, Kenneth Wherry, linked homosexuality to any type of subversive attitude, claiming that "you can't hardly separate homosexuals from subversives. Mind you, I don't say every homosexual is a subversive, and I don't say every subversive is a homosexual. But [...] they are all tied together" (cited in Savran 1998, 4–5). Wherry also call for measures to avoid "sabotage" in cities by "subversives and moral perverts" lurking in the government (cited in Cuordileone, 532). His petition resulted in an investigation by the Senate—the "Employment of Homosexuals and Other Sex Perverts in Government"—which reported that homosexuals were morally weaker due to their sexual indulgence, and their unacceptable affliction made them socially vulnerable and prone to corruption by Communism and other totalitarian regimes. All this brought about a feeling that if one, especially a man, did not behave according to the normative model of masculinity, he was probably a latent homosexual (Ehrenreich 1987, 24) or a communist (Kimmel 2006, 155).

In view of this, it should come as no surprise that one of the main characteristics of the 1950s was its "self-conscious preoccupation with masculinity"

(Gilbert 2005, 2) and, more particularly, to any trace of "waning masculinity" (Loftin 2007, 577). This eventually caused a state of "panic" among men (Gilbert, 9), since "there was room only for straight gender identity—straight and narrow" (Filene 1974, 180), as homosexuality was regarded as a "national security risk" (Corber 1997, 2). Thus, to avoid the taint of Communism and homosexuality, U.S. citizens conformed to the prevailing social norms, embedded in the concept of maturity as theorized by R.J. Havighurst (cited in Ehrenreich 18). He claimed that men and women could prove their normative heterosexuality and achieve happiness in their (early) adulthood if they were able to "mature" and "settle down." To accomplish this, he created a series of tasks clearly based on traditional gender roles which, if followed, would lead to maturity, whereas failing to complete them was associated with either immaturity or a subversive nature (Ehrenreich, 24), and would therefore lead to, as explained earlier, suspicions of homosexuality and pro-communist tendencies. The tasks were as follows: "(1) selecting a mate, (2) learning to live with a marriage partner, (3) starting a family, (4) rearing children, (5) managing a home, (6) getting started in an occupation, (7) taking on civic responsibilities and (8) finding a congenial social group" (quoted in Ehrenreich, 18). It was this pressure and anxiety that led Norman Mailer to claim that the men and women of the 1950s were living in "one of the worst decades in the history of man" (quoted in Castronovo 2004, 13).

Jobs, Manliness and Michael's Decadence

One of the key aspects of normative masculinity in the 1950s was the notion of the breadwinner—being a provider has traditionally been regarded in America as the "natural" role of man (Armengol 2013, 31). The intertwinement of jobs and manliness became tighter than ever especially since women, after the end of the war, were expected to go back to their role as housewives instead of working outside the home (Anderson 1981, also 2002; Collins 2003; Friedan 1963; May 1981; Meyerowitz 2002). As a result, jobs became the main source of identity for men (Filene, 184). Consequently, their manliness depended on the type of job they had. To perpetuate capitalism and expand their power, the U.S had an interest in increasing consumerism as much as possible (Cuenca 2011, also 2013; Ehrenreich 1987; Halliwell 2007). Therefore, high-salary jobs were portrayed as the ones men should aspire to in order to prove their worth as breadwinners and as men, with the result that white-collar jobs were considered the only ones which provided men with enough income and prestige to be regarded as truly manly (Cohan 1997, xii; Cuenca 2013, 42; Hoberek 1997). Conversely, blue-collar jobs were often looked down on, partly because of their low wages, but also because the manual labor and muscular body associated with them created uncomfortable parallels with the Great Depression (Cuenca 2013).

As C. Wright Mills explains in his study of the 1950s, white-collar workers were divided into three types of salesmen: stationary, mobile, or absentee:

Stationary salespeople—now about 60 per cent of the white-collar people involved in selling—sell in stores, behind the counters. Mobile salesmen—now about 38 per cent—make the rounds to the houses and offices of the customers. They range from peddlers walking from door-to-door, to "commercial traveler" who fly to their formal appointments expertly made weeks in advance. Absentee salesmen—admen, now 2 per cent of all salespeople—manage the machineries of promotion and advertising and are not personally present at the point of the sale, but act as all-pervasive adjuncts to those who are [Mills 1951, 165].

Men tried their best to become absentee salesmen not only because of the extra money it provided, but also because of the enormous prestige they had in society and the higher status it provided within the company. This is perfectly portrayed in novels such as *The Man in the Gray Flannel Suit* (1955), and *The Space Merchants* (1953), which shows its protagonist, Mitchell Courtenay, as a member of the "star-class" due to his position as an adman. Conversely, the mobile salesman, even though it was still a white-collar profession, was often looked down on and, to some extent, considered a failure, especially if he did not succeed in selling enough, as happens to Willy Loman in *Death of a Salesman* (1949).

In *Young Hearts Crying*, after marrying Lucy, Michael soon finds himself in a clash between his desire to become a writer so that he can have his name engraved in literary history, and his need to prove his manliness through the role of the provider. On their honeymoon, Lucy confesses that she has a fortune "between three and four million dollars" (Yates 2008; 1984, 12). This is news Michael should receive as a blessing, since the thing he needs most to exploit his artistic skills is time, as he claims repeatedly throughout the novel. However, Michael quickly refuses to hear anything about Lucy's money. Initially, he attributes ideological reasons which seem to be related to the reigning hope of the 1950s that the American Dream was, once again, possible to accomplish. Indeed, he explains to Lucy that "[h]e was a middle-class boy and he had always assumed he would make something of himself on his own. Could he really be expected to abandon that lifelong habit of thought overnight?" (13). He also argues that "[l]iving off her fortune might only bleed away his ambition, and might even rob him of the very energy he needed to work at all" (13). What he does not tell Lucy is the actual reason he refuses to use her money, which is that he is certain "that to accept her money would jeopardize his 'very manhood,'" and would eventually "emasculate" him (14).

Michael's fear suggests that his conception of his own masculinity does not depend on whether he personally feels manly, but rather on how his actions and behavior display heteronormative manliness. Indeed, following the ideology of the 1950s, he knows that if he accepts Lucy's money and becomes maintained by her, he will be seen to be swapping gender roles in the eyes of society; being a provider was a condition sine qua non for normative masculinity whereas being maintained was considered a trait of femininity (Ehrenreich 1987, 24). Moreover, refusing to carry out the role of the provider would prevent him from fulfilling one of the basic tasks of maturity/normative masculinity, resulting in him being considered an immature (i.e., homosexual) or a subversive (i.e., communist). This, in part, explains Michael's fear of emasculation, and the reasoning behind his claim that they are going to do things his way (14). He is adamant that they will keep to the plans he made "for them long before the wedding"—going to New York to start working "in some advertising agency or publishing house" and "live on his salary like an ordinary young couple" (13).

Initially, Michael plans to work at a white-collar profession—a job that would allow him to become part of the prevailing hegemonic masculinity and, at the same time, give him time to focus on his artistic work—and so he looks for a vacancy as an absentee salesman in an advertising agency. However, he realizes that this job would soon "drive him out of his mind" (5) and thus has to settle for a job as a stationary salesman in the "permissions" department of a publishing house (15). This becomes another burden for him because the salary he earns is barely enough to pay the bills. In this context, Lucy's money becomes, for Michael and his conception of masculinity, a constant reminder that if he continues to be unable to provide for his family, he might eventually need to accept her wealth, which would make him feel completely emasculated.

His only hope to make a break and earn decent money is by having his own work become successful, but to do that he needs time he cannot afford due to his job. As a result, the poems and plays he creates barely catch people's attention, with the exception of "Coming Clean"—a key poem in his development, as I will explain later on. Not surprisingly, the money he receives for his work is as shameful as the pay he earns from his job. As if to rub salt in his wounds, the parties he attends with other artists triggers in him the feeling that everyone else is earning more money than him, both as artists and workers (35). Indeed, he realizes that the money he got from his first work is the same or even less than the money Tom Nelson gets for a twenty-minute painting (53). As a result, instead of celebrating the publication of his work, he feels humiliated as a man by Nelson's success. These examples show that Michael also perceives his manliness as being in competition with that of other men. This competitiveness is, as Brannon and David stated as early as 1976, a common trait of the traditional model of normative masculinity; the ultimate goal is to be regarded as manlier than the rest, either at the workplace, sports, etc. As Michael Kimmel pointed out in a recent interview, the main problem of competitiveness is that no man can embody the perfect ideal of manhood, as he will always be lacking in some aspect or have some flaw (Kimmel 2011). Therefore, this trait is bound to bring about disappointment and dissatisfaction, as well as a feeling of one's manliness being constantly threatened, often causing violent outbursts in an attempt to reaffirm one's manhood.

This is exactly what happens to Michael at a party with Paul and Bill, where he feels his manliness shrink in comparison with other more successful men, and as a result, challenges Al Damon to a game consisting of hitting the opponent as hard as possible in the stomach. Maggie McKinley's theories on men's violence in the 1950s become especially relevant for Michael's apparently random, and poor, decision. Borrowing from Bourdieu and Arendt's studies on how society has justified and accepted male violence, McKinley argues that men who felt emasculated in some regard by other men tended to use violence as an attempt to both subdue others' manliness and enhance and reaffirm their own (McKinley 2015, 4). However, as McKinley points out, by using violence to break free from a situation that jeopardizes their manliness, men are actually becoming part of the hegemonic masculinity that is subduing and emasculating them, which eventually leads them to "a deepened sense of conflict and emasculation" (8). Michael perfectly portrays this irony as his punch knocks Al down, causing a scene which makes him abandon the party in profound shame, leaving him "humiliated –even emasculated" (88) and "eaten with anxiety" (89). In the end, the constant unintelligent actions Michael performs to prove his manliness and his capability as provider, combined with his incapacity to accept her money, takes its toll on Lucy. She thus decides to divorce Michael because she realizes she has never been able to agree with him (115) and because he is "intimidated by her money" (227)—an attitude she considers immature. This separation triggers a downward spiral for Michael, who eventually loses his mind and is institutionalized in an asylum. After this, there follows "a year of melancholy and regret" (265), which increases when he sees how his actions and attitude have created an "infinite sadness" in his daughter (265). He eventually realizes that he would have been happier—and would have made his family happier—had he swallowed his pride and accepted Lucy's money (280).

Once again, Yates uses a trait—madness—traditionally regarded as feminine or emasculating as the outcome of a pursuit of manliness. As in other novels and short stories, such as *Revolutionary Road* or "The B.A.R. Man," Yates attempts to present the pernicious effects of blindly trying to conform to the normative model of masculinity. In doing so, Yates is actually denouncing hegemonic masculinity by showing how, ironically, it can lead men to feel unmanly, repulsed and ridiculed by their own actions. Yates implies that new models and practices are indeed needed, which is what he provides in the third part of the novel in terms of caring and nurturing practices of fatherhood.

Fatherhood, Masculinity and Michael's New Hopes

Traditionally, fatherhood has been seen as a way to prove to society one's virility and manliness (Brannon and David 1976). As Fasteau notes, however, what confers manliness is the act of having offspring—which leads to the role of the provider—rather than the act of fathering or having a nurturing or caring attitude to one's children (1976). In fact, fathers have traditionally avoided getting involved in their children's emotional development as that was regarded as the realm of mothers (Rotundo 1994; Tanfer and Mott 1999; Wall and Arnold 2007).

Models of fatherhood which go beyond the role of the breadwinner, embracing instead a closer and more nurturing relationship with children— what has been labeled as "caring fatherhood"—have recently been explored as practices of alternative masculinity (Requena 2014). Defining caring fatherhood has become a point of debate between scholars. In a 2012 seminar given at the University of Barcelona, Victor J. Seidler argued that practices of caring fatherhood are not just about how much time men spend with their children, but rather the quality of the time (Seidler 2012). Similarly, Marsiglio and Pleck claim that what constitutes caring fatherhood is not "simply the amount of involvement" but rather "the nature and quality of the involvement" (254). In this line, LaRossa argues that the new "conduct of fatherhood" includes "routine activities of men when they are trying to act 'fatherly.' Changing a diaper, feeding a baby, monitoring a child, playing with a daughter or son, being accessible [...] and mental engagement" (LaRossa 2012, 39–40).

As historian Steven M. Gelber argues, being a husband and a father in the 1950s did not simply mean being a provider but also taking care of the home (Gelber 1997, 66). Indeed, throughout the 1950s there was an "exaggerated emphasis on family life" (Anderson 1981, 178) by which men were supposed to be "companions" and providers for their wives (Gilbert 2005, 79) as well as "warm and nurturing" fathers (Gelber 1997, 94). Men would show their maturity as husbands and fathers only if they were able to make their families reach "togetherness" (Filene 1974, 186; Gilbert 79). This meant that families were supposed to be a "democracy" where the "decisions were to be made jointly" and disagreements were to be "resolved by consensus"

(Filene, 186). This focus on companionship and on spending considerable time at home made men feel that they were adopting, to a certain extent, the domestic role which had traditionally been played by women (Gelber, 94). Thus, there was the fear that this enforced domesticity of men would eventually emasculate them (Filene, 187). As a result magazines, as well as some films and TV sitcoms, criticized this domesticity and promoted traditional patriarchal models of husband and father in which men became absentee fathers and violence against their wives and children was acceptable, as shown in sitcoms such as *Father Knows Best, I Love Lucy,* and *The Adventures of Ozzie and Harriet.* This traditional and misogynistic model dominated throughout the 1950s.

Fatherhood has been a prominent, yet conflicting, topic in Yates's fiction. What has been common, however, is that all characters have regarded fatherhood, whether desired or not, as a means to prove their manliness, and more often than not, they follow the stereotypical 1950s model. Indeed, Frank Wheeler, although despising fatherhood and unable to tolerate being with his children (77), decides to become a father because the idea of abortion or, apparently, becoming childless, is regarded as a "threat" to his masculinity (379). Similarly, Fallon, the protagonist of "The B.A.R. Man," is more than willing to become a father so that he can prove his manliness. Michael becomes a unique character in Yates's fiction in as much as he is the only one to regard caring fatherhood as a desirable model, seeing in it a redeeming quality for traditional masculinity. Indeed, in Chapter 5, when Sarah tells him she wants to have a baby, Michael is more than willing to become a caring father so that he can "have a chance to atone for all the aching mistakes he'd made over the years with Laura" (354).

His first opportunity to redeem himself comes when his daughter Laura phones him in need of help, as she is stranded in the middle of nowhere, without money, and possibly pregnant. For the first time in his life, Michael decides to leave behind his job and his writing to try and save his daughter. When recollecting the journey he has just undergone, Michael is filled with an extreme sense of pride in his actions and attitude and almost unconsciously begins to recite his most successful poem, "Coming Clean." This moment symbolizes his change to caring father and practitioner of alternative masculinities through which he is purging himself of the damaging effects traditional manhood has inflicted on him. As Michael tearfully describes his journey to Sarah he claims:

> the main thing is I'm proud of myself for the first time in—first time in years. Oh, Jesus, baby, she was all alone out there and she was lost—she was lost—and maybe I've never done anything right in my whole life, but son of a bitch, I went out there and found her and got her and brought her home and now I'm fucking proud of myself [363].

Caring fatherhood is, therefore, not portrayed as an emasculating process, but rather an invigorating one beyond compare. Moreover, it is also acknowledged by others, as both Lucy and Sarah congratulate Michael and feel proud of his actions (367). He also becomes very involved in the upbringing of his son, showing no reluctance to change his diapers or spend quality time with him (389).

Interestingly, Richard Yates seems to make a connection between new practices of manhood and the possibility to transcend. "Coming Clean" is the key poem of Michael's career as a writer, the one which has enabled him to be popularly recognized as well as the one which has received the better criticism. To some extent, "Coming Clean" is the poem that has allowed him to partially achieve his desire to "transcend" as even in his old age he finds people who consider it one of the best post–World War II poems (396). The relationship between new fatherhood and this poem, established in the aforementioned reciting of "Coming Clean," seems to suggest that these alternative practices can actually lead to some sort of transcendence. This is further emphasized by Michael's writing, which increases in quantity and quality throughout the first year of his son's life, while he changes diapers and becomes deeply and happily involved in his upbringing (388).

Likewise, this renewed force and hope within him makes him open up and reveal weaknesses that the traditional model of masculinity would otherwise make him hide because they were considered a failure. He decides he has to write about his time at the asylum and about his sexual problems, including his experience of impotence with Mary Fontana. Both experiences had been taboos in the normative model of masculinity and have, moreover, often been related to the feminine, in case of madness, or even latent homosexuality, as in the case of impotence. Also, he believes this writing to potentially be as good if not better than "Coming Clean" (390), which will presumably increase his chances of becoming a recognized writer, thus linking, once more, new alternative practices of masculinity and their benefits with transcendence.

Surpassing the Sex Malady

In a seminar given at the University of Barcelona in 2013, Lynne Segal explored the relationship between manliness and sex. She argued that normative masculinity teaches men that "the sexual conquest is the affirmation of masculinity." As a result, Segal argues, "to be a man [becomes] synonymous with the functioning penis. The two become inseparable. Powerlessness is related to impotence" to the extent that "erectile dysfunction" or "the fear of

not being able to 'get it up'" is ultimately related to a sense of becoming "fragile, more like women" (Segal 2013).

After his break-up with Lucy, Michael sees sexual conquests as a means
to demonstrate his manliness. Thus, he looks for exceptionally pretty girls to
"show [them] off to other men" so that their "face[s] would go slack and weak
with envy" at the sight of them (Yates 2008; 1984, 272). Sex also plays a key
role in defining his manhood, becoming a "determined venereal questing
[that] had taken the place of ambition in his life" (276). The problem comes
when Michael is unable to get an erection and have sex with Mary Fontana.
Michael regards this failure as an inability to be a man (281), and that "revulsion and disdain" are "appropriate feelings to have about a man who couldn't
get it up" (283). The silence surrounding problems of a dysfunctional penis
becomes another burden, as he wonders if other men also suffered and why
"was it so seldom discussed except in jokes?" (283). Thus, he tries to bury
this experience deep within himself, becoming a deep-seated trauma that
sometimes resurfaces, rendering him "terrified of impotence," a "self-deceiv-
ing, self-defeating man"(296).

The process of "coming clean" prompted by his new fatherhood leads
Michael to talk about his problems with impotence for the first time. He
expresses his desire to write about it, to make other men realize that it is
more common than it might seem, and that it should not be regarded with
such fear (390–1). In doing so, Michael shows how the alternative practices
of masculinity he has been following allow him to surpass the fears embedded
in the hegemonic model of masculinity. Likewise, talking about it becomes
a healing process which enables Michael to heal himself from a trauma for
which he thought he would never find a cure.

Old Habits Die Hard: Antifeminism and Michael's Return to the Hegemonic Model

Despite Michael's many changes, there is still one aspect of hegemonic
masculinity he cannot overcome: his disdain for feminism or any attempt to
liberate women. In his extensive research on the behavior of pro-feminist
men, Bob Pease argues that one of the main problems for alternative practices
of masculinity and gender equality is "whether or not men can and will
change" (Pease 2014, 17). Pease claims that the patriarchal system, even if
it sometimes puts too much pressure on them, allows men to exercise a
power and control over the rest of the population which grants them benefits
which just might be too good to give away. Even if men decided to carry out

alternative practices of masculinity, Pease doubts they can in any way actually challenge the structures of patriarchy. However, he believes that what men do have are "choices as to whether they accept patriarchy or work collectively against it" (17). Borrowing from Michael Kimmel's concept of "democratic manhood" (Kimmel 2000, 335), Pease advocates educating men not to see gender equality as an end to the benefits a patriarchal society provides without something in exchange, but rather as a means to obtain what he calls "relational interests"—the benefits a more egalitarian society would give to men and to men's relationships with their wives, daughters, sisters, mothers, etc. (Pease 2014, 18). He thus concludes that if men can learn to favor these relational interests over "their egotistical interests" then changes towards gender equality can actually take place (18).

Michael's dilemma in changing his model of masculinity is his unwillingness to completely give up his privileges as a patriarchal man, and his consequent fear of feminism and its ensuing liberation for women. Macarena García-Avello, analyzing the representation of 1950s gender problems in *Revolutionary Road*, argues that Frank, and American society for that matter, expected April and all women to behave like the "Angel in the House"—that is, to be blindly supportive and avoid upsetting her husband (2013). Elements of García-Avello's theory can be seen in *Young Hearts Crying*, since Michael's relationship with women, including his partners, seems to be for the most part of the novel one of possession rather than affection. Indeed, he does not see women as his equal, as his patriarchal attitude expects them to submit to him, conforming to their allegedly natural role.

As a result, he sees traces of non-traditional behavior or lack of support as the "evil" consequences of the feminist movement which, he believes, is brainwashing women to leave their husbands (Yates 2008; 1984, 393) and "open [their] legs for a different man every Saturday night" (411). This irrational thinking is what causes Michael's relationship with Sarah to fall apart. When Sarah refuses to be considered the possession of any man, including Michael, and questions his idea of male ownership of women, Michael feels his masculinity threatened and proceeds to abuse her psychologically. He tells her to stop with her "feminist horseshit" and to come with him, but she refuses, leaving Michael alone again (410). Thus, the happiness and pride Michael felt as a result of his change evaporates as soon as he succumbs to his more traditional side. This reversion brings back Michael's desperation and fears, making him realize that his misogynistic and patriarchal attitude has isolated him (422). The ending of the novel, therefore, attempts to show that a partial adoption of alternative practices is not sufficient, suggesting a need for deeper change. It follows what Carabí and Armengol argue—that men cannot change their lives and the lives of those close to them until they fully recognize their "false entitlements to unequal power" (2014, 1).

Conclusions: Yates's Third Space

There is no doubt of the dominant presence of normative masculinity in *Young Hearts Crying*. As it occurs with Yates's other male characters, Michael is the embodiment of the 1950s patriarchal man obsessed with proving his manliness through the role of the breadwinner, displays of violence, both physical against men and psychological against women, and with a strongly antifeminist attitude. However, it is precisely through this accurate and detailed representation of the hegemonic model of masculinity that Richard Yates constructs his fierce critique. Focusing on the aforementioned three pillars of traditional manhood, Yates subverts their alleged benefits—their capacity to enhance one's manliness and the pride and admiration obtained from them—showing how they can actually lead to exactly the opposite outcome. By pinpointing these flaws, Yates is trying to deconstruct the popular and idyllic conception of the normative model of masculinity and of patriarchy to ultimately denounce it. The tragedy Michael lives because of his need to prove his masculinity seeks to make readers realize the futility of his actions, and thus lead them to consider the relevance of adopting alternative practices of masculinity.

Contrary to his earlier works, Yates actually offers a new path for men by focusing on the benefits of a caring and nurturing fatherhood. The renewed hope and energy, the symbolic link with transcendence implied in Michael's "Coming Clean," and the significant improvement in the productivity and quality of his artistic work, suggest that these models, and presumably others not explored, can bring about genuine happiness and also the possibility of actually doing something for which to be remembered. In this line, Yates, almost as if following Bob Pease's theories on how to advance towards more gender-egalitarian societies, encourages men to choose relational interests, which can also benefit women, over their own egotistical ones. Similarly, Yates also seems to be advancing Lynne Segal's claim that to create a better society, men need to realize that their lives must be constructed on how they care for others rather than how they can get more benefits (Segal 2013).

Thus, even if his work might not be regarded as feminist per se, it cannot be considered antifeminist either inasmuch as it essentially denounces, very much like feminism does, the roots of patriarchy. Therefore, Yates and his oeuvre does seem to belong to a third space, a niche wherein his novels and short stories deconstruct the hegemonic masculinity and advocate for alternative practices of being a man, tiptoeing around the borderline of feminism. Consequently, I believe that Yates's reputation as antifeminist should be reconsidered. His capacity to position himself in this third space makes him, in my opinion, worthy of inclusion in the texts studied in the fields of anti-hegemonic masculinities, and possibly even feminism, not as an activist or practitioner, but as an ally in their fight.

BIBLIOGRAPHY

The Adventures of Ozzie and Harriet. TV Series. Stage Five Productions, 1952–1966.
Anderson, Karen. 1981. *Wartime Women: Sex Roles, Family Relations, and the Status of Women During World War II.* London: Greenwood Press.
_____. "The Great Depression and World War II." 2002. In *A Companion to American Women's History*, edited by Nancy A. Hewitt, 366–381. Malden: Blackwell.
Anderson, Robert. (1953) 1983. *Tea and Sympathy.* New York: Samuel French.
Armengol, Josep Maria. 2013. "Embodying the Depression: Male Bodies in 1930s American Culture and Literature." In *Embodying Masculinities: Historicizing the Male Body in U.S. Fiction and Film*, edited by Josep Maria Armengol, 31–48. New York: Peter Lang.
Bailey, Blake. 2009. "Richard Yates' Real Masterpiece: What Kate Winslet doesn't tell you about Yates and women." *Slate.* 5 January. (Accessed 10 June 2013). http://www.slate.com/articles/arts/books/2009/01/richard_yates_real_masterpiece.html.
Bannon, Ian, and Maria Correia. 2006. *The Other Half of Gender: Men's Issues in Development.* Washington, D.C.: The World Bank.
Brandt, Stefan L. 2007. Introduction to *The Culture of Corporeality: Aesthetic Experience and the Embodiment of America, 1945–1960.* Heidelberg: Universitätsverlag.
Brannon, Robert, and Deborah David. 1976. *The Forty-Nine Percent Majority: The Male Sex Role.* New York: Random House.
Bremmer, Robert H., and Gary W. Reichard. 1982. *Reshaping America: Society and Institution, 1945–1960.* Columbus: Ohio State University Press.
Carabí, Àngels, and Josep Maria Armengol. 2014. Introduction to *Alternative Masculinities for a Changing World*, edited by Àngels Carabí and Josep Maria Armengol. New York: Palgrave Macmillan.
Castronovo, David. 2004. *Beyond the Gray Flannel Suit: Books from the 1950s That Made American Culture.* New York: Continuum.
Cenamor, Rubén. 2013. "Son of Depression, Man of Anxiety: Frank Wheeler's American Patriarchal Masculinity in Richard Yates' *Revolutionary Road.*" Master's Thesis. Universitat Autònoma de Barcelona. http://ddd.uab.cat/record/144982.
_____. 2015. "Advancing the Feminine Mystique: 'The Problem That Has No Name' in Richard Yates' *Revolutionary Road.*" Plenary Session at the Reexamining the 1960s: Media, Politics, Culture Conference on Texas Christian University, Fort Worth, Texas November 6–7.
Charlton-Jones, Kate. 2014. *Dismembering the American Dream: The Life and Fiction of Richard Yates.* Tuscaloosa: University of Alabama Press.
Cohan, Steven. 1997. Introduction to *Masked Men: Masculinity and the Movies in the Fifties*, edited by Steven Cohan. Bloomington: Indiana University Press.
Collins, Gail. 2003. *America's Women: 400 Years of Dolls, Drudges, Helpmates, and Heroines.* Glasgow: HarperCollins.
Connell, R.W. 1987. *Gender and Power: Society, the Person and Sexual Politics.* Cambridge: Polity Press.
_____. 1995. *Masculinities.* Cambridge: Polity Press.
Corber, Robert J. 1997. Introduction to *Homosexuality in Cold War America*, edited by Robert J. Corber. Durham, NC: Duke University Press.
Cuenca, Mercè. 2010. "Lectura, homosexualidad y resistencia a la homofobia: el caso de los Estados Unidos (1945–1965)," in *Homoerotismos Literarios*, edited by Rodrigo Andrés, 109–127. Barcelona: Icaria.
_____. 2013. "Invisibilizing the Male Body: Exploring the Incorporeality of Masculinity in 1950s American Culture." In *Embodying Masculinities: Historicizing the Male Body in U.S. Fiction and Film*, edited by Josep Maria Armengol 49–62. New York: Peter Lang.
Cuordileone, K.A. 2000. "'Politics in an Age of Anxiety': Cold War Political Culture and the

Crisis in American Masculinity, 1949–1960." *The Journal of American History* 87, no. 2: 515–544.

Daly, Jennifer. 2014. "'Emily Grimes Is Me': Anxiety, Feminism, and the Masculinity Crisis in Richard Yates's *The Easter Parade*." *Irish Journal of American Studies* 3. (Accessed 20 May 2015). http://ijas.iaas.ie/index.php/emily-grimes-is-me-anxiety-feminism-and-the-masculinity-crisis-in-richard-yatess-the-easter-parade/.

Dick, Phillip K. (1959) 1999. "The Father-Thing." In *The Father-Thing*, n.e., 101–110. London: Clays Ltd.

Ehrenreich, Barbara. 1987. *The Hearts of Men: American Dreams and the Flight from Commitment*. New York: Bantam Doubleday.

Fasteau, Marce Feigen. 1976. "Men as Parents." In *The Forty-Nine Percent Majority: The Male Sex Role*, edited by Robert Brannon and Deborah David, 60–65. New York: Random House.

Father Knows Best. TV Series. Warner Brothers Burbank Studios, 1954–1960.

Filene, Peter G. 1974. "The Long Amnesia: Depression, War, and Domesticity." In *Him/Her/Self: Gender Identities in Modern America*, edited by Peter G. Filene, 158–190. Baltimore: The Johns Hopkins University Press.

Finney, Jack. (1955) 2015. *The Body Snatchers*. New York: Simon & Schuster.

Ford, Richard. 2000. "American Beauty (Circa 1955)." *New York Times Book Review*. 9 April. (Accessed 20 June 2015). http://www.tbns.net/e_evenkinds/richardford.html.

Fraser, Nick. 2008. "Rebirth of a dark genius." *The Guardian*. 17 February. (Accessed 15 February 2013). http://www.guardian.co.uk/books/2008/feb/17/biography.fiction.

Friedan, Betty. (1963) 2010. *The Feminine Mystique*. London: Penguin Classics.

García-Avello, Macarena. 2011. "'I've Always Known...': La Mística de la Feminidad en *Revolutionary Road* de Richard Yates." *Odisea* 12: 289–305.

_____. 2013. "The Angel in the House Revisited in Richard Yates' *Revolutionary Road*." *Corps, Pays, Maison* 5: 139–154. (Accessed 15 June 2015). http://e-crit3224.univ-fcomte.fr/download/3224-ecrit/document/numero_5/7.-pays_the-angel-of-the-house-revisited-in-revolutionary-road_139–54.pdf.

Gelber, Steven M. 1997. "Do-It-Yourself: Constructing, Repairing and Maintaining Domestic Masculinity." *American Quarterly* 49, no. 1: 66–112.

Giardina, Anthony. 2007. "An Emotional Journey Down *Revolutionary Road*." *NPR Books*. 17 July 2007. (Accessed 20 June 2015). http://www.npr.org/templates/story/story.php?storyId=11913039.

Gilbert, James. 2005. *Men in the Middle: Searching for Masculinity in the 1950s*. Chicago: University of Chicago Press.

Halliwell, Martin. 2007. *American Culture in the 1950s*. Edinburgh: Edinburgh University Press.

The Hoaxters. Directed by Herman Goffman. 1952. USA: Metro-Goldwyn-Mayer, 1998. DVD.

Hoberek, Andrew P. 1997. "The 'Work' of Science Fiction: Philip K. Dick and Occupational Masculinity in the Post–World War II United States." *Modern Fiction Studies* 43, no. 2: 374–404.

I Love Lucy. TV Series. Desilu Productions, 1951–1957.

Kimmel, Michael. 2000. *The Gendered Society*. New York: Oxford University Press.

_____. 2006. *Manhood in America*. Oxford: Oxford University Press.

_____. 2011. "Interrogating Racialized Masculinities." http://www.ub.edu/ubtv/en/video/interrogating-racialized-masculinities-michael-kimmel.

LaRossa, Ralph. 2012. "The Historical Study of Fatherhood: Theoretical and Methodological Considerations." In *Fatherhood in Late Modernity: Cultural Images, Social Practices, Structural Frames*, edited by Mechtild Oechsle, Ursula Müller, and Sabine Hess. Leverkusen-Opladen, 37–58. Berlin: Barbara Budrich Publishers.

Loftin, Craig M. 2007. "Unacceptable Mannerisms: Gender Anxieties, Homosexual Activism, and Swish in the United States, 1945–1965." *Journal of Social History* 40, no. 3: 577–596.

Marsiglio, William, and Joseph Pleck. 2004. "Fatherhood and Masculinities." In *The Handbook of Studies on Men and Masculinities*, edited by Raewyn Connell, Jeff Hearn, and Michael Kimmel, 249–269. Thousand Oaks, CA: Sage.

May, Elaine Tyler. 1998. *Homeward Bound: American Families in the Cold War Era*. New York: Basic Books.

McCormick, Thomas J. 1989. *America's Half-Century: United States Foreign Policy in the Cold War*. Baltimore: John Hopkins University Press.

McKinley, Maggie. 2015. *Masculinity and the Paradox of Violence in American Fiction, 1950–1975*. New York: Bloomsbury.

Meyerowitz, Joanne. 2002. "Rewriting Postwar Women's History, 1945–1960." In *A Companion to American Women's History*, edited by Nancy A. Hewitt, 382–396. Malden: Blackwell.

Miller, Arthur. (1949) 1998. *Death of a Salesman*. New York: Penguin Classics.

_____. (1953) 2003. *The Crucible*. New York: Penguin Classics.

Mills, Wright C. (1951) 2002. *White Collar: The American Middle Classes*. Oxford: Oxford University Press.

My Son John. 1952. Directed by Leo McCarey and Ray McCarey. Paramount Pictures, 2012. DVD.

Oakley, J. Ronald. 1986. *God's Country: America in the Fifties*. New York: Dembner Books.

Pane, Sal. 2009. "Unflinching, Uncomfortable, and Unsettling: *The Easter Parade*." *Hot Metal Bridge*. 25 January. (Accessed 2 June 2013). http://hotmetalbridge.org/2009/01/unflinching-uncomfortable-and-unsettling-the-easter-parade/.

Pease, Bob. 1997. *Men and Sexual Politics: Towards a Profeminist Practice*. Adelaide: Dulwich Centre Publications.

_____. 2000. *Recreating Men: Postmodern Masculinity Politics*. London: Sage.

_____. 2002. "(Re)Constructing Men's Interests." *Men and Masculinities* 5.2: 165–177.

_____. 2010. *Undoing Privilege: Unearned Advantage in a Divided World*. London: Zed Books.

_____. 2014. "Reconstructing Masculinity or Ending Manhood? The Potential and Limitations of Transforming Masculine Subjectivities for Gender Equality." In *Alternative Masculinities for a Changing World*, edited by Àngels Carabí and Josep Maria Armengol, 17–34. New York: Palgrave McMillan.

Pohl, Frederik, and C.M. Kornbluth. (1953) 2011. *The Space Merchants*. New York: St. Martin's Press.

Requena, Teresa. 2014. "Fathers Who Care: Alternative Father Figures in Annie E. Proulx's *The Shipping News* and Jonathan Franzen's *The Corrections*." In *Alternative Masculinities for a Changing World*, edited by Àngels Carabí and Josep Maria Armengol, 115–130. New York: Palgrave Macmillan.

Riemer, James D. 1987. "Rereading American Literature from a Men's Studies Perspective: Some Implications." In *The Making of Masculinities: The New Men's Studies*, edited by Harry Brod, 289–300. Boston: Allen and Unwin.

Rotundo, Anthony. 1994. *American Manhood: Transformations in Masculinity from the Revolution to the Modern Era*. New York: Basic Books.

Savran, David. 1998. *Taking It Like a Man: White Masculinity, Masochism, and Contemporary American Culture*. Princeton, NJ: Princeton University Press.

Segal, Lynne. 2013. "Aging and Masculinities." Lecture at the University of Barcelona. 26 September. http://www.ub.edu/ubtv/video/aging-and-masculinities-lynne-segal (Accessed 5 May 2016).

Seidler, Victor. 2012. "Alternative Masculinities." Lecture at the University of Barcelona. 22 November. http://www.ub.edu/ubtv/es/video/alternative-masculinities-victor-seidler.

Tanfer, Koray, and Frank Mott. 1999. "Appendix C: The Meaning of Fatherhood for Men." Prepared for NICHD Workshop "Improving Data on Male Fertility and Family Formation" at the Urban Institute, Washington, D.C. January. http://fatherhood.hhs.gov/cfsforum/apenc.htm.

Wall, Glenda, and Stephanie Arnold. 2007. "How Involved Is Involved Fathering? An Exploration of the Contemporary Culture of Fatherhood." *Gender & Society* 21, no.4: 508–527.

Wilson, Sloan. (1955) 2002. *The Man in the Gray Flannel Suit*. Cambridge: Da Capo Press.

Yates, Richard. (1961) 2009. *Revolutionary Road*. New York: Vintage Books.

_____. (1962) 2008. In *Eleven Kinds of Loneliness*. London: Vintage Classics.

_____. (1975) 2007. *Disturbing the Peace*. London: Vintage Classics.

_____. (1976) 2008. *The Easter Parade*. London: Vintage Classics.
_____. (1984) 2008. *Young Hearts Crying*. London: Vintage Classics.
_____. (1986) 2008. *Cold Spring Harbor*. London: Vintage Classics.
Young, William H., and Nancy K. Young. 2004. Introduction to *The 1950s*, edited by William H. Young and Nancy K. Young. Westport, CT: Greenwood Press.

About the Contributors

Chloé **Avril** is an assistant professor of English literature at the University of Gothenburg, Sweden. She is the author of a book about Charlotte Perkins' utopian novels, as well as articles on Gilman and motherhood, the portrayal of riots in American detective fiction and Black Panther autobiographies, among other works.

Rubén **Cenamor** is a Ph.D. candidate at the University of Barcelona. He is a member of the European Association of American Studies (EAAS) Women's Network Steering Committee, and its treasurer. He is also a member of the European Society for the Study of English (ESSE) Women and Gender Studies Network and of the Constructing New Masculinities (http://www.ub.edu/masculinities/).

Kate **Charlton-Jones** is the author of *Dismembering the American Dream: The Life and Fiction of Richard Yates* (Alabama University Press, 2014). The *Times Literary Supplement* called it "an impressive piece of scholarship" and Monica Yates wrote that "*Dismembering the American Dream* is strong and true and deeply felt.... [Dad] would have been honored by her careful attention."

Rona **Cran** teaches twentieth-century American literature and culture at the University of Birmingham (UK). She is the author of *Collage in Twentieth-Century Art, Literature, and Culture* (Ashgate, 2014). She writes for the *Times Literary Supplement* and *New Walk* magazine.

Jennifer **Daly** completed her Ph.D. on masculinity in American fiction at Trinity College Dublin in 2016. Her research looks at issues surrounding the validity of the masculinity crisis narrative in the 20th and 21st centuries. She has published work on Richard Yates, and Richard Ford, and is actively involved in the Irish Association for American Studies.

Sophie A. **Jones** received her BA from the University of Manchester, her M.Phil. from the University of Cambridge, and her Ph.D. from Birkbeck, University of London. She has held research fellowships funded by the AHRC and the Wellcome Trust and is a postdoctoral researcher in the School of English at the University of Leeds.

Rory **McGinley** completed his Ph.D. at the University of Glasgow. His thesis on Yates adopted a revisionist position to argue for the socio-historic significance of

Yates's work. He is particularly interested in 1960s American literature's engagement with suburban studies, medical humanities and constructions of masculinity.

Helen **Turner** has a Ph.D. in literature from the University of Essex. She has presented papers at a number of conferences including the joint conference of the Irish and British Associations of American Studies Conference in 2016 as well as the last three International F. Scott Fitzgerald Conferences. She is working on a number of articles on twentieth century American literature.

Joanna **Wilson** is working towards a Ph.D. in English literature at the University of Edinburgh. Her research examines relationships between American literature of the 1960s and anti-psychiatric theory. She also works as a student coordinator and reader for the James Tait Black book prize.

Karl **Wood** holds a Ph.D. in history from the University of Illinois at Chicago. He is an associate professor at Kazimierz Wielki University, Bydgoszcz, Poland, where he has been on the staff since 2003. His interests include American suburbia and masculinity studies, as well as leisure studies and the cultural history of medicine.

Index

www.ingramcontent.com/pod-product-compliance
Lightning Source LLC
Chambersburg PA
CBHW050335110726
47899CB00007B/2511